Everyday humanitarianism in Cambodia

Manchester University Press

HUMANITARIANISM
KEY DEBATES & NEW APPROACHES

SERIES EDITORS: BERTRAND TAITHE AND REBECCA GILL

This series offers a new interdisciplinary reflection on one of the most important and yet understudied areas in history, politics and cultural practices: humanitarian aid and its responses to crises and conflicts. The series seeks to define afresh the boundaries and methodologies applied to the study of humanitarian relief and so-called 'humanitarian events'. The series includes monographs and carefully selected thematic edited collections which cross disciplinary boundaries and bring fresh perspectives to the historical, political and cultural understanding of the rationale and impact of humanitarian relief work.

Humanitarian aid, genocide and mass killings: Médecins Sans Frontières, the Rwandan experience, 1982–97
  Jean-Hervé Bradol and Marc Le Pape

Calculating compassion: Humanity and relief in war, Britain 1870–1914
  Rebecca Gill

Humanitarian intervention in the long nineteenth century
  Alexis Heraclides and Ada Dialla

The military–humanitarian complex in Afghanistan
  Eric James and Tim Jacoby

Reconstructing lives: Victims of war in the Middle East and Médecins Sans Frontières
  Vanja Kovačič

Global humanitarianism and media culture
  Michael Lawrence and Rachel Tavernor (eds)

Aid to Armenia: Humanitarianism and intervention from the 1890s to the present
  Jo Laycock and Francesca Piana (eds)

Humanitarianism and the Greater War, 1914–24
  Elisabeth Piller and Neville Wylie (eds)

A history of humanitarianism, 1775–1989: In the name of others
  Silvia Salvatici

Humanitarian extractivism: The digital transformation of aid
  Kristin Bergtora Sandvik

Donors, technical assistance and public administration in Kosovo
  Mary Venner

The NGO CARE and food aid from America 1945–80: 'Showered with kindness'?
  Heike Wieters

The Red Cross movement: Myths, practices and turning points
  Neville Wylie, James Crossland, Melanie Oppenheimer (eds)

Everyday humanitarianism in Cambodia

Challenging scales and making relations

Anne-Meike Fechter

MANCHESTER UNIVERSITY PRESS

Copyright © Anne-Meike Fechter 2023

The right of Anne-Meike Fechter to be identified as the author of this work has been asserted by them in accordance with the Copyright, Designs and Patents Act 1988.

Published by Manchester University Press
Oxford Road, Manchester M13 9PL

www.manchesteruniversitypress.co.uk

British Library Cataloguing-in-Publication Data
A catalogue record for this book is available from the British Library

ISBN   978 1 5261 7210 5   hardback
ISBN   978 1 5261 9132 8   paperback

First published 2023
Paperback published 2025

The publisher has no responsibility for the persistence or accuracy of URLs for any external or third-party internet websites referred to in this book, and does not guarantee that any content on such websites is, or will remain, accurate or appropriate.

EU authorised representative for GPSR:
Easy Access System Europe – Mustamäe tee 50,
10621 Tallinn, Estonia
gpsr.requests@easproject.com

Typeset
by New Best-set Typesetters Ltd

To Lilja and Annika, as promised

Contents

Acknowledgements	*page* viii
Introduction	1
1 Making scales and relations	24
2 The part and the whole	42
3 Every person counts	63
4 Distance and proximity	81
5 Desire to connect	103
6 Humanitarian kinship	121
7 Affinities and shared biographies	144
Conclusion	166
References	178
Index	191

Acknowledgements

This book is the result of collective efforts. First and foremost, my thanks go to those in Cambodia and abroad who generously helped with information and insights; who participated and let me join as they went about their everyday humanitarian activities, in some cases over a time span of several years. While they need to remain anonymous, it is only through their openness, patience and goodwill that any of this material has been gathered. I hope my rendering of it does their efforts justice. Over its gestation period the book has benefited from many exchanges with academics and practitioners, including colleagues and students at the University of Sussex, which has provided a lively and supportive research environment. At a critical stage, Alice Wilson and Anke Schwittay were key interlocutors which helped bring this text into its current shape. Further afield, fellow researchers Silke Roth and Allison Schnable offered comments and support as our respective projects took shape. I also sincerely thank the discussants at several workshops and conference panels, held at universities in Goettingen, Zurich, Oxford, Berlin and Lisbon for their critical and productive comments, including members of the Anthropology of Humanitarianism Network (AHN). The feedback of four anonymous reviewers has been crucial at manuscript stage, as well as Bertrand Taithe's enthusiasm for the project as series editor. Sina Emde has been a constant sounding board on research in Cambodia. Closer to home, Perpetua Kirby offered insightful readings of the manuscript, not infrequently while paddling off the East Sussex coast. Friends and family have been a source of sanity. Finally, my profound thanks go to Paul Basu, fierce critic and therefore most reliable tester of ideas one might ask for.

Introduction

Having grown up with a single parent, struggling in the aftermath of the Khmer Rouge regime, Piseth set up a day-care centre to support local children as soon as he could afford to. Located on a small plot on the outskirts of town, neighbourhood kids would drop in for classes in English and Computing, help with homework and exam revision. Piseth partly relied on his own wages from a job in the hospitality sector; local and international supporters paid for school uniforms, stationery, and transport to ensure the two dozen children he looked after completed their education. Occasionally Piseth travelled to other, rural schools on his motorbike, laden high with supplies. Supporters of the project from other parts of the world, visited and taught English; advised on the curriculum, helped renovate the compound, and bought building and other materials. Piseth often found his day-to-day operations a struggle, but whenever a student received their high school diploma, or one of them landed a good job in town, he felt *'all smiles'* and that it had been worthwhile. In the same town, Irena, originally from Malaysia, surveyed several enormous cooking pots in the backyard of her house, stirring a vegetable curry. Together with a dozen international volunteers and local supporters, she prepared hot lunches to be distributed to families living in the area. As she explained, *'this is often their only proper meal a week'*. Irena and the volunteers knew most of the families whom they handed the meals to; in her words, *'we are giving just a bit of care, because nobody looks out for them'*. Beth, a British citizen, used to work for an international aid agency, heading up country offices in Africa and Asia. While in Cambodia, she and her husband were looking after a young woman, estranged from her family, who lived in their neighbourhood. While their relationship had its challenges, taking on this role in Chantha's life was as important to Beth as her day job managing aid budgets – and often more rewarding, as *'you can see exactly the difference you are making'*.

All of them aim to improve the lives of others. They do so through modest interventions, targeted at small communities. These are examples of everyday humanitarianism, privately funded aid activities, set up and run by individuals, and typically funded through the founders' social networks. Founders are foreigners or Cambodians, often working in close collaboration with each other. While some of these projects are registered as NGOs, they operate on the margins of the formal aid sector. They offer educational programmes, vocational or leadership training, provide food donations, disability support, or further income generation and livelihoods. What fascinated me about them was, on the one hand, a sense of scepticism about institutional aid. Researching and teaching on overseas development assistance had left me with little conviction that this was a sustainable way forward, with its documented flaws including paternalist, neo-colonial and racist attitudes. I was also mindful that remittances by migrants dwarf the volume of overseas state aid by a multiple. At the same time, private charity I had encountered among foreigners in Southeast Asia (Fechter 2007), often among female partners of highly paid executives, seemed both pitiful in scope and tokenistic. How to understand these thriving aid initiatives in Cambodia? Were they not equally futile gestures, drops in the ocean? Did the sheer modesty of their operations discount them from systematic consideration? I wanted to explore, in the first instance, my own nagging sense of their futility. What was their significance in a world of big challenges? Second, they embodied a persistent concern I had been unable to resolve, how the supposedly 'small', such as local actions and singular interventions, connected to the so-called 'larger picture'. In the face of seemingly sluggish, self-serving institutions, had the time for grassroots action finally arrived? While they have a long history, was now the moment where simultaneous, if not collective action by small groups of people could eschew bureaucracy and professionals, harnessing a do-it-yourself spirit, to make advances where those had not? I pursue these questions in the case of everyday humanitarians here. Where to put one's efforts, and how small acts figure in a global crisis, however, matters for all of those who want to transform the world. At this particular moment of rupture, where action in the face of the climate crisis is ever more urgent, where to start?

In this case, when faced with the enormity of inequality and poverty, one question is whether to start at all, given the spectre of partial reach and futility that hangs over any such attempt. Among all humans who need support, where to put your effort? Who to care for, and what shapes these choices? These questions are at the core of this book. It traces how, through their actions, everyday humanitarians challenge entrenched ideas and values of what matters. They upend the notion that the large-scale is inherently important – and even the notion what 'large' means in the first place. It explores the social relations which motivate the support that is being offered. In so doing, the book tackles a problem that the philosopher Peter Singer, among others, has articulated as 'who are we responsible for?' (1972). He answered this radically and entirely theoretically: everyone, he argued, was in principle responsible for everyone else, no matter how socially distant or close, or how geographically nearby or far away. Following extensive debates among philosophers of ethics, Frances Kamm (1999) admitted that these had come to an impasse – and that in finding a way forward, rather than continued controversies about what humans should be doing, one should turn to empirical data to see what they were actually doing. This book does just that. Rather than mounting a prescriptive answer to the question of moral responsibility, it asks what some people do when faced with seemingly insurmountable challenges and their limited capacity for supporting others. How do they decide where to put their efforts, and what actions follow from this?

Beyond a descriptive account, the book argues that everyday humanitarians exemplify a challenge not unique to humanitarianism, but characteristic of those seeking social change more broadly. It demonstrates how people negotiate the inevitable partial-ness of their efforts. This partial-ness refers to their limited reach, given the scope of the problem. They address this through skilfully operating with scales of their own making, which give meaning to, and guide, their actions. From this partial-ness follows the necessity to decide where to intervene, and whom to support. Here, I suggest that in contrast to the aspired-for impartiality of formal humanitarianism, these everyday practices are fundamentally partial. The decisions on whom to support are deeply embedded in the social relations that are created in the context of offering assistance to others. Indeed, as such a relational lens makes visible, providing support can become a vehicle to establish such relations in the first place. In contrast to the trope of the distant stranger so prominent in literature on humanitarianism, these relations are often couched in the idiom of kinship. Finally, a key modality are affinity ties, which bind everyday humanitarians to particular communities or causes. Biographical similarities or shared histories can determine and drive their interventions.

Beyond making everyday humanitarians more visible, the insights gained here have broader significance. First, despite partial-ness being a fundamental challenge for all forms of humanitarianism, there has been no empirical account of how those involved negotiate this challenge, and maintain their efforts. Adopting a scalar approach unsettles established notions of what counts as small and large, domestic and public, or being trivial and worthwhile. Instead, the approach taken here makes visible how practitioners produce scales that make their actions meaningful. They often operate with multiple and sliding scales, and moving between different scales of size or space is fundamental to negotiating the fact that their interventions are always limited, given the overall scope of the issues they are facing.

Such challenge of partial-ness applies much more widely to anyone aiming to effect change on a human or global scale. Whether this relates to environmentalism, changing the way the global economy works or fighting the climate crisis, the question of how one's own endeavours and achievements sit within what is required, is a practical and theoretical one in need of investigating. This is not least because understanding how people negotiate this can help to valorise their efforts, and make their practice more sustained in the long term. Its theoretical significance lies in how this changes our understanding of what constitutes humanitarianism. Bringing such everyday humanitarian practices to light vernacularises dominant notions of humanitarianism. Rather than being the preserve of trained professionals and recognised institutions, humanitarian practices can be, and are, carried out by ordinary people, in the context of their daily lives.

Such partial-ness engenders its own challenges, such as where to place one's limited resources. Considering everyday humanitarianism is instructive here. I argue that rather than being determined by formal and ethically reflected needs assessments such as medical triage, the actions of many everyday humanitarians are profoundly driven and shaped by individually based, partial priorities. They are not aiming to be impartial in the sense of not favouring one equally needy group of beneficiaries over another. Instead, a relational lens – paying attention to how social relations matter in everyday humanitarianism – reveals them as central to such decision-making, whether they are consciously reflected or not. Rather than being considered a problem that is due to inherent biases, being partial – favouring one group of people to support over another – constitutes a necessary guide to action. It may enable intervention rather than leading to an ethical impasse. For theoretical significance, raising awareness of how such partialities matter upends notions of what is considered good humanitarian practice. In order to foster interventions, recognising how much partialities matter offers valuable operational knowledge. Rather than branding partiality as opposed to impartiality as a problem, recognising its role in directing intervention provides a more honest and accurate account of what shapes humanitarian action.

Discovering everyday humanitarianism

Talking with Dara in his taxi on a trip to the outskirts of Phnom Penh, he explained to me how he had worked for many years as a staff driver for a succession of international aid organisations which had sprung up across the capital. While this provided a steady income for him and his family, it also involved long hours, with little control over his schedule. He had, however, become friendly with many of the foreign staff members he worked with. He remembered one consultant, Marco, fondly: *'He goes with me all the time, when he arrived at the airport, I pick him up and drive him around.'* When Marco's assignments in Cambodia came to end, *'he said to me, you keep the car you are using at the moment. I pay it for you, and you can have your own taxi.'* With the donation of the car, Dara set himself up as an independent taxi driver, and had been working successfully for a number of years when I met him. Dara was keeping in touch with Marco, sending him updates and driving him around on his occasional visits back to the country. Such acts of spontaneous giving do not seem particularly noteworthy in themselves. They are, however, the visible outcrop of a much more widespread practice. Beyond a manifestation of individual charity, paying attention to this offers fundamental insights about humans' understanding of, and construction, of assistance to others. Dara's situation encompasses a number of features of everyday humanitarianism which made me aware of it in the first place. These were Dara's enduring relationship with Marco; the donation of the car; the circumstances of Marco's decision which changed Dara's livelihood; Marco's dual role as a development consultant and individual donor, making him a professional as well as everyday humanitarian: all of this prompted my curiosity, and made me take note whenever I became aware of such spontaneous donations and relationships.

Going back further to trace my understanding of such practices, I was researching corporate expatriates in Jakarta (Fechter 2007), when I realised that among the mobile professionals attending 'expatriate'-focused events were those working for international aid agencies. Their journeys to work involved a taxi or driver who took them from their air-conditioned apartments in Jakarta's high-rise tower blocks to their well-appointed offices, the headquarters of a multi-or bilateral agency, or a large international NGO. In their free time, they played tennis, visited spas and massage parlours, attended networking events and work receptions. Aid work did not necessarily mean, as I had imagined rather naively, living in remote, rural areas, busily installing water wells. What did it mean to do aid work if it took place in tower blocks and consisted of meetings and report writing, interspersed with occasional forays to local government offices? I was intrigued by what I saw as the mundane side of something that looked both adventurous and possibly heroic from the outside or from the distant view of someone in their home countries. Understanding contemporary aid in its humdrum, office-based form was to look at aid as a form of work. That did not mean that issues of morality and good intentions did not come into play: rather, it meant trying to understand how they did. This project was about understanding how, what I assumed to be, at least partly, a roundabout way of caring for others would manifest, or be transformed, when carried out in settings and taking forms that seemed, on the surface, indistinguishable from those of the business expatriates I was studying at the time.

Yet later again, having spent time with those aid workers in Cambodia, I realised that many of them found fulfilment and a sense of reward not only, or not all in their office work, but in private aid activities they engaged with on the side (Fechter 2018). It is difficult to pinpoint when exactly I became aware of the veritable underbelly of the formal aid sector in Cambodia. Having set out to study the lives of international aid workers, I noticed how several of the people I was talking with had set up their own aid projects, alongside their daytime, paid work for international aid agencies. The story of Marco and Dara was among the first that I encountered. A Dutch couple I interviewed mentioned that they were spending much of their weekends at a Buddhist-run home for teenage girls, supporting them with mentoring and financial support through their high-school education. On another occasion, I met two international aid workers in a cafe in a provincial town, which was run as a social enterprise by a Cambodian monk. It emerged that the aid workers were deeply involved, from choosing the fabric of the seat cushions and designing the menu to taste-testing the coffee beans to be used. At first I was surprised – were these people not busy enough in their day jobs? I began to realise just how numerous such projects were, and wherever I took a closer look, more emerged. It also became clear that this was not limited to international aid workers with a sideline in charitable projects, or 'MONGOs', short for 'my own NGO' (Polman 2008). There was a multitude of private aid projects, initiated by foreigners and Cambodians, many without training or previous interest in formal aid work. These follow a reverse trajectory from those of professional aid workers. They often have their beginnings in the everyday, in the lives of ordinary citizens who set up their own initiatives alongside their daytime jobs or careers. To look at them means to trace how the will to intervene travels not just from the top down, from established agencies, but from the bottom up, from the margins and from outside the established aid sector.

Aid, development and humanitarianism

What constitutes everyday humanitarianism, and how does it relate to the established aid sector? The terms aid, development and humanitarianism are often used rather loosely and even interchangeably. For the most part, I adopt these flexible conventions as I engage with the relevant bodies of literature. 'Aid' as an overarching notion can encompass both development and humanitarianism. Conventionally, 'development' refers to long-term support, assistance and cooperation, whereas 'humanitarianism' is used to describe emergency-related, short-term missions and interventions. Having said that, the boundaries between the two are not always clearly delineated, but are becoming increasingly blurred. In practice, this means that organisations which consider themselves 'humanitarian' find that they are drawn into more long-term, development interventions in sites where they operate. At the same time, some NGOs, for example, provide support in emergency situations in areas where they normally engage in 'development' activities. The existing literature on the privately funded, informal support that is at stake here overwhelmingly favours versions of 'humanitarianism' (Fechter and Schwittay 2019). This captures the human-centred nature and spontaneous response to need that characterises these activities. In comparison, the term 'do it-yourself' development has gained less traction – arguably because 'development' invokes degrees of formalisation and professionalism which these informal aid activities do not display. I use the term 'everyday humanitarian' here to draw on the meaning of humanitarianism, less in terms of delivering emergency relief but capturing a compassion for humanity. That is the impetus to support others in need, no matter how dramatic or mundane, short-lived or intractable their situations are. There is now a substantial body of literature on what I call 'everyday humanitarianism', which I discuss in more detail in Chapter 1.

Broadly, with regard to terminology, people involved in informal aid activities have been called 'freelance altruists' (Swidler and Watkins 2017), 'aid amateurs' (Schnable 2021) and 'volunteer humanitarians' (Sandri 2018). These and similar terms distinguish them from the conventional aid system, notably highlighting their perceived lack of formal qualifications and professionalism ('amateurs'), and their unpaid, not formally employed status ('freelance altruists'). From this we can derive the contours of the conventional aid sector, which everyday humanitarians do not necessarily see themselves as part of. As it has developed since the end of the Second World War, the sector is constituted of formal institutions and organisations, including bi- and multilateral, governmental and non-governmental ones. It is characterised by particular funding mechanisms, guided by formal policies, implementing long-term programmes, deploying established monitoring and evaluation mechanisms, and so forth. Histories, and especially criticism, of this sector abound, including a lack of efficacy, transparency, downward accountability and its increasing reliance on private sector providers, to name but some. It is against this backdrop that everyday humanitarianism emerges, not as a consciously devised alternative, but as an often spontaneous reaction to situations of need, sometimes triggered by the absence of formal aid organisations or state interventions.

What does it involve in practice?

While the range of everyday humanitarian activities is wide, they do not straightforwardly mirror those of the formal sector. Rather, and for obvious reasons, there are many areas where everyday humanitarianism is much less, if at all, involved, such as large infrastructure projects like roads. Areas such as urban planning, labour rights, environmental protection or animal conservation are similarly left to formal national and international organisations. In contrast, there are examples of everyday humanitarians setting up healthcare projects, but as these tend to require medical qualifications, the barriers to entry and operation are relatively high. This, of course, does not prevent people from fundraising for large, privately run clinics, or for individual Cambodian children in need of medical treatment. The building of schools, clinics, community centres and houses, especially in rural areas, can also be part of their work. Generally, however, everyday humanitarians tend to focus on direct support of people, and in particular youth. In Cambodia, this ranges from regular provision of food, clothes or school supplies, to setting up education and training schemes. A common model are projects which complement state school teaching through additional English language and IT classes. Foremost is perhaps support for any kind of schooling or learning activity, as is working with women, children, those living with disabilities or HIV/Aids, and vulnerable groups more generally. Everyday humanitarians are involved in improving livelihoods, such as training women in handicrafts and helping them to market their products, or supporting small enterprise schemes aimed at lifting disadvantaged people out of poverty. As Schnable (2021), Berman (2017) and others illustrate, schemes that involve leadership or mentoring are common, alongside soup kitchens and emergency food banks, especially in the aftermath of COVID-19, as well as programmes that involve arts, sports or even circus skills training. Beyond working with communities or neighbourhoods, a substantial part of everyday humanitarianism can involve support of particular individuals. This might take the shape of one-off gifts, such as Dara's taxi, bikes or regular payments of tuition fees to see one or more young people through school.

Who are everyday humanitarians?

The existing literature on development and on everyday humanitarianism tends to foreground those from the Global North, whether professional aid workers or freelance altruists. Much of the literature (Berman 2017; Kinsbergen 2019; Schnable 2021), maintains the impression that everyday humanitarianism is carried out by people who are white, or not local to the places, or different from the people where they intervene. Existing research often divides those involved into categories of donor or beneficiary, with donors cast as foreign, and beneficiaries as local. If local people are accorded any agency, it is through the third category of 'broker' (Swidler and Watkins 2017) or 'gatekeeper' (Kinsbergen 2019). They are portrayed as facilitating humanitarian efforts, but not envisioning or driving them. The material presented here challenges this, and offers a more complex picture, where humanitarians are not necessarily white or foreign, and do not neatly fit into categories of donor, founder, broker or beneficiary. Instead, my research shows how people may inhabit more than one category at a time, and they can move through them as time progresses. Approaching everyday humanitarians with this degree of nuance is important because the spectre of white saviourism looms particularly large. It is all too easy to associate 'voluntourists' and visitors from the Global North, as well as everyday humanitarians, with the 'white saviour industrial complex' (Cole 2019), as I discuss in Chapter 7. While voluntourists and other, often white, 'do-gooders' have been pervasively criticised, this has in practice had the effect of downplaying or ignoring the work of Cambodians and non-white foreigners altogether.

Everyday humanitarianism is by no means the preserve of individuals from the Global North, or others who are foreign to Cambodia. Instead, the everyday humanitarianism discussed here is carried out by a diverse group of people, often acting in collaboration. They include native Cambodians and, to a lesser extent, those who left the country during the civil war and later returned. A substantial group of humanitarians originate from neighbouring and more affluent countries such as Singapore, Malaysia, Japan and South Korea, who scarcely get a mention in the relevant literature. They constitute a hugely important, but largely overlooked segment. Others arrive from North American and European countries, as well as Australia. Their humanitarian practices often emerge as a result of very partial understandings and knowledges of the other, and do not neatly fall into categories of either 'local' or 'global', but often emerge in interaction, or contestation, of these. Their diversity is defined not only in terms of nationality and ethnicity, even though there are clearly patterns.

While my research suggests that people at various life stages are active humanitarians, there are also, perhaps unsurprisingly, certain patterns. There are younger people, college and university graduates, who often begin as volunteers and then become attached to projects or set up their own. Some of the foreign ones hand over operations to their Cambodian partners and gradually reduce involvement as they return home for work or family reasons. There are also those who, mid-career in a higher-income country, visit Cambodia as tourists and decide to return, leave their jobs, and become involved in supporting others. While families with younger children are relatively rare, Cambodians in mid-life, supporting not just family members but also others in their neighbourhood or village, are common. A sizeable group are those from the Global North who have retired, but are keen to find renewed purpose in life.

This book focuses less on the impact on 'beneficiaries', who are conventionally defined as the 'targets' of the humanitarian interventions. One reason for not foregrounding recipients' perspectives is that this research aims to understand the practice of everyday humanitarianism in the first place. An important next stage will be an analysis of recipients' experiences of these kinds of grassroots interventions. Rather than focusing on beneficiaries as traditionally understood, I propose much more diverse notions of who donors, supporters, founders and 'beneficiaries' are in the first place. As the book makes clear, in many cases, everyday humanitarians have themselves been previous recipients of aid, while others are keen to 'pay it forward'. Who is a recipient, and who benefits, is thus an important question which the book poses. It complicates simplistic divisions of 'humanitarians' and 'recipients', as people can be and have been both. As I document throughout the following chapters, Cambodians are not confined to roles as gatekeepers or brokers. Some start as 'beneficiaries', then move on to become founders, brokers or donors themselves. Others have never been beneficiaries, but are strongly motivated to support others due to their own experiences of deprivation. Some are visionary founder figures, drawing on transnational networks of supporters to realise their ambitions. Chapter 7 explores these issues in more depth. Given such diversity of humanitarians, a question is where they locate themselves in relation to the established aid sector. One way of exploring this is through looking at the trajectories, particularly of foreign aid workers who have transitioned from institutionalised aid to everyday humanitarianism.

Locating everyday humanitarianism

In order to understand how everyday humanitarianism is situated in the wider aid sector, we can trace how those involved understand their positionality and motivation. Their perspectives cover a wide range, from close involvement to conscious distancing, to an apparent lack of interest in the aid sector altogether. At one end of the spectrum were those whose views of aid are cautiously critical, but who were at the same time full-time staff members of aid agencies. Arising from their long-term experience, some found that the shortcomings of their everyday work, often office-based, are alleviated through engaging in private aid initiatives. At the same time, these two kinds of engagements need not be mutually exclusive. Rather, both their professional and private commitments to aid can be understood as serving their overall imperative to support others, albeit in different modalities, and with different kinds of personal involvement and reward (Fechter 2018).

Some of these aid workers grow increasingly discontent with their paid work and commit themselves to their private aid projects on a full-time basis. This was the case, for example, for Moritz, a video producer by training. He set up a small vocational training project with a Cambodian friend and collaborator, alongside his paid work for an aid agency. As the project slowly grew, it demanded more of their time, while he also felt it was a more effective and rewarding way of investing his efforts. Consequently, he decided to leave his paid job and dedicated himself to their project full-time. He undertook occasional consultancies in order to retain an income, while his wife maintained her salaried job. Other, similar trajectories to Moritz's include those who previously held a job with an established organisation and, having become frustrated with their ways of working, set up their own projects. Charlotte for example, a UK-trained artist in her forties, had been employed by a large international NGO in Phnom Penh for several years. As the aid sector in Cambodia grew, she found that,

NGOs became more businesslike … you could have a career with it, and it all turned into a circus. I didn't like their attitude towards Cambodians … people came here to develop their CVs. They pity the Cambodians, the staff don't listen, and then things go wrong. I realised that the NGOs have such a neoliberal structure, the ways that they are organised, if you have ideas outside of that, then that's not wanted.

Instead, Charlotte found that those who came with a long-term commitment to a place, such as post-conflict Cambodia, had a substantially different attitude than 'career-minded' development workers. She recounted her experience:

I worked in the refugee camps in 1992. I think there is a big difference with people who have humanitarian ideas, a cause, or a faith, or who go into development as a career. At that time, there was still a civil war going on. In 1997, lots of foreigners left the country. You had to want to stay here. When it was more stable, more people came in with well-paid jobs.

In contrast, Charlotte set up a small-scale handicraft project, training women from disadvantaged backgrounds, and living in rural areas, to produce locally inspired handicrafts, in order to sell to overseas tourists. Charlotte also acted an informal broker, being approached by acquaintances and visitors for information on worthy causes to give small sums of money to, which she happily provided.

People like Moritz and Charlotte made a journey away from the established aid sector, towards private initiatives on the margins of it. Others arrive at citizen aid from successful careers in the corporate sector. One was Laura, an American in her early thirties, who left a career with a logistics firm, evidently on the spur of the moment, in order to start her own aid project. As such, Laura might arguably fall into the category of 'accidental aidworker' as described by Pollet et al. (2014). Their spirit is captured well in Charlotte's description, who had witnessed many of them in Cambodia: *'there are some people who come with benevolence – they have no aid or development background – they have seen something and think, I can do this. It's an emotional experience, they just happened to be there.'*

One might query to what extent such trajectories are at all accidental. In many cases, the person concerned talks about 'stumbling into it' or 'being drawn in' and finding themselves returning to a particular cause or community even if they had meant to leave them behind. In Laura's case, this meant that she left behind a successful and well-paid corporate job, without having had previous exposure to development agencies. This aspect of her trajectory is fairly common among those doing everyday humanitarianism. Having come to development from the outside, she was not an ardent critic or conscious dissident. She declared with a shrug, '*I would see myself as part of development, sure*' – on the basis that she was engaged in a similar kind of service delivery. She was disappointed by the lack collaboration with formal development actors, and how they were reluctant, in her words, to '*share down*':

> *once they* [a UN agency] *had a big campaign here about de-worming, they were handing out thousands of tablets. So I got in touch asking, can we have 200 please for our kids, that would be great ... and we heard nothing from them, absolutely nothing. They never even acknowledged the email. So the big guys, they don't share down, they don't even communicate with us. We could be their arm on the ground. But they ignore us.*

Everyday humanitarian initiatives do not primarily consist of people who keep their distance from the established sector because of their dissatisfaction with their ways of operating. Many of the foreign founders I spoke to did not have strong views on the established aid sector, negative or otherwise. Their attitudes most closely resonate with the 'do-it-yourself' paradigm put forward by Kristof (2010). They were not necessarily interested in deep reflection on existing development practices. Instead, their attention was almost exclusively focused on their own projects, the people they were supporting, and their donors, local and overseas. Such apparent lack of interest in professional development means that everyday humanitarianism cannot necessarily be understood as a set of consciously alternative practices. Rather, the diversity of actors and trajectories provides a more complex picture. It includes disenchanted current and former employees at large agencies who shift, more or less deliberately, towards less formal aid initiatives; those who arrive at aid from careers in other sectors and intentionally remain on the margins of what they see at the aid establishment; and those who are unconcerned with 'professional' aid, focusing instead on what they consider their private initiative. In their own understanding, they occupy positions vis-à-vis formal development which are, in turn, cautious, critical or uninterested, but at any account removed and distinct from established organisations. Since what they do, however, can arguably be considered 'aid' or 'development' in a broader sense, I refer to them as 'everyday humanitarians', occupying perhaps a marginal niche in the overall aid ecosystem, but being part of it nevertheless for the purposes of our understandings of aid more broadly.

Cambodia, kingdom of charity?

The insights arising from Cambodia resonate in other places across the world. And yet sites of everyday humanitarianism do not spring up at random. Particular circumstances enable these practices to thrive. At the outset there is human need that is not addressed, whether by humanitarian agencies or relevant government authorities. In the case of the informal refugee camps in Calais, France, following the surge of migrants fleeing conflict in the Middle East, or the maritime rescue of migrants in the Mediterranean, this may be the result of political decisions rather than practical limitations or oversights (Rygiel 2011; Anderson 2014). In addition to such need, and a lack of service provision by established actors or agencies, there are alternative providers – in this case, Cambodians and foreign everyday humanitarians. It is boosted by the relatively loose oversight of visitors to the country, and their ability to set up their own projects, unfettered by inordinate institutional control or bureaucracy. This holds especially while they remain under the government's radar, operating unobtrusively and in accordance with local authorities. It is therefore no coincidence that forms of everyday humanitarianism are particularly prominent in Cambodia. Indeed, there are structural conditions which make it more likely for such projects to be sustainable.

Two sets of circumstances make it more likely for such practices to take place. The first is the demand for such interventions; and the second is that implementation is enabled by a relative lack of bureaucracy and regulatory oversight. Both have occurred since the turn of the twenty-first centurys in Cambodia. Having emerged in the 1990s from a prolonged period of genocide and civil war from 1975 onwards (Kiernan 2002; Hinton 2005), Cambodia is among the 'least developed countries' (UNCTAD 2020). After

UN-administered elections in 1993, and the establishment of a democratic government, the country began receiving substantial amounts of overseas foreign aid, to the extent that Ear identified it as substantially dependent on overseas aid (Ear 2013; Springer 2015). This sets it apart from some of the more affluent countries in the region, such as Thailand and Vietnam, though it shares its relative poverty status with Lao PDR. Having received substantial amounts of overseas aid since the end of the civil war in the late 1990s, as well as a steadily increasing stream of tourists, both institutionalised forms of development, as well as everyday humanitarianisms have been flourishing there.

While economic growth has accelerated, levels of inequality have, too. It combines high levels of precarity, a low level of state provision of services such as education and healthcare, with a relatively unregulated third-sector environment. These circumstances have allowed Cambodians and foreign nationals to set up aid projects and small NGOs, often without much interference or oversight from government authorities. While such civil society space has been shrinking, for the past two decades Cambodia has proved a fertile ground for such privately funded aid initiatives, both because of the need for them, and the relative ease of establishing such projects. This sets Cambodia apart from its more tightly regulated neighbouring states such as Vietnam, Lao PDR or even China, and partly explains the high prevalence of such initiatives there.

When I began research on international aid workers (Fechter 2011) I came across a poster in the office of one of the NGOs that had sprung up all over the capital, Phnom Penh. It showed a map of the distribution of NGOs in different parts of the country, declaring it the 'Kingdom of NGO', a play on the country's official name of 'Kingdom of Cambodia'. This signalled that the country's population was in need of assistance, but also that the government did not put strict limits on the setting up of such organisations. This changed with the introduction of a controversial law in 2018 (Curley 2018). For over two decades, the growth of local, national and international NGOs, as well as the presence of bi-and multilateral agencies in Cambodia has been substantial. In addition, it remains relatively easy for non-Cambodians to enter the country on a tourist or business visa, which enables frequent travel in and out of the country without much formal scrutiny. These conditions, the relative lack of government regulation of the NGO sector, as well as the possibility of short and mid-term residence in the country for foreigners, constitute the conditions for many people, Cambodians as well as foreigners, to set up and run their own projects. Such relative room for manoeuvre sets the situation in Cambodia apart from to its neighbouring countries such as Vietnam, which retains a much stronger oversight of its third sector. In short, Cambodia's relative poverty, loose regulation of the NGOs sector, and ease of travel to the country, created conditions where demand for, and possibility of, everyday aid interventions coalesced for forms of everyday humanitarianism to thrive.

As a recipient of high levels of overseas aid, Cambodia was the workplace of numerous international aid workers and consultants (Fechter 2018). In addition, steadily increasing streams of tourists from Asia-Pacific, Europe and North America, have provided a reliable source of income for many aid initiatives and projects, through their involvement in tour guiding, hospitality or educational opportunities. In the context of Cambodian towns that draw significant numbers of foreign visitors, foreign and Cambodian brokers engage tourists in order to forge sets of transnational connections. These enable the flow of money, goods, stories, and even further visits and ongoing commitments. Partly sustained by the tourist presence in town, private aid initiatives are successfully making use of such connections in order to channel resources towards the local people they are supporting. In addition, amenities that draw tourists also make it easier to be a foreign everyday humanitarian. These include affordable and comfortable accommodation, good travel and internet connections, and small but thriving networks of like-minded residents.

This also raises the question in what ways, if at all, is everyday humanitarianism distinct from forms of local charity? Whether inspired by Buddhism or otherwise, local charity and philanthropy, diaspora giving and acts of supporting others have long traditions in Cambodian society, albeit perhaps being more contested through the disruption during the civil war (Zucker 2013). Notions of local charity and solidarity may be contested in relation to Cambodia, such as the claim that 'every household is an island' and solidarity practices have not existed there for a long time (Trankell, Ovesen and Ojendal 1996). Nevertheless, local notions of virtue and gift-giving, and Cambodians helping others are not dependent on, or need to be mediated by foreigners (Kent and Chandler 2008; Guillou and Vignato 2013). In the context of a country where support for the poorer populations is to such an extent shaped by overseas, outside agencies, as well as national and international NGOs, and the formal aid sector, I consider some of these expressions of local charity as forms of 'everyday humanitarianism', simply because they belong to a set of practices which is informal, and exists at the margins or outside of the formal and institutional aid sector.

Approaching research

My own approach to development was that of an outsider. I was initially fascinated by international aid workers as mobile professionals; as migrants with a mission to facilitate social change. Studying 'professional' aid workers first, and then everyday humanitarians, was underpinned by a perspective on development as a social field that offered a window on how people thought about responsibility for others; their interest in social relations, and how they conceptualised and initiated social change. Everyday humanitarianism provides an opportunity for exploring this. On a personal level, I have been quizzed, usually by students of development, how I feel about aid. Can it be done ethically? What is the right way of going about it? Is everyday humanitarianism a solution, or is it doing more harm than good?

My own forays into the world of aid began with a stint of volunteering with a local NGO in Ghana. There, I had a memorable encounter with Helmut, a German development worker who had been tasked with running a carpentry apprentice scheme for local youth. That morning, he had found his tool shed broken into and valuable materials gone. With a sigh he explained to us, a group of volunteers, how the young trainees kept squatting on top of the workbenches, rather than standing next to them as instructed. Some of the European women volunteers in my group appeared to be just as keen on romantic encounters as digging holes for the school latrine. All this fostered a sound scepticism about what 'development' was and how it was trying to achieve its aims, who was involved and what their interests were. At the same time, I was continually impressed by some Ghanaians and long-time foreign residents who ran projects, by their commitment and their dogged insistence that change was possible. Nevertheless, Helmut's disappointment concerning the stolen tools and his despair about the squatting trainees stayed with me. It left me with the question of how people dealt with what I saw as the fundamental futility of their efforts. What difference did they make? And how did they keep going? These issues, arising from these singular moments, but leading to broader questions about how people envisage and implement change, animate this book.

Researching everyday humanitarians can be seductive. They often radiate optimism. They tell you they are working with wonderful people; that they have learnt so much; they love what they are doing. They feel that fate is on their side, offering chance encounters which lead to wonderful things. This is often less gushing and more tempered among Cambodians, but they also talk about how their lives have changed; how they met good people; what they achieved together with others. Foreigners, especially, felt that doing good can be 'infectious', that it spreads and multiplies. As a researcher, this is refreshing, not just after working with privileged but often jaded foreigners who did not necessarily want to live abroad. It also marks a departure from 'professional' aid workers who may struggle with motivation or purpose in their jobs but have not necessarily found answers. Becoming hooked on these narratives is problematic not just for analysis. I was wary of being washed away by their optimism. But giving their efforts a good look-in, trying to withhold judgement and keeping an open mind, with some sympathy for local and foreign outsider efforts who were located on the margins of the established aid system, seemed a reasonable approach.

The ethnographic material I draw on here is based on a research project investigating alternative actors in aid.[1] Its objective was to engage with a range of individuals and their networks who operate at the margins of the established aid sector, with the aim of supporting Cambodians who they perceive to be in need. These individuals include foreign nationals as well as Cambodians, and range in age from their mid-twenties to late sixties. Their countries of origin comprised North America, Australian and European countries, as well as Japan, Malaysia and Singapore. Research participants were actively involved in citizen aid, including local and foreign project founders, local partners, overseas supporters and recipients. All names and some personal details have been changed in order to maintain confidentiality and anonymity. The material was gathered in a series of field trips, with the bulk being gathered during a series of fieldwork trips between 2013 and 2015. Follow-up visits were made to gather more longitudinal data in 2018 and 2019.

The research took place in Cambodia across a range of sites including the capital city, Phnom Penh, and a provincial town. Methods included participant observation; interviews and conversations with founders and supporters, staff, volunteers and visitors. Participants included Cambodian founders and partners in these projects, but only to a limited extent those who receive such aid. All names are pseudonyms, and in some cases, I have altered personal details and identifiers to preserve anonymity as far as possible. The long-term, if intermittent, nature of the research made it possible to follow individuals and projects over the span of several years. I was able to trace the trajectories of projects from their inception and how they developed; decisions to stay small or to grow; charting relationships, some of which had broken down and others which were going strong many years later.

Many of these humanitarian projects were run as partnerships, with Cambodians and foreigners worked together. While some projects were set up by foreigners, others by Cambodians, most intensely relied on collaboration between both of them. Some of the foreign founders resided in Cambodia on a long-term basis, others stayed there for periods ranging between a few weeks and months per year. Their income sources varied, with some being financially self-sufficient, at least for a time, for example after having taken early retirement from a job in the global North. Others were earning money through occasional consultancies, or a part-time work, especially in the case of Cambodian nationals. Fieldwork was carried out initially in Phnom Penh, and most of it in a provincial town with a considerable tourism sector. In addition to informal interviews, methods included conversations and participant observation at project sites, attending fundraising and networking events, as well as drawing on content and debates as they appeared on people's social media sites. This study is distributed across different locations, and draws on work with more than thirty private aid projects, their founders, supporters and communities in which they worked.

The question what constitutes everyday humanitarianism extends to what projects count as 'small' in size. On one side of the spectrum there are minute gestures, such as people giving a friend travelling to Cambodia ten or twenty dollars, asking them to put it to good use, or for a specific project that they knew of. On the other side of the spectrum, there are projects which I have followed over a period of several years, witnessing their growth.

Starting sometimes in people's living rooms, or through handing out food to street children, they developed into small NGOs, progressively expanding to several sites in Cambodia, and even across national borders to Thailand or Laos. While some prefer not to formalise their projects, others choose to do so as it facilitates private donations, specifically with regard to tax relief. Such incorporation is not considered important in order to achieve recognition by the Cambodian authorities, as some anyhow find it easier to operate, in their words, 'under the radar'. Meanwhile, for others it becomes necessary to enable their interactions with local government authorities.

Regarding the quality and longevity of work between initiatives that incorporate and those that do not, no straightforward correlations were evident. Rather, the sustained commitment of the founders, whether locally present or not, was key, independent of the formal status their projects had. Where on this spectrum everyday humanitarian practices are positioned, and by what measure they are too large or institutionalised to count as 'everyday', remains debatable. Drawing on Lewis's notion of the NGO as an 'unstable category' (Lewis and Schuller 2017) means that their registered status and size is not the only feature that defines it an aid initiative. Furthermore, its shape may vary considerably over time, expanding, shrinking or even ceasing to exist (Fechter and Schwittay 2019). For this book, I captured initiatives at a particular stage in their trajectory. Some remained in a steady state; others grew, while yet others were struggling to survive. These questions, namely whether to stay small or 'scale up' and how this matters, are among those at the heart of the book.

Overview of the book

Constituting the first half of this book, Chapters 2, 3 and 4 focus on themes which are central for many aid practitioners, but are particularly pronounced for everyday humanitarians. These include the problem of partial-ness, that is, how people conceive of their own limited efforts in relation the size and scope of the challenge they are facing. The insistence that 'every person counts', and how people adopt and make sense of such focus on the individual, underpins many such initiatives. This is followed by practitioners' constant movement between geographical distance and proximity to people in need in determining when, if and how to intervene.

Chapter 2, 'The part and the whole', tackles 'the problem of the singular' (Ticktin 2015). While aimed at the entirety of suffering humanity, its efforts, whether carried out by large organisations or lone individuals, can only ever have a partial reach. The situation of everyday humanitarians in Cambodia is no exception to this predicament. This chapter traces their often acute awareness of the bigger picture, such as the socio-political landscape of Cambodia, and how they feel positioned and act within this. Some arrive at what they are doing after having become disenchanted during careers in large aid organisations. Others have had less linear trajectories, but are ambitious for the future of their projects, such as bringing their activities to a larger group of beneficiaries. For either process, the making of scales is crucial: their insistence that 'small is beautiful' provides an ongoing source of inspiration and assurance for some, and their actions become meaningful within this particular scale. Others are clear that their attention remains fixed not on a whole nation but on members of a particular community, such as training a group of single mothers, to help improve their livelihoods. A key practice to making and sustaining everyday humanitarianism is the adoption of temporal, spatial or numerical scales which best express their priorities, manifest in the popular mantra, 'changing the world, one village at a time'. This does not imply ignorance or neglect of other forces that shape the lives of their beneficiaries, and often affect them adversely, but means articulating their position within this context.

Chapter 3, 'Every person counts', picks up on a slogan which was displayed, among other places, in a cafe run by a small NGO, dedicated to people with disabilities. Such emphatic commitment to the value of the single person is not unique to this constituency. The belief that 'every person counts', or the 'logic of the one' (Malkki 2015), drives many of the initiatives at the heart of this book. This insistent focus on the individual, and on improving the lives of small groups of beneficiaries, often shape their activities. What makes their work meaningful to them is creating a visible difference in the life of a particular person, while accommodating the challenge of their limited efficacy in the context of widespread poverty. This matters not least because a focus on the small scale runs counter to much development policy that favours 'scaling up', relying on large-scale approaches rather than localised interventions.

Everyday humanitarians accommodate the partial-ness of their endeavours through deploying a particular scale of the single individual. The practices carried out under this logic contain singular acts of care, as well as lives being transformed. This may consist of distributing weekly hot meals to those at the margins of society; helping a handful of young people pass their high school exams and make their way into further education, or setting up a cafe to provide training and employment for people living with disabilities. Importantly, other scales are brought into play, such as a person 'paying it forward' by supporting others in turn, and effecting change in wider society. Rather than leaping from a scale of 'the one' to 'the many', humanitarian practitioners continuously interlink these. As a result, what appears as a limited, 'mere' act, offers pathways into the future.

Chapter 4, 'Proximity and distance', addresses the notion of humanitarianism as predicated on distance, that is, geographical scale. This is prominently embodied in the figure of the distant stranger, a trope ubiquitous and simplistic in equal measure. In this context, what role does distance play for people's desire to intervene in the lives of others? What compels people to support those nearby, regional neighbours, or across nation states and continents? The chapter illustrates how people create and respond to distance, how this shapes their personal and professional trajectories, and interventions in the lives of others. This matters not least because the notion of distance, physical and social, looms large in how philosophers and ordinary people construct responsibilities towards others. An advertisement for the US Peace Corps, for example, confidently declared that 'the difference between a career and a purpose is about 8,000 miles', asserting that service is most meaningful undertaken far away from home.

Unravelling these tropes, everyday humanitarian practice shows how distance is not fixed, but dynamic and flexible. Those who intervene outside their own country are attracted to help in faraway places not least by a desire for travel and adventure. When faced with street children or begging veterans on a daily basis, some find they need to keep poverty at bay. They move between immersing themselves, and withdrawing when it becomes overwhelming. Embedding themselves in local communities of need or retreating, sometimes for good, to more comfortable surroundings, requires constant negotiation and raises moral quandaries. As practitioners are using sliding scales, humanitarian distance emerges not as fixed, but segmented into mobile, interlocking and dynamic scales, which they adopt as it suits their situation.

Chapter 5, 'Desire to connect', revolves around the purpose of humanitarian aid defined by the desire to help. This chapter argues that it leaves a key motivation out of sight: how aid is animated by its twin desire to connect. The chapter explores what everyday humanitarians mean by 'making a connection'. This can include experiential, face-to-face contact with those they support, such as bringing food or teaching supplies to schools. It can mean direct experience of aid activities and their tangible efficacy. Establishing personal relationships across national, ethnic and cultural differences, while potentially challenging, is a key motivation for those involved. These connections are often sought with people in need who are separated by geographical distance, and may be considered 'other' in some ways from everyday humanitarians themselves. The 'impulse of philanthropy' (Bornstein 2009), is here conjoined with a parallel, anthropological impulse to know and connect with an Other.

The importance of relationships for institutionalised aid, and the shaping and implementation of policy has, at least partly, been recognised. More than social relations being merely instrumental to successful aid practice, the chapter suggests that providing assistance to others can be a vehicle that facilitates the making of these desired relations. Rather than assisting distant strangers, forging these connections means making relationships personal. This can lead to long-term connections between individuals, regular visits and contact in the case of overseas supporters. Acknowledging the desire to connect unsettles notions of the 'distant stranger' as the archetypical humanitarian object, highlighting the wish for familiarity and closeness being just as important for motivating assistance to others. This offers a surprising insight: a core target for everyday humanitarianism, contrary to popular assumptions, a driver is the support for people who are familiar, or with whom we create relationships.

Chapter 6, 'Humanitarian kinship', argues that while geographical distance is not central for driving humanitarianism, as documented in Chapter 4, neither is the strange and socially distant other discussed in Chapter 5. Rather, this chapter argues that a vast amount of private financial assistance across the globe flows along kinship networks. While remittances from migrant workers to their families are a well-documented example, the allocation of overseas aid, via taxpayers or private donors, is not meant to be bound by kinship ties, given the aspiration of impartiality underpinning institutionalised humanitarianism. In practice, the chapter shows that everyday humanitarians do precisely this: crafting kin relations with the people they support. Indeed, such partial relations are in many ways central to their way of operating. This is because kinship, other that friendship, does not demand or imply equality. For professional aid workers who feel alienated by aid bureaucracy, 'adopting' a young person allows them to be embedded locally in a way difficult to achieve otherwise.

For everyday humanitarians, both Cambodians and foreigners, making others into kin creates social relations which entail responsibilities. They allow for inequality to be accommodated, while calling for the provision of assistance. This can take the form of sponsoring an adopted son or daughter through school; supporting a Cambodian family that they have become part of; or perceiving a group of children at an after-school club as one's children or family. Such humanitarian kinship matters because it runs counter to the principle of impartiality. On the contrary, what motivates humanitarian support, on this evidence, is the creation of partiality through kinship ties. Rather than presenting an obstacle, being partial provides a rationale for whom to support, thus solving the problem of resource allocation posed by the limited-ness of their efforts. In addition to connecting with an Other and making humanitarian kin, the final chapter reveals the importance of similarities and shared biographical ties.

Chapter 7, 'Affinities and shared biographies', argues that not all support relations take the form of kin. In motivating assistance, a key driver concerns affinity ties (Ho 2017). These ties are commonalities between those offering support and those to whom it is aimed. Recognising the role of such affinities challenges the trope of the 'white saviour' (Cole 2012), which reiterates the importance of interventions by the actors of the Global North, while making others invisible. While its critique resonates in the aid community, this chapter argues that a wide range of people navigate difference and affinity on multiple grounds, to justify interventions. It nuances the the 'white saviour' narrative in so far as it makes visible the wealth of aid relations that derive from affinity ties, based on similarity and shared biographies. Such commonalities can include shared experiences of hunger or deprivation while growing up, or experiences of abandonment, displacement, illness or bereavement. It surfaces in notions of shared 'Asian-ness' and historical trajectories shared by everyday humanitarians from other Asian countries.

This chapter shows that even as founders or supporters from the Global North are foregrounded on the websites and social media of their aid projects, this often serves the purposes of fundraising and networking with potential donors. Such prominence is furthered by their memoirs, feeding into a 'white saviour' narrative, but obscures the often fundamentally cooperative nature of such initiatives. In fact, everyday humanitarian ventures often rely on close collaborations between Cambodians and foreigners from other parts of Asia, Australia, Europe and North America, and are by no means the prerogative of those from the Global North. Documenting Cambodians' and foreigners' perspectives and interactions, the chapter argues that the figure of the 'white saviour' should not only be critiqued, but the mechanisms through which it is continuously reinvigorated needs to be made visible. This makes it possible to appreciate the complexity of interactions at stake, and understand who is offering support to whom, how and with what consequences.

The conclusion highlights the significance of everyday humanitarianism in a broader context. People who seek to instigate social change, are inevitably challenged to consider their own, limited actions with what they regard as the wider context or causes. I suggest that beyond a reflexive understanding, a scalar approach can provide a blueprint for action. Making and operating within a set of interlinking scales, consciously or not, can offset doubts about lacking significance. It provides a sense of how one's own actions matter in a wider world, and those of others. Challenging scales and the values associated with them, has wider applicability. People seeking social change consider how their own, limited actions link with wider issues including social injustice, environmentalism or the climate crisis.

Note

1 The research was carried out as part of a project on 'Alternative Actors in Aid', funded by the Leverhulme Trust (RF-2013-535), whose assistance is gratefully acknowledged.

1

Making scales and relations

Accounts of humanitarianism, including its critiques, have long been preoccupied with its established, institutional forms, driven by governments and multilateral organisations (Barnett 2011; Bornstein and Redfield 2011). Such emphasis often equates the large-scale with the significant. This book argues that engaging with humanitarianism's informal manifestations disrupts this equation. Drawing on ethnographic research with everyday humanitarian practitioners in Cambodia who run their own, privately funded aid projects, the book demonstrates how they make their own scales with regard to size, space and social relations, unsettling associations of importance with the 'large-scale'. They offer radically different understandings of what actions are meaningful, and who counts.

Such a perspective casts core tenets of humanitarianism, and of social change more generally, in a different light. It suggests that everyday humanitarians operate with multiple, interlinking scales of their own making. Rather than being dismissed as 'small-scale', they demonstrate how they render people and causes meaningful, regardless of numbers or size. They reject the much-vaunted centrality of distance for the constitution of humanitarianism, revealing a more nuanced interplay of proximity and distance to those in need. Unsettling the valorisation of the large-scale or far-away extends to social relations. The distant stranger as the archetypal object of humanitarianism is replaced by a desire to get to know an Other through the act of assistance. Idioms of kinship are being drawn on to orient support. In de-centring the trope of the 'white saviour', everyday humanitarianism is characterised by a multiplicity of affinity ties between actors from the Global North and South, which direct and motivate humanitarian action.

Scholars of humanitarianism tend to focus on its institutionalised forms (Barnett and Weiss 2008; Fassin 2012). Adopting a scalar approach challenges its narratives, central among them being distance to defining humanitarian action, and the prominence of the 'stranger' and the 'white saviour' which are often part of these narratives. Bringing a scale-making approach to social relations in humanitarianism demonstrates that interventions are not necessarily motivated by those who are geographically and socially distant (Boltanski 1999; Chouliaraki and Orgad 2011). Rather, humanitarian distance is being modulated to suit people's purposes, making strangers familiar through the act of supporting them. Being partial is, in fact, fundamental to their way of operating. It means providing support not to those most deserving according to abstract principles, but to those with whom one has a connection. Such connection can take the form of crafted kin relations, or affinity ties (Ho 2017). Being partial, rather than an obstacle and deviation from humanitarian norms, emerges as a driver for action.

Recognising humanitarian forms beyond the institutionalised ones also makes it possible to dislodge assumptions and critiques which have become associated with the latter. Key among those is Fassin's preoccupation with the 'saving of an individual life' which, he argues, has become the 'definitive humanitarian gesture' (Robbins 2019). This is problematic as, in his view, the focus on saving a single life distracts from the more urgent question of justice. Rather than pursuing an 'ethics of rescue', more important is a 'structural politics that aims at the transformation of collective life' (Robbins 2019). In short, if humanitarianism – or the particular version which Fassin's work is grounded in – culminates in the 'single rescue', this disconnects if from the struggle for structural change. Nothing less is required to address the conditions of 'planetary inequality' (Fassin 2018) which lie at the root of the problems, and which the 'single rescue' can never fully address. As Robbins explains, 'these conditions remain linked to a set of planetary problems that require planetary solutions. Humanitarianism, which has largely claimed this scale as its own, must be supplanted, or at least inflected, by politics' (2019).

One objective of this book is to understand the efficacy of the conviction that a single life matters. This does not mean that everyday humanitarianism is devoid of what Fassin calls 'politics', or struggles for structural change. On the contrary, while the idea that 'every person counts' is a strong model for everyday humanitarians, the following chapters illustrate how practices and imaginations focused on identifiable people are being connected to the larger issues, which are at the root of their inequality, through a process of making and interlinking scales. Rendering humanitarianism, especially a particularly narrow version of it, as antithetical to politics is a mistake. The case of everyday humanitarianism documents how single gestures of rescue and structural change are not separate, but how people connect one to the other, both in practice and in their imaginations which drive their actions. Chapter 2 documents this in more detail.

Indeed, other research has shown much the same. It has been recognised that there is no particular version of humanitarianism which is subversive as such, but that many forms have the potential to undermine governmentality, rather than being complicit in it. They illustrate how humanitarianism is not disconnected from politics, but – especially in its grassroots and everyday forms – has solidarian or transgressive dimensions which challenge existing regimes of governmentality. This goes against the grain of the 'humanitarian reason' which has so often been foregrounded (Fassin 2012). Such a narrative has profoundly constrained wider perspectives of what constitutes humanitarianism, and how it relates to governmentality and politics respectively. There is now a substantial body of research, mainly on pro-migrant activities in the European context, which details persuasively how everyday humanitarians resist incorporation into institutional humanitarian regimes. They skilfully, even in small acts, carve out spaces for activism and solidarity in their efforts (Vandevoordt 2019, 2021; Vandevoordt and Fleischmann 2019; Vandevoordt and Verschragen 2019: Fleischmann 2020). Recent work on care and activism (Jupp 2022; Altman 2022) demonstrates how seemingly 'domestic' care activities contain political efficacy. A broader argument here is not about particular kinds of humanitarianism and their efficacy in tackling structural inequality, but a broader question about how apparently 'small acts' hang together with larger, structural problems. The case of small environmental gestures, and the required 'system change', is just one such example.

Another rendering of this 'single humanitarian gesture' and its limited reach is the notion of the 'Mere' (Malkki 2015). In a nutshell, it contains the question of how ostensibly small-scale activities matter within their broader context. Studies of such 'vernacular humanitarianisms' (Brkovic 2019) and their proponents face the challenge of how to attribute meaning to activities that are characterised by their fundamentally partial reach. This book argues that framing this limited reach as 'Mere' equates the 'small', domestic and private with insignificance. Instead, the book argues that making their own scales is how everyday humanitarians render the notion of the 'Mere' as misguided. Using and interlinking multiple scales and associated values is a way of dealing with the partial-ness of all social change and sustains their practice.

The philosophical and anthropological construction of moral responsibility for others which is at stake here, is intertwined with social relationships – how they are being envisaged, and how they are considered to matter (see Trnka and Trundle 2017). Taking a radically rationalist perspective, the philosopher Peter Singer proposed that the scale of their relatedness should be immaterial to people's responsibility towards others (Singer 1972). In going beyond what has become a philosophical impasse, and considering what people actually do, a more complicated picture emerges. Through the study of everyday humanitarians, this book furnishes long-standing philosophical debates about responsibilities to others with empirical substance.

In place of an impasse of abstract imperatives of what humans should be doing, and whom they should be helping, we learn that people find innovative ways of dealing with the overwhelming nature of their tasks, as well as drawing on social relationship to decide who to support, and why.

Among all humans who may need support, the question driving this book is who to extend help to, and why. Perhaps curiously, scholars of development and humanitarians studies, with some exceptions, have not dwelt on these questions extensively or explicitly. This is partly because humanitarian studies continue to espouse its formally adopted principles. Notable among these are 'humanity' – the imperative to serve all those who are suffering; and 'impartiality': that is, not to favour certain populations over others, and act on the basis of their needs alone. In practice, these principles remain unattainable, no matter how comparatively large, well-funded or comprehensive in scope such operations are. A further reason is that humanitarian studies tend to be concerned with interventions on the level of institutions, eschewing personal quandaries when it comes to interventions. More recently, however, there has been a distinct broadening out from established histories, actors and practices of humanitarianism. Indeed, in the wake of more diverse forms of humanitarianism becoming visible, one might now speak of humanitarianisms in the plural.

This is not equivalent to a new set of actors thrown into the mix of existing ones, such as philanthrocapitalists, the military or new state donors (Sezgin and Dijkzeul 2016). More significantly, it involves a different way of looking at both humanitarianism and development, and recognising a multitude of ways in which people support others. These practices I here refer to as 'everyday humanitarianism'. A closer, more systematic account of these forms yields analytical dividends, such as understanding how partial-ness is managed via making scales; and that partiality is a driver, not an obstacle. I suggest that the study of everyday humanitarianism offers empirically grounded answers to questions of moral responsibility for others, in terms of dealing with the potentially enormous scope of the task, and the social relations that help deal with it. There are several reasons why the opportunity to answer these questions has arisen. Other forms of humanitarianism are now offering new theoretical perspectives on long-debated ethical questions. One is a growing awareness that the history of humanitarianism, as often recounted, was embedded in Northern-centric and Judaeo-Christian frameworks. This shift has been further accelerated by the recognition of Islamic traditions of humanitarianism (Benthall 2007; Barnett and Stein 2012; Mostowlansky 2020). These are not just changes in scholarly sensitivities. In the wake of a series of migration 'crises', in the Middle East and Europe, as well as at the US-Mexico border, there has been a well-documented rise in pro-migrant interventions by individuals, local communities, and civil society actors (Fleischmann and Steinhilper 2017; Rozakou 2017; Sandri 2017; Vogt 2018; Vandevoordt 2020; Yarris, Garcia-Millan and Schmidt-Murillo 2020). Local, mutual aid efforts have sprung up in the context of the COVID-19 pandemic (Springer 2020).

It is no coincidence that even though such 'demotic humanitarianism' has a long history (Taithe 2019), one of the most prominent manifestations both empirically and analytically, has emerged in regions of the Global North which have more recently turned into sites of humanitarian intervention. These are the sites of makeshift refugee camps on the Greek island of Lesvos; squats in the city centre of Athens; or near Calais in France. Prompted by their geographical proximity, ordinary citizens and residents, who often had no prior involvement in such activities, have found or placed themselves on the frontline of such aid scenarios. This was especially the case where intervention by state or multilateral agencies was insufficient or entirely absent thus creating a need, as well as a space, for such initiatives to take hold. This is taking place in the historical context of the rolling back of the state during neoliberalism, and the expectation that 'the big society' will step in. In parallel to such activities, there has also been a steady increase in everyday humanitarianism in its long-distance forms, as evidenced by the substantial rise in small registered charities which are active overseas beyond their national borders, including those based in the USA, Europe and elsewhere (Clifford 2016; Appe and Schnable 2019; Kinsbergen 2019; McKay and Perez 2019; Davis 2020). Other humanitarianisms are often characterised in counterdistinction to more conventional forms, such as multilateral organisations, international NGOs and state agencies, that is, formally organised, 'professionally' trained, and publicly funded humanitarian activities. In contrast, what unites research and data on 'other' humanitarianisms is a focus on their grassroots, amateur, vernacular, domestic and private manifestations.

In mapping this terrain, it is paramount to note that various denominations of humanitarian practice do not necessarily constitute separate categories of humanitarianisms. This holds even though the terminologies employed are slippery and may suggest such an approach. It is more productive and appropriate to think of these as traits and characteristics that pervade many practices, and provide lenses to better understand them. Rather than declaring a range of reified, distinct humanitarianisms, these are better understood as different ways of conceiving of and delivering support to others, which may be dispersed and cutting across a range of humanitarian practices.

To begin with, it is useful to consider the notion of the 'everyday' nature of humanitarian action. One might indeed argue that the work done by professional aid staff employed by organisations also has an everyday dimension: the routine of meetings, field trips, drafting reports and meeting stakeholders. This holds, however, for all human occupation, describing the routine, mundane, expected and minute aspects of carrying out one's tasks. The 'everyday' nature of the humanitarian action discussed here is more akin to the 'ordinary ethics' described by, for example,. Lambek (2010) and Stafford (2013). This refers to ethical decision-making which is embedded and implicit in ordinary, daily life, rather than to explicit or codified ethical beliefs and actions. Further, the notion of everyday invoked here refers to the often spontaneous inception of such humanitarian efforts. These tend to be not drawn up in strategy group meetings or derive from high-level policy imperatives. Instead, they often arise from spontaneous encounters, sometimes described as 'fate' or 'destiny' by those involved, even though one might argue that deeper needs and structures are driving them.

Finally, 'everyday' also captures the fact that while some of these initiatives are driven by people with professional training – say, nursing, teaching sign language, engineering or photography – they are not necessarily carried out as part of their main day-time work, although they may draw on relevant skills and capacities. Instead, especially at the beginning, they are often undertaken in people's spare time, and on the edges of their other life activities, though this can and does change over time as initiatives develop. While 'everyday' is a necessarily imprecise descriptor, it provides a useful starting point to identify other forms of humanitarianism which have long remained invisible in comparison to its dominant, Western-liberal, institutional manifestations. The following themes capture more of these analytical attempts.

Grassroots

While research on 'other' forms of humanitarianism has generated a range of theoretical concerns and insights, the problem of the scale of humanitarian efforts, and the social relations that underpin them, have mostly been addressed indirectly and obliquely. Considering some of these emerging debates, I render them more visible. The growing literature on 'other' humanitarianisms has to some extent defined itself in terms of what sets them apart from its institutionalised forms. Several themes are emerging in this vein, the first, notable one being a 'grassroots' practice. These are defined as bottom-up, responding-to-demand interventions. Their emergence is very much related to the absence of activities that should arguably have been carried out by state or institutional aid actors. One argument arising from research on those sites is that the absence of state and multilateral agencies has created spaces where interventions by ordinary people, and spontaneously set up organisations, are required and thriving (Rygiel 2011; Sandri 2017). The mobilisation and activism of volunteers who undertake these informal interventions challenge what Fassin and others have argued is an inherent governmentality of humanitarianism, the 'humanitarian reason' which 'governs precarious lives' (Fassin 2012:4; see also Feldman and Ticktin, 2010). In contrast, scholars of grassroots activities suggest that these have the potential to challenge the state or local municipalities in their handling – or control – of migrants and refugees, if only temporarily (Fleischmann and Steinhilper 2017; Vandevoordt 2019; Vandevoordt and Verschraegen 2019), giving room for what they call 'subversive humanitarianism'. This might include acts of civil disobedience, but also the creation of social spaces and personal bonds, which is mirrored in the centrality of relationships to everyday humanitarians.

Such grassroots pro-migrant activities, whether in Southern Europe (Cabot 2016; Rozakou 2016) or North America (Vogt 2018; Yarris, Garcia-Millan and Schmidt-Murillo 2020), are already confronted by the limited scope of their efforts in relation to the extent of demand. The way in which such limits are conceptualised mostly takes the form of their interfacing with state and multilateral agencies. If the pressure on their makeshift services can only bring temporary relief to migrants, how do such grassroots interventions interlink, or even collaborate with state agencies and thus harness their potentially wider reach? Their relationships are often characterised by tension, to the extent that migrant solidarity actions or maritime rescue operations are being criminalised (Fekete 2018), or that both volunteers and migrants in makeshift refugee camps are exposed to police violence (Doidge and Sandri 2018). While this raises the important prospect of humanitarianism being a subversive rather than an inevitably governmental practice, this does not address the problem of the limited reach of grassroots interventions as such, which is the main issue that I want to discuss.

Amateur

A second set of issues emerging from other humanitarianisms revolves around the distinction between 'professional' humanitarianism and development, and amateurs, volunteers or 'do-it-yourself' aid workers. These overlap with those raised by grassroots practices, but are concerned with the fact that many volunteer, 'amateur' humanitarians are not professionally trained in what they are doing, or do not act in a paid and formal capacity, even if they possess relevant training. These do-it-yourself humanitarians include the US college graduates originally giving name to the concept, who set up their own aid projects in countries of the Global South (Kristof 2010; McLennan 2017). Their evident lack of professionalism is also central to

Schnable's (2021) analysis of grassroots international NGOs, registered in the USA and active internationally. They are usually funded through social, communal or religious networks and have grown since the 2010s, partly enabled by affordable long-distance travel and communication. Schnable argues that these 'amateurs without borders' represent a new form of international interventions which tend to lack the training, organisational capacity and experience of larger-scale international NGOs.

Similar accounts of 'aid amateurs' or more charitably, citizen aid initiatives describe such projects and initiatives in the context of Europe, many of which are stage their activities in the Global South. For while the small initiatives documented by Schnable and Clifford are formally registered as charities, Schnable suggests that the way in which they operate sets them apart from professional, formalised non-profit organisations. A view of everyday humanitarians as amateurs points towards the lack of scope and reach of their activities, and with the quality of their implementation (Appe and Schnable 2019; Schnable 2021). A similar concern with legitimacy, lack of effectiveness and even damaging consequences is evident in Berman's account of them as 'contraband' humanitarians (Berman 2017:77). In contrast, the material discussed here shows that the boundaries between 'amateurs' and 'professionals' are fluid, given that everyday humanitarians often have professional skills that they deploy in their pro-bono work, not least since some of them work in the formal aid sector in their daytime job. Research on those conceived of as amateurs, however, recognises the importance of social relations, particularly the personal connections between founders and donors of such small projects, and those whom they are assisting. I take these insights further by asking how these relations are made; what forms they take, and what significance for assistance they have.

Vernacular

A third theme revolves around these forms of humanitarianism as vernacular, local or alternative practices (Brkovic 2016a, Ho 2017; Horstmann 2017; Carruth 2021). This pitches them in contrast to the international, and indeed global nature of humanitarian actors, such as the UN and other multi- and bilateral agencies. These latter promote standardised and formalised ways of carrying out humanitarian intervention. In contrast, vernacular humanitarianisms are locally emerging forms of intervention which arise from communities' and individuals' beliefs and practices. Vernacular or local humanitarianism can include a wide range of actors, such as residents of a Bosnian town who respond to calls for financial help for children to be sent abroad for urgent medical treatment (Brkovic 2017) or therapeutic rehabilitation, such as children from Chernobyl recuperating in Italian host families (Zhukova 2019, 2020). Horstmann describes the 'Free Burma Rangers' a group operating in Myanmar in a Christian missionary context. It relies on national volunteers, often religious converts, and offers medical support to civilians affected by conflict (Horstmann 2017). More broadly, local humanitarianism can include a 'philanthropy of the poor' (Wilkinson-Maposa 2005), local charity (Bornstein 2012; Osella and Widger 2018), local social protection practices (McCarthy 2016), and locally based disaster responses by and for community members (Solnit 2010).

Again, in the context of migration, among the vernacular and local humanitarian and development interventions are Islamic-inspired notions of neighbourliness and hospitality that underlie refugee support in Lebanon, Jordan and Turkey (Zaman 2016; Fiddian-Qasmiyeh, Ager and Greatrick 2021). In short, these practices do not derive from internationally agreed norms, but are rooted in local sets of beliefs, either religious or based in a shared locality. Highlighting the vernacular makes visible the importance of social relations, especially through what Elaine Ho calls 'affinity ties' (2017). These are shared religious, geographical, ethnic and historical connections, which may motivate community members – in her case, Chinese nationals who live across the border with Myanmar – to offer support to their co-ethnic group, the JingPo, on the other side. These Myanmar citizens have been displaced by conflict and find it hard to access support normally offered to refugees. Their affinity ties with their co-ethnic group residing in China becomes the basis on which help is offered. I return to the notion of affinity ties as a driver for intervention in Chapter 7, which critically engages with the idea that vernacular humanitarianism is based on the belief that all humans deserve support 'irrespective of their particular identities (including, for example, their race, class, citizenship, ethnonationality, gender, age, and sexuality)' (Brkovic 2020). The 'vernacular' bent of these activities is grounded in different national cultural contexts. In contrast, while everyday humanitarians accept this in principle, in practice they often choose to support others on the basis of their particular identities, and the affinities with which they identify.

Domestic and private

Finally, a key distinction made in the research on other humanitarianisms is between those forms which are publicly recognised, and those which are considered 'private' or even 'domestic' in character. In the first instance, 'private' refers to how these interventions and projects are financed, that is, through private rather than public means. While many large aid organisations receive donations from individuals, the privately funded projects discussed here are usually smaller in scope, and may not be set up as formal organisations or registered as charities. Instead, some are spontaneously emerging initiatives, responding, at least initially, to short-term needs. The private aid initiatives studied by Kinsbergen and Schulpen (2010) are one such example, where Dutch citizens raise funds from among their social networks to carry out development projects in the Global South, such as setting up schools or nurseries in sub-Saharan Africa. Such private aid is also at the centre of Nina Berman's work on the charitable activities among German residents of Diani county in Kenya. Having arrived as travellers, instituting charities there becomes part of their engagement with their chosen location (Berman 2017; Richey 2018).

In a related mode, Malkki labels such humanitarian forms 'domestic' (2015). This refers less to their finances, but to their ostensibly domestic motivations, and modes of interventions. In Malkki's case, this involves Finnish volunteers who undertake craft activities in the context of Finnish Red Cross campaigns, as well as professionals, such as nurses and doctors, whose motivation to help is driven by their personal need for recognition, for a sense of purpose and the alleviation of loneliness. Altman's work on 'domestic humanitarianism' describes how Australian volunteers make refugees welcome by distributing food and furniture, and enabling them to make a home in defiance of the Australian government's explicit efforts to prevent them from doing so (Altman 2020). A question posed by Malkki is to what extent this domestic and private character further underscores its marginality as a form of humanitarianism, or how it can challenge state discourses and practices, and even fire a 'politics of the imagination' (Malkki 2015) to overcome such limits. In Altman's view, the domestic arts are resolutely political, as they enable 'a political care ethics', making invisible labour public, and settle people seeking asylum into a 'national space' (Altman 2020).

All of these approaches – grassroots, amateur, vernacular and domestic – offer correctives to existing accounts of humanitarianism, and make visible the multitudes of global resource flows. And yet despite, or perhaps alongside, their growing importance in academic debates and public awareness, practitioners and ethnographers have wrestled with the implications of the very approach that sets them apart from more institutionalised forms of aid. This is their ostensibly limited reach, their amateur nature and the partial-ness of their efforts. Malkki has expressed this as the problem of the 'mere', meaning that such forms of humanitarianism can never adequately address the enormity and size of the challenges they are facing (2015:199). In response, I suggest a radical reframing of this problem through adopting a scalar approach.

Scaling

Studying scale means 'to examine how the ideals of social life stand in tension with notions of what is practically achievable' (Carr and Lempert 2016:10). This neatly captures the archetypical tension characteristic of humanitarianism, between certain 'ideals of social life' – such as the wish to save everyone – and the practicality of what one person, or a small group of individuals can achieve. People respond to this situation through making scales. One result of this scale-making concerns value statements. The scales that are being made – for example, that every person counts, or that the single life is worth saving – justify, valorise and frame the ensuing interventions. They are a way for everyday humanitarians to make sense of and guide their actions. Scales are useful because 'they help people orient their actions, organize their experience, and make determinations about who and what is valuable' (Carr and Lempert 2016:9). While everyday humanitarians are not using explicit terms of scale, they articulate their own scale-making to themselves and others, through semiotic labour. Expressions such as 'every person counts', or 'changing one village at a time', are examples of this (see Chapters 2 and 3).

It is useful to point out here that the tenet that 'everyone matters' does not imply, in theory or practice, that everyone matters equally in the context of humanitarian efforts. Rather, as I discuss, everyday humanitarians make scales – of social closeness, for example – that guide them in whom to support. Such decisions engender their own exclusions, and it would be wrong to suggest that everyday humanitarian support is by and in itself any less hierarchical, or less suffused with structures of power and privilege. It will be important to identify and map these structures in future work. The 'every person' of this mantra rather confirms a commitment to the singular. It means that no gesture is too small, no person not worthy of attention or support; an assurance that there does not need to be a critical mass, a particular minimum number or size reached before humanitarian efforts count.

It is important to remember that the evident limited-ness of other humanitarianisms, whether framed as being grassroots, amateur or vernacular, is not unique to them. This is a feature of any humanitarian activity, irrespective of whether it is formalised, state-funded and carried out by professional staff in aid agencies, or informal, privately funded and operating through volunteers. The problem of the 'mere' is inherent in any such intervention. It becomes more prominent, and indeed may offer grounds to dismiss grassroots humanitarianisms more readily because it becomes more visible among them. This book is based on the premise that bringing a scalar approach to humanitarianism – that means recognising that the scales we use are not given, but made – enables us to question and let go of particular scales and the values associated with them. As a consequence, we can recognise one such distinction between 'large-scale' and 'small-scale' humanitarianisms. The former is often associated with formal programmes and interventions, implemented by multinational organisations, state institutions or high-net-worth philanthropic foundations. The latter, in contrast, refers to a plethora of support practices carried out by and for individuals and a handful of beneficiaries, often funded through private social networks. These are driven by personal sensibilities and can be seen as lacking accountability, but especially efficacy, precisely due to their 'small scale'. One contribution of this book is to understand these in more nuanced ways. This makes visible a broader range of humanitarian practices, of the people carrying them out, and ways of defining and effecting change. Such nuancing includes questioning established notions of what matters, and who counts in people's efforts to support others.

Scalar perspectives have been employed in a range of anthropological contexts (Wastell 2001; Comaroff and Comaroff 2003; Tsing 2012; Bristley 2020). Marilyn Strathern warned that 'scale has been a headache for anthropology' (1995:15), on the basis of her sense that 'the potential for complexity remains constant no matter what the scale' (Holbraad and Pedersen 2009:374). This holds, and may indeed make it a particularly appropriate way of thinking through the range of humanitarianisms. Carr and Lempert remind us of the perhaps obvious insight, worth restating, that 'scale is process before it is product' (2016:8–9). Inspired by the semiotics of making scales, they explore 'how, why, and to what ends people and institutions scale their worlds' (2016:4). The framework of scale-making, paying attention to what scales are made, how this happens, and what use these scales are put to, is particularly productive in understanding how different forms of humanitarianism are being conceptualised, and with what consequences.

A scalar approach has not been applied wholesale to studies of humanitarianism (see Brkovic 2016), though there are substantial benefits in doing so. Such absence is even reflected in Carr and Lempert's collection, which does not envisage this possibility, and similarly in the steadily growing literature on 'other' humanitarianisms. This is odd, in so far as the very idea of humanitarianism has ambitions of scale at its core. Its imperatives are based on a shared humanity; it aims to support all those in need; it is meant to apply universally and globally. And yet, all forms of humanitarianism – whether labelled 'large' or 'small' – grapple with the same challenges. They must always fall short on their ambition to address suffering wherever it occurs; interventions are limited in time and place; and even where one challenge can be addressed – such as eradicating polio – this stands among many others that cannot. As a result, humanitarian practitioners, policymakers and researchers must constantly negotiate issues of scale. An approach that puts practices of scale-making at the centre of enquiry is therefore productive, if not for solving those challenges, but for making them explicit and their negotiations visible. In the first instance, we should therefore not dismiss small-scale humanitarianism because of its limited reach, but recognise that all humanitarianism grapples with issues of scale and limitations. The bigger point is, though, to recognise and dissociate scales from particular valorisations, and instead pay attention to what scales people make and use, and to what effect.

Increasing attention has been paid to forms of humanitarianism described as vernacular (Brkovic 2016; Horstmann 2017), everyday or quotidian (Richey 2018); grassroots (Sandri 2018), demotic (Taithe 2019), domestic (Malkki 2015; Altman 2020), private (Kinsbergen and Schulpen 2010), or indeed, small-scale or grassroots international (Clifford 2015; Schnable 2021). This range of attempts at grasping their character, which I have discussed previously (Fechter and Schwittay 2019), raises the question of how these forms of humanitarian are defined. I suggest that one intrinsic feature can be unlocked through an approach of scale. In one form or another, their descriptors are placed along sets of scales. These are temporal ones, such as juxtaposing 'everyday' humanitarianism with the millennium goals of global programmes; the scale of formal validity, which place the vernacular, the indigenous or local in contrast to the globally deployed and generically valid. Finally, they might sit on scales with the domestic at one end, and the scale of policy relevance or public recognition on the other.

Perhaps the most eye-catching manifestation of these is the scale of 'small' versus 'large'. The literature does not usually refer to 'large-scale humanitarianism', this being the default, but to 'small-scale' forms as its marked case. While notions of humanitarianism are underpinned by particular scales, they tend to remain implicit. Instead, making these scales visible brings to light how they are being made, what values are associated with them, and what use they are being put to. The adoption of a scalar approach allows us to let go of the micro–macro binary, and its associated valorisations. One of these consequences is that adopting a binary scale of 'small' and 'large', and valorising the latter over the former, has meant that 'small-scale' forms of humanitarianism have struggled to find their place in academic and policy literature; despite the fact that 'unlike the large-scale humanitarianism that makes headlines, a great deal of humanitarianism is spontaneous, informal, unmediated, and habitual' (Bornstein 2012:174). The reason why they have not been paid attention to is not just because of their small scale, but also because they do not conform to the norms of the humanitarian industry in more than one way. The purpose of this book is not to revalorise other humanitarianisms, or their analyses from the outset. Even though, as Judith Irvine argues, 'off-the-shelf versions of "scale", such as "micro–macro" that assume social life takes place on a single dimension of bigness (or smallness)', are problematic not least because 'the value of an analysis is similarly scaled, so that the bigger the picture, the more worthwhile the analysis' (2016:215). Rather, the book argues what can be gained from paying attention to scale-making is an understanding how everyday humanitarians negotiate the challenge of the partial-ness of their efforts.

Scaling relations

In the second part of the book, Chapters 5, 6 and 7 extend this scalar approach to social relations and demonstrate what kind of relations are made, to what purpose and how they upend conventional narratives of humanitarian objects. Together, they furnish an understanding of how limited reach and partiality constitute not an obstacle, but a condition that makes humanitarian action possible. As will be discussed in Chapter 4, geographical distance – or more specifically, the role of distance and proximity – has been declared irrelevant in principle for how we should construct responsibility to others (Singer 1972). This extends to social distance. Singer's radical normative position implies that everyone is responsible for everyone else, irrespective of geographical proximity or degree of social relatedness. Turning from the normative to the empirical, the first question at the heart of this book is how people handle the inevitable limited-ness of their actions.

Following on, the second question is: if only a limited number of people can be offered support, who to choose? Where to start, and on what grounds? As Bernard Williams reminds us, we should not think it 'an accident or a limitation or a prejudice that we cannot care equally about all the suffering in the world: it is a condition of our existence and sanity' (2006:147). Having to be selective about whom to care for is unavoidable, and not unique to everyday humanitarianism; but such challenges emerge more starkly in this context. The book offers insights into how such partiality operates in practice. This resonates, among others, with Christian beliefs, emblematically rendered in the story of the Good Samaritan. In a public exchange with Jesus, 'a certain lawyer stood up and tested him, saying, "Teacher, what shall I do to inherit eternal life?", and received the response that "You shall love the Lord ... and your neighbour as yourself." [...] But he, desiring to justify himself, asked Jesus, "Who is my neighbour?"' (Luke 10:25–29). The question of 'who is my neighbour', beyond its Christian connotations, is among those that this book explores.

What does it mean to apply a scalar approach to social relations? As Strathern reminds us, 'when anthropologists talk about relations, it is persons who most often come first to mind; that is, beings inevitably enmeshed in a relational world [...] they also put in relational work to support, deny, reconfigure, or transform their relations with one another' (Strathern 2018). Such relational work is evident among everyday humanitarians, foreign or Cambodian, who are threading ties with others across national, cultural, ethnic and other differences, as well as along lines of similarity or sameness. The result of this relational work is the scaling of social distance, turning others from unrelated stranger into humanitarian kin; from cultural other to friend, collaborator or supporter. The resulting social closeness and proximity becomes both a product of, and motivation for, humanitarian connection and intervention. As discussed earlier, research on alternative humanitarianisms recognises how social relations matter for grassroots forms of intervention (Brkovic 2016; Rozakou 2016; Schnable 2021). While their role is recognised, such relations are not always considered central. This is not to say that they do not matter in the institutionalised forms either. They do, in the form of partnerships between individuals within and between organisations. Despite often being disavowed, or hidden as unprofessional, Eyben argues that they are central even in the formal aid sector for enhancing effectiveness (Eyben 2006, 2011a, b). Others have argued that friendships in the field (Heuser 2011) and between staff and 'beneficiaries' (Girgis 2007) are an overlooked but important feature of how aid and development work.

This does not mean that the humanitarian practices at the centre of this book should be described as, or be turned into a separate category of 'relational humanitarianism', as done by some (e.g. Otegui 2022). Rather, as suggested, social relations matter in all forms of humanitarianism, institutional or informal. Their relevance, however, becomes much more visible in its everyday manifestations. One reason for this is that these relations are not hidden or downplayed, but on the contrary, made central and visible – by founders, supporters and, to some extent, by those that are being supported, too. One of this book's aims is to document which social relations there are, how they are made, and how they matter. The question is what the answers tell us not just about humanitarianism, but more broadly about how humans respond to the challenge of not being able to care for, and support equally everyone who is in need.

The scaling of social relations provides people with a way through this impasse. Scaling relations, in practice, means turning 'strangers' into people who are known. Those being supported become people with whom one shares a past, discovers or creates commonalities, or indeed become kin. Scaling relations brings people closer and reduces some social distance: this creates responsibility, justifying as well as calling for support. De Jong echoes this, drawing on Massey's 'hegemonic geography' of responsibility (2004:9). This assumes that 'a feeling of responsibility correlates with proximity and that therefore a sense of responsibility for "distant others" only comes secondarily, as opposed to those who have direct contact with target groups' (de Jong 2014). The scaling of relations make one humanitarian imperative – to attend to all those who are suffering – commensurable with what humans can do, that is attending to a select few. The relations that are made explain and shape the kinds of humanitarian interventions that ensue. The distant stranger, it turns out, is not perhaps a figment of the imagination, but certainly an expression of a very particular, historically and politically contingent form of humanitarianism, namely its relatively recent, Western-liberal institutionalised form. One insight arising from this book is the need to radically rethink, and re-appreciate, other forms of supporting others which predate – and may yet outlast – this particular version which has come dominate understandings of what is considered 'humanitarianism' in the twentieth and twenty-first centuries altogether.

More recently, two pertinent ethnographies further furnish dimensions of this argument. These are Louise Olliff's *Helping Familiar Strangers* (2022), and Lauren Carruth's *Love and Liberation* (2021). Both document humanitarian aid and support that is extended from members of the same group or community, towards others in the same or similar situation. While Olliff focuses on the work of refugee diaspora organisations, Carruth examines the interrelation of locally embedded forms of care with the international aid system in Ethiopia. This provides an excellent illustration of one aim of this book, namely the role that being connected – socially, culturally, through ethnicity or migration experience – plays in extending support to others, locally or translocally. Olliff documents how these diaspora organisations support refugees around the world. In her account, refugee diaspora humanitarianism is about 'how groups of people come together to try to do good that goes beyond – or perhaps sits between – acts of caring for kith and kin and acts of caring for an abstract and distant other' (2022:177). Refugee-led humanitarianism is thus part of the 'rich tapestry' of care which studies of everyday humanitarianism aim to make visible. In Carruth's work, the notion of *samafal* – a Somali term – corresponds to the English term 'humanitarianism', but also to a multiplicity of local care practices, which are extended to kin and fellow sufferers, as well as those who are targeted by more formal interventions.

Taken together, these bodies of research tell an arguably older story of how, and on what basis, humans support others and each other, independent of, and alongside, the formal humanitarian assistance system. They offer additional evidence of how humanitarian efforts are not extended to all of humanity, but to those who are related, nearby, or with whom ones shares a history. This is significant, as it shifts narratives of humanitarianism: it documents how the institutional forms favoured by organisations of the Global North are a recent occurrence, a mere blip in the history of care. Instead, a much richer and more diverse 'tapestry of care' (Olliff 2022) emerges, of which everyday humanitarianism forms a part.

Such social ties that make up a care fabric, such as love, kin or shared migrations, have also been described as 'affinity ties' (Ho 2017). There are similarities with others, based on ethnicity, religion, co-location, shared biographies or histories, which become the basis for, and call for support of those with whom one shares those ties. Such affinities are not just a defining feature of everyday humanitarianism, but their role unsettles the understanding of humanitarianism as primarily a mode of giving or resource distribution. Instead, everyday humanitarianism can be understood as constituted of the twin desires to give, as well as to connect. The reason why social relations become more visible in accounts of everyday humanitarianism is because the objects and modes of their interventions are often highly partial and personal. As such, they disregard the tenets of humanitarianism mentioned, the aspired-to impartiality. This stipulates supporting humans according to their needs, not on the bases of other ties, motivations or preferences on the part of the donors. Not adhering to these tenets is not unique to everyday humanitarians, as institutional interventions can be similarly driven by geopolitical, security or diplomatic preferences and priorities instead.

Forms of everyday humanitarianisms thus reveal that they operate not on the principle of impartiality, but of partiality. Rather than carrying out formal needs assessments, everyday humanitarianism is fundamentally characterised by philanthropic particularism. People choose to support those with whom they have, or can create, a relationship. What are the bases on which people make these connections? If social relations drive and direct support, what kinds of relations are they? Chapter 5 focuses on the desire to connect as well as to help, where personal connections with an 'Other' are made spontaneously and sometimes apparently at random. Chapter 6 examines a most pervasive form of recognising relations, those of humanitarian kinship, and Chapter 7 explores affinity ties, based on commonalities and shared biographies.

In line with the recognition that support extends differently in everyday humanitarian practice than in its more institutional forms, I avoid using the term 'beneficiary' here, for several reasons. The most important is, as Malkki (2015) and others have argued, that those who are often unthinkingly classed as 'donors' or 'aid practitioners' usually themselves benefit in significant ways from the aid or support activities they are undertaking. Many of the humanitarian practitioners were at pains to stress that their own needs were being met in this process. This may be a need to help, or to belong, to make a difference or to make friends. Reserving the term 'beneficiaries' for those who are nominally being supported – with activities, money, goods or acts of care – therefore makes invisible the inevitably two-sided nature of these aid interactions. This matters, not least in relation to questions of power, privilege and vulnerability, and how these shape, and are shaped by everyday humanitarianism. Differentials of power and privilege are undoubtedly ingrained, and partly drive these activities, but not always in straightforward ways.

Those who are being supported are vulnerable in many ways, whether as a result of pre-existing discrimination, their socio-economic marginality, or as a result of gendered and ableist structures of inequality. But thinking of them as vulnerable only, misrecognises the more complicated nature of who is involved in everyday humanitarianism. As discussed especially in Chapter 7, there is often no clear boundary between former 'victims' or survivors – of genocide, hunger or neglect – and becoming an everyday humanitarians who supports those from similar situations or backgrounds. As hopefully becomes evident throughout the book, humanitarians include Cambodians as founders, visionaries and practitioners who want to drive change. They sometimes draw on outside resources, such as foreigners' social networks, funding capacities, communication and representational capital, to achieve their aims. For the same reason, I do not treat the figure of the 'white saviour' as a particular group of people, and a distinct category of actor in everyday humanitarianism. Rather, white saviourism can also be described as an attitude, underpinned by ethnic or racial privilege, and paternalistic attitude towards those they are purporting to support. Such an attitude can cut across different forms of humanitarianism, including its institutional and everyday manifestations (I discuss how this can play out in more detail in Chapter 7). This does not deny the risk and reality of abuse of power in informal humanitarianism, which needs to be treated with vigilance both in practice and academic analysis. It should hopefully fundamentally reorder, however, entrenched notions of who is a 'beneficiary' of aid, and highlight the fluid nature of being a survivor, humanitarian or outside supporter who is actually in need. This points towards necessary future work with a greater focus on legitimacy and accountability than can be carried out here. To begin with, I turn the attention to the primary problem facing those who want to support those in need, namely the apparent impossibility of their task.

2

The part and the whole

One weekend morning in Phnom Penh, I was talking with Pamela, a medical trainee doctor from the UK. Pamela enjoyed a day off from the medical charity that she had come to work with for several weeks of her summer holidays. Most days, their team of medical volunteers would go to informal settlements in the city, where people were living in shacks perched on the edge of rubbish-filled canals, and ran basic health clinics for the residents. Pamela sighed as she described the activities of volunteers around her: *'When I see these people trying to rescue a poor kid, it reminds me why I've chosen my specialisation, going into public health.'* She vividly remembered a lecturer in her first year at university, who presented them with a scenario she recounted as follows:

> there are masses of people falling into a river. Downstream, scores of rescuers are trying to fish them out, one by one. He said, 'public health is about preventing people from falling into the river in the first place'. That made total sense to me, so that's why I don't want to be doing these slum rescue missions in the long run.

The scenario described by Pamela could be considered as a fairly accurate account of the efforts of everyday humanitarians: rather than tackling root causes, such as preventing people from falling into the river, they expend endless energy fishing out individuals, one by one. Indeed, when I talked to people about my research, comments ranged from the pitiful, 'these people are doing no more than sticking on a band-aid', to the more drastic, 'they are just pissing in the wind', pointing to the apparent futility of their endeavours. Such dismissiveness and accusations of wilful neglect of the so-called 'bigger picture' is not unique to the public imagination. Academic accounts of such singular gestures and rescue missions, share a deeply rooted, if perhaps unreflected conviction that because some acts appear 'small', or limited in their reach, they must by definition lack significance. Liisa Malkki cannot quell a sense of absurdity when she describes how elderly Finnish citizens are sending hand-knitted toys in order to comfort children in disaster zones. While she valiantly claims that such acts represent the 'power of the mere' (2015:199), it never quite becomes clear what this power consists of. Instead, the reader is left with the lingering sense that these acts remain 'mere' – well-intentioned, but invariably ineffectual. The accusation routinely levelled at everyday humanitarian practitioners is that they are operating on the level of the 'micro' – having finite resources and reaching limited target populations. This means being unable, or uninterested, in scaling up. This is understood here as expanding their operations; increasing their fundraising; cooperating with larger, formal organisations, or feeding into government policy.

Such critiques are underpinned by what Carr and Lempert define as the distinction between the macro and the micro, combined with the 'tendency to assign political economy to the former, face-to-face interaction to the latter' (2016:8). Malkki documents how volunteers for the Finnish Red Cross are knitting aid bunnies. What she finds troubling, and aims to resolve theoretically, is a nagging sense that these initiatives can easily be dismissed by 'real' humanitarians as something less 'real', less impactful or serious, something that barely counts as humanitarianism. To counter this, she ascribes an 'imaginative politics' to this power of the mere, to claim a place for it in the realm of 'real' humanitarianism. The problem of the 'mere' is an articulation of the limited reach and scope not just of everyday but of all forms of humanitarianism, whether they are considered large-scale, governmental and professional, or informal, individual and thus 'small-scale'. By virtue of their fundamental rationale, all these forms strive to address suffering and offer support to all who need it, while, at the same time, never being able to fulfil these aspirations. The 'mere' makes this insufficiency more visible. But it cannot be dismissed on this basis, because both the small and large scales fail in their aspirations. It therefore does not serve as a fundamental distinction between small and large-scale forms of humanitarianism.

I suggest that the fallacy that prevents Malkki from attributing significance to such acts is importing pre-existing sets of scales, inherent in humanitarian studies, which equate conventionally defined small or domestic acts with being 'mere'. The problem with such equations is that they make it impossible to grasp how scales mould social acts. These scales must be understood as constructs, which are devised and used by practitioners to suit their needs. I suggest that rather than wrestling with the 'mere' as an epistemological problem – how to attribute power to something one thinks of as limited and little by definition – a more productive approach is to ask how everyday humanitarians themselves conceive of their efforts. Are they wrestling with the problem of the 'mere', and possible futility of their efforts, and do they consider them in that light? And by extension, what do their beliefs and practices tell us about how scale-making is efficacious in structuring social life and thought, and specifically actions to improve the world, or parts of it?

The problem that this chapter addresses is how everyday humanitarians think of their work not as mere, but how they are conceiving of and dealing with its limited reach, their efforts inevitably partial and incomplete. While they inhabit the partial-ness of what they do, this does not make it 'mere' in their view. This chapter details ways in which this is being dealt with. This consists of, first, by defining their 'part'; and second, through devising strategies that link their part with the whole. There are no fixed notions of what counts as 'part' and 'whole'. Rather, the scales of part(s) and the whole, nested and interlinking, emerge from their semiotic and concrete practices. Many everyday humanitarians handle their partial-ness through the making of multiple scales. This involves, first, a focus on the part by necessity and choice; and second, ways of connecting the part with a whole, through practices of chunking, nesting, engaging with futurity and policy. This chapter thus provides the link between 'doing good in the world' and 'doing good in order to change the world'. In the context of orangutan conservation work, Chua argues that support acts through online social activism are 'small, quotidian ways by which people seek not to change the world, but to do their bit of good within it' (Chua 2018:11). The aim of this chapter is to explore ways in which these two are not distinct, but interlinked spheres.

Beyond everyday humanitarianism, this has wider implications. The question of how apparently small acts are linked, if at all, to what is defined as the 'bigger picture', affects all those who are trying to make social change happen. This includes, at one end of the spectrum, curt dismissals of the small, individual acts in the context of tackling the climate crisis, to 'forget shorter showers', and focus on system change instead (Jensen 2009). At the other end is the emphatic insistence that the two, the small and the large, must be linked. The conviction that the only meaningful and feasible place to start is in one's own life, is expressed in the dictum to 'think global, act local'. Rather than dismissing the 'small' as inherently insignificant, the theoretical upshot from the ethnographic material presented here is to describe these not as distinct or polar opposites, but as a part and a whole. There is a range of ways to define and focus on the part, by necessity or choice, and different ways of linking the two. These comprise the core of this chapter.

The first section focuses on those who stay focused on the part but valorise it, through insistence that 'small is beautiful', without linking it explicitly to a bigger picture. The focus remains on quality, staying small out of necessity or out of conviction, in order to maintain the quality of their work. The second section documents how people connect the part with the whole. This means making multiple and often interlinking scales. It involves breaking a problem into smaller parts, and changing things 'one at a time'. This serial approach, with a focus on 'one village' or 'one child' at a time, introduces a temporal scale which links the singular unit to a future multiple, and as such parts to the whole.

The part: 'That's all we can do'

Through paying attention to what scales everyday humanitarians make and deploy – in this case, in relation to the apparent partial-ness nature of their endeavours – this chapter unsettles the assumption that their practices and projects accord with a pre-existing micro–macro binary. Rather, for many, the 'micro' and the 'macro' are not self-evident and given scales; neither do they understand their activities as forms of 'micro' or 'mere' humanitarianism. Ralph, who oversaw an umbrella of projects supporting people with disabilities, summed up an attitude among fellow practitioners, in response to my question what impact their work was having, *'I ask myself, have I made a difference? I say that most of the people I know don't seem to be too bothered by it, because its's kind of obvious. Do they worry about scaling up? I guess they mostly worry about sustainability.'*

The model of sustainability that Ralph was referring to was not necessarily along the 'teaching people how to fish' logics, that is, making one's interventions superfluous, as those assisted would be able to support themselves in due course. Rather, sustainability here refers to the income and lifespan of people's projects, that is, raising sufficient income on an ongoing basis to continue their operations in the mid- to long term. Political questions about tackling the production of poverty, rather than the fact of poverty itself, were bracketed out of these conversations (an issue I return to). Ralph's comment picked up on distinct, but interrelated issues – the scope, in his words, of their 'obvious' impact, which unfolded in a tangible way in front of them, and its inevitably limited nature in the sense of not being able to support everyone who needed it. With this came the question whether they would aim to grow their projects. Rather than understanding themselves as 'micro' operators in a realm of 'macro' humanitarianism, such scales, and associated values (or dismissals), were not necessarily relevant to them. Instead, many everyday humanitarians situate their efforts in multiple scales of their own making.

Indeed, many did not routinely lament or think of their work as inconsequential or 'mere'. This does not mean that they were unaware of the limited reach, or partial-ness of their efforts. Rachana for example, a Cambodian working as a tour guide, had shown Leslie, then a tourist, the necessarily limited support activities she was able to offer to local schoolchildren. These were funded almost entirely through resources provided by her own family members. 'Leslie ask me, why don't you help all the kids that need it? I said, I am bankrupt! She said, Rachana, I won't let you go bankrupt.' At that stage, Leslie began helping Rachana to professionalise their fundraising and put her project on a more sustainable financial footing. When I talked to them about the possibilities and risks of growing their project, they both remembered this being an issue right from the outset of their collaboration. Indeed, it was Leslie's input that helped transform Rachana's activities from a one-person endeavour to an organisation employing multiple staff, with fundraising extending well beyond Rachana's immediate family. When I first spoke with them, Leslie had moved to Cambodia permanently and their after-school programmes had substantially expanded over the course of several years. Nevertheless, Leslie explained to me at that point, that they had reached their ceiling in terms of fundraising, which determined the scope and reach of their operations. They could not widen their outreach programme any further after realising their constraints:

> we figured, after a few years and I went through the accounts quite carefully, $6,000 is all we can raise in year, among local people here, and overseas donors. No matter what, that's all we can get. So we have to size what we do: that's all we can do.

This expressed an awareness of their financial and other capacity limits; of course, such awareness is not a unique constraint for everyday humanitarians, but also applies to formal aid organisations. It is important to recognise that for many of the everyday humanitarians the question of whether to grow, or expand what they were doing, was materially not an option.

This was also the case for Leo. When they were in the early stages of their after-school care project, he explained that

> for us, at the moment, it's all from day to day. We are so small. I was lucky to get some sponsorship from the travel industry when I started out. So now, a possible next step is planning to build a secondary school in [a village in a remote area]. But there is much we can't do anything about.

When I asked Leo how he was envisaging the future of their project, he responded: 'I want to see our kids [at their drop-in centre] all at school. I want to see the school in [village] happen. I want Chek to be a nurse. I want to have four kids in university ... maybe five.' Leo's expectations were modest. When I talked again with Visal, his Cambodian project partner, a couple of years later, he explained that Leo, who was still involved in the project, had taken a paid job in the hospitality industry to keep himself financially afloat, while Visal was able to draw a small salary from the work he was doing with the after-school club. However, they were not in a position to include all the young people who could have benefited. Visal regretted that he had to turn away children who came to his house asking for help, as their programme could only sustain a limited number. This raises the issue of responsibility and sustainability; being aware of their financial constraints and having to limit the number of individuals they could support without risking the stability of the overall project.

A problem that follows on from the constraints of their assistance is, if only a limited number of children can be supported, who to choose, and why? I return to this problem in more detail in Chapters 5 and 6. These constraints were sometimes more pronounced among projects founded and run by Cambodian nationals. Several of them had very limited access to international funders, compared to some of the foreign or jointly led ones. Bunroeun for example, a Cambodian man in his thirties, had set up a small children's home in a concrete bungalow, housing a dozen children on his family's small plot of land. Despite his valiant efforts to fundraise abroad, which he did with occasional success, Bunroeun was acutely aware of, and worried about, the precarity of his situation. In this case, expanding their project was not an option, despite the evident need of children who came to them asking for help. Sustaining their current activities, and their continued existence, was all they could reasonably aim for. Here, sustainability required matching their income to what they could offer in the mid-term. Even so, their position remained insecure, especially in so far as they depended on charitable donations related to the tourism sector.

While they were keenly aware that the needs were greater, they accepted that they could only do so much without endangering support for existing students. Notably, this did not deter them from their efforts, while it might others who would, in these limitations, see futility. The decision, despite their wishes to support more children, was grounded in the sense that this would have been irresponsible. Like others, Bunroeun was living from hand to mouth in regard to his project. The need to operate according to their limits was painfully clear to them. One outcome of making scales is keeping to an existing project, recognising its practical limits, and positioning oneself within them.

Focus on quality: 'We're not looking for numbers'

There were also those humanitarians who focused on their part alone, and did not expand as a choice, even though they would have had the financial and organisational capacity to do so. They remained focused on their part in order to preserve the quality of relationships that they had created, and nature of the work they wanted to maintain. In contrast to Malkki's thought of the mere as a problem, they did not consider this as an issue to be solved. Rather, such reasoning risked misrecognising what they were doing. Joshua for example, with his wife Lynn, supported a group of five Cambodian women, mostly single mothers, who lived in a cluster of wooden houses on the outskirts of town. This support included frequent visits and trainings to produce handicrafts. Lynn helped them design items made from recycled materials, while Joshua was involved with marketing their wares. These were put up for sale online, for distribution in Singapore and at a local craft market aimed at tourists. When I joined them as the women were sitting on the tiled floor of a small communal building, I asked them about their plans or about increasing the scope for the project. Joshua shook his head in response: '*We're not looking for numbers*', he told me firmly. '*We're just doing work with communities that we know. We allow doors to be open for us, to go through. We are not here to build a nation. We're here to help a community. It's got to be all connected.*' Their vision for the future of this project was not for it to grow, because, Joshua explained, '*when projects get too big, people become numbers*'. They envisaged the project eventually being taken over by the women themselves, with progressively less input from Joshua and Lynn. As Joshua outlined,

> *The road to evolve is that we go back to Singapore, but we come here for extended periods. Sending the kids* [of the women] *to the school – it's a long-term engagement, but we don't need to be here to oversee things. They have to take ownership of it. At the end of the day, this is not just a job for us.*

Joshua rejected a utilitarian perspective on what they were doing. Insisting that 'it was not just a job' for them, their activities did not have to conform to particular notions of efficiency, or producing quick results. They cherished moments such as the women successfully running their new market stall, increasing their sales online and overseas, and sending their children to schools. The fact this involved only five women – and in the long run, only one of them, Chantrea, managed to do this successfully – was immaterial to them. Their focus on this particular community, and especially Chantrea, maintained the quality of their work and the relationships they aimed for. I return to such attitudes, dismissing superficial notions of efficiency in favour of taking care of individuals, in Chapter 3.

Approaches which prioritised quality over quantity, and the gains from this, were shared by others. They reiterated the value of this particular scale of the individual, or of the 'small things'. As Aiko, who ran an art school for young people, explained, '*I want to support children. I can't take every child. Only a few can become artists, only a few have those special skills needed.*' When I asked her if she considered herself as 'doing development', she made it clear that

> *our purpose is not to teach thousands. We collaborate with other organisations, we get lots of requests. There is an American-run school, they would like us to deliver art workshops to their school. Some requests we get from far away, like Svay Rieng. So we can't go there and help more people.*

Aiko and her Japanese assistant, Emiko, were unanimous in their resolve not to grow their project. Emiko was particularly wary of this, as she had worked for a large international NGO in the USA before joining Aiko in Cambodia. In Emiko's view, one drawback of such organisations was that

> *you have many different opinions. They have lots of money, lots of staff. But with education, it is hard to scale up. We are managing as a small team ... our decision making is very simple! It is just me, Aiko, and the interpreter. In a big organisation, you have to decide on one level, then ask for approval on another level, another manager, it gets very complicated. We have flexibility, no bureaucracy, less mistakes. In an NGO – you have limited time to meet the beneficiaries. There would not be enough time to be with the art students. So that's why we keep the size limited. Otherwise, mentally, physically, it would be too much stress. Your mind is switching. You're constantly chasing big grants. We want to keep our minds focused. We are consciously keeping it simple. If we were bigger, we would struggle.*

Further, Aiko mused on the possibilities they would have to extend the reach of their operations, for example through affiliating with a company as a sponsor: '*there is a Japanese telephone company, they built ten schools in Cambodia*'. They could have done that, but she decided not to, stating specifically: '*I don't want to make an NGO... I want to stay small. To keep the vision.*' Wrapping up our conversation, Aiko added with a wry smile, '*that is why it's called "small" art school. We don't expect too much. I started this by myself. If I lost my ways then it would all be gone.*' Summing up her stance, she reiterated, with a friendly nod towards me, '*small activities are very important*'.

For some, emphasis on the 'small' emerges from their previous experience in the formal aid sector, which made them aware of its downsides and keen to keep control over their activities, as well as the possibility for personal relationships. Lynn for example explained that,

> *I had a lot more stress working with a big NGO in Singapore. The amount of politics that is going on in organisations, that is just offputting. It's not about scale. It's about the community. Places like UNICEF, they have not given their lives, they have the integrity question.*

Apart from putting one's values into practice in small operations under one's control, Lynn remembered relationships with people she had supported through tough times, and who had found their feet as a result of their intervention:

> *there was also the Malay lady, and long after we left, she was running her own business, she was doing so well, and still, every Christmas and Easter – and she wasn't even Christian – she would come to our house and bring us these amazing cakes that she made herself. She never forgot us.*

Success is not defined in terms of size, but the quality of relationships. A recurring theme is the question of accountability and close contact with the people who are being supported, which large organisations do not generally enable. I return to these issues in Chapter 5, in the context of personal relationships which are at the heart of everyday humanitarianism.

The sense that there would inevitably be losses if a project were to grow, was shared among several informants. Ralph, together with others, set up a fair-trade handicraft workshop. He thought that if they expanded their operations, they would '*lose something*' in the process. He went on to explain, '*Yes, Leakena can now send $30 back to her mum from what she earns. Is that scaleability? If you grow, you lose something. What works – you lose what works.*' One might ask what it is that 'works', depending on their vision for their project. For Ralph, this was less about expanding what they were doing, but letting people move through their projects. They had rented a plot of land on the outskirts of town, which provided housing and gardening space for two families, some members living with a disability. They were able to keep chicken and grow vegetables there, mostly for their own use, with a modest surplus to sell. He considered this a halfway house to their independent living:

> *these guys will need to move on. Is it scaleable? Yes ... but not in the traditional sense. What will it take – the original family living there moves on, a new one comes in; that scales it. I don't need to open another outfit in Singapore or Hanoi. I'm interested in these people in their own way. So scale and sustainability? That's not our model – but we are trying to increase numbers of people who have full bellies.*

Ralph explained why he thought expanding the smallholding model would be a mistake: '*If there are too many families, it spells trouble, we've already seen that; it only works when there is no more than 5, 6 people, otherwise they quarrel. This here is manageable; it works.*' The scale that Ralph was deploying involved numbers not in parallel, but as extending into the future: there may be only a handful of people on this plot of land, but over time, there would be succession of them living there, benefiting from it, and then moving on. As mentioned, Ralph did not reject scale completely, but defined it in his own way:

> *I don't think that what we create could be replicated on a larger scale. We can stay in a small state, but people within it will move on. Like a Mom and Pop corner store, it's being passed on. It doesn't have to grow, no, that's a bad idea. The risk with scaling up is that you break it. There is the micro and the macro level – our work is not going to change the macro level much. But it all depends on your motivation.*

The sense that there was a balance to be struck between wanting to increase the number of people being fed, supporting more, while not losing 'what works' was shared among other everyday humanitarians. Abby, from RiceFirst, acknowledged that they were perhaps teetering at the edge of this balance. As they had around 200 children attending their after-school club on different days, she thought that they were still *'small enough to be a family, but big enough to have a real impact'*. At the point when I talked to her, they were looking to set up a second club a short distance from the existing one, even though she and her team were at times struggling to keep their fundraising to the levels required. As she explained to me, they held around three months of reserves – if they ran out, they would have to cut down their operations. This illustrates the tension between the desire to expand, and their limits in terms of financial or organisational capacity.

This tension was also an issue for Leslie, as she was reflecting on the size of their programmes, and how to achieve such balance: *'across five schools, we are responsible for 2,600 kids all the way through their schooling. We go as deep as we can, go into that community, but still we need to start going wider ... but we have to avoid being too big for oversight – you double the size, and that starts happening. But for now, that's right here – a success story.'* Such a balance did not only relate to how many children to take on, but also applied to one of their fundraising models. This involved a 'breakfast round', where visitors could sponsor the cost of a breakfast for a whole school for one morning, and accompany the team in preparing and handing it out. However, she was aware that *'you have to keep the line between giving people this experience, and gawping at kids; and just taking their money without giving them involvement. Everybody struggles with balancing that.'* Considerations on how to balance feeding the few and the many, were thus very much a part of running their project.

In contrast to people like Ralph and Aiko, who were keen on 'staying small' to preserve the quality and integrity of their work, others think more enthusiastically about growth in terms of numbers. This involves expanding the reach of their project, but stopping short of policy influence. At that end of the spectrum were people who were fired up, such as Sabine, and her programme of writing workshops. As she explained, she was once pushed to reflect on the question of growth in a conversation with a friend, a coach for corporate executives. '*She said, what do you want? What is your ambition? And said, I want this to be nationwide policy! I want this to be global! I want to do a TED talk and be in Davos!*' Sabine laughed. It may be no coincidence that this happened in a conversation with an executive coach, and reflects on her ambitions possibly to become an 'aid celebrity' – another facet of charismatic founder figures that I explore elsewhere (Fechter 2023).

During the year when I talked to Sabine, her writing programme had become established in a range of locations across Cambodia, and she had recently been invited to run workshops in Vietnam as well as in Laos. She reflected:

> *this programme works. Writing through Cambodia, Laos, and the rest of the world! I want this to be all over the developing world … but I'd have to raise ten million dollars. If you can't do that, you can't go global. I guess if it works, you don't need to push it, like I was approached by schools in Lao and Nepal. But you need to let it happen, slowly.*

People like Sabine wanted to scale, or were thinking about it, not because they saw staying small as a failing. They believed what they were doing was worthwhile, and wanted it to reach more people. The 'small' here has both value in itself, as well as containing the seed of expansion, such as in Sabine's case. Abby, from RiceFirst, was similarly exuberant in principle about her project's future: '*I want to create a blueprint for others. When we started, we had no know-how, no special expertise, no money … Our model should be all over the world, not a one-man show, a thousand-man show!*' Such optimism prevailed even though in practice, their project had been running for the past five years, sometimes teetering on the brink of downsizing, if not collapse. Mostly reliant on donations, Abby had been propping up the project with her wages as an English language teacher at private tuition centres. While they had been steadily expanding the number of children they were supporting, and at one point were considering a second site, this was not necessarily underpinned by a strategic plan for growth. Abby, as a result, was 'running herself ragged', in the words of a friend, to keep the project going. Such tensions and efforts at sustainability can be alleviated by building up, for example, a Cambodian leadership team, so responsibility would not rest solely on Abby as the founder, but this did not necessarily happen – a situation not unique to humanitarian projects.

Linking the part and the whole: 'One village at a time'

Apart from deploying numbers in the form of writing workshops delivered, children taught or breakfasts handed out, there were other ways in which everyday humanitarians were making scales to deal with the enormity of the issues they were facing. One such way was about imagining oneself as 'taking a chunk out of a problem', bolstered by the thought of other people doing the same. Ralph for example, when I asked him about the discrimination faced by people with disabilities in Cambodia, explained,

> *I normally choose not to get angry. I say, the problem is big, but not too big so I can't take a chunk out of it, and then it will be smaller. It's what I believe ... be the change you want to see in the world.*

The semiotic labour of 'chunking' here consisted of linking the part and the whole: if one person 'took a chunk' out of the problem, less of the problem would be left. In this scale, embracing even a partial approach, as they must, has the effect of reducing the overall problem, no matter by how much. A similar form of semiotic reckoning was carried out by Stella, describing her agency and her project as part of a broader division of labour:

> *We are a very tiny project in a very huge problem, a problem that is getting worse in Cambodia by the day. We reach some 550 out of 25,000,000 people with AIDS in the world. Fortunately there are other people out there. Our concern is with doing what we can as well as we can and learning as much as we can from the doing. Remember, there is also a division of labour: you don't have to do everything.*

Stella's reasoning was not just addressing a small chunk, but also knowing that her team were not the only ones dealing with this. This way of linking one's own part with the whole relies on collective activities – not necessarily in actual collaboration with each other, but achieving efficacy through simultaneously pushing in the same direction (Dessewffy and Nagy 2016). For this, too, semiotic frameworks exist, such as 'small streams making a big river', invoked by Norwegian founders of humanitarian projects in the Gambia (Fylkesnes 2016).

Another way of linking the part and the whole, signalled in this book's title, is the segmenting of efforts along a temporal scale. Some everyday humanitarians created a scale extending into the future through a serial model, changing the world, one step – or pen, book, child, village – at a time. Through expanding the time scale, considering problems not in their overwhelming entirety, but rather pared down, and 'one by one'. If one cannot, or does not want to, grow or feed into policy; a way of expanding one's reach is to see it unfolding serially. The semiotics of making this temporal scale were visibly widespread among projects in Cambodia, provided mottos, emblazoned on websites, and titles of memoirs, such as *Healing Cambodia, One Child at a Time* (Duchâteau-Arminjon 2012). A related version appeared as, 'One child, one teacher, one book, one pen can change the world.' In the way that 'a journey of a thousand miles begins with one step' (Dao De Jing, ascribed to Laozi), this envisaged how small projects would unfold into the future. While not being able to expand immediately, people who had received support would accumulate, one by one, as time moved on. Rachana's project website declared that their aim was to educate Cambodia, 'one child at a time'. The motto for Sabine's writing workshop was, *'we save minds, one poem, one story at a time'*. China Scherz recognised a similar process of temporal scale-making in the charity work of Ugandan nuns. When challenged by conventional development frameworks, they insisted that they were not beholden to those, and in contrast were 'living according to God's time' (Scherz 2013). This serial approach dovetails with the focus of Chapter 3, the belief 'every person counts'. The semiotic model of 'one at a time' interlinks the single with the many, and the part with the whole, through the vehicle of time.

Discussing the very limited and particular timeframes characteristic of the formal aid sector, Boris, who had built up an athletics team for people with disabilities, was deeply disdainful of such practices. Comparing his long-term involvement with the team, and the group of female athletes he coached, he exclaimed scornfully,

> *Aid? That's basically esoteric social experiments designed in the West and executed to a short timeframe. It took eight years to grow that person* [one of the athletes he supported]. *You don't know what you're going to achieve. If we had walked out after a year, that would have been it.*

Everyday humanitarians often invoked not just a long-term, but an open-ended time frame. Brigitta, a medical doctor at a privately funded hospital insisted that in so far as time was involved, for her project, *'this is not a Millennium Development Goals thing, but an attitude to life … that is how you do things, not to have impact in a given timeframe'*. Making their own temporal scales, or dispensing with temporal frames altogether in favour of an attitude or a commitment, was emphasised by many. One might argue that an open-ended time frame makes it difficult, by certain standards, to declare a project a success. In cases where someone's initiative had not progressed as much as had been hoped, I was often told that the project was 'just beginning to take off'. Using an open-ended temporal scale was not unique to everyday humanitarians. Talking to international aid workers whose projects were coming to the end of their allocated time, or were cut prematurely, a common response was that these projects 'were just about to fly'. Audrey for example, working for a Catholic charity, had been working in tertiary education in Cambodia for more than two decades. Most early mornings, she steadfastly took her ageing scooter to her office in the university grounds on the other side of town to carry on her work. I asked with awe and disbelief how she kept going, over so many years. Her answer was that she was sure that it would happen: *'it is happening slowly – it's a new generation – I can see it coming'*.

Even the people engaged in policy processes adopted such long-term tenacity tethered to the everyday. Maxim, for example, explained this modus as a source of hope in spite of sluggish government or aid donors. He remarked of a well-known American national and long-time advisor to the Cambodian government: *'yes but people like Scott Leiper, they are not frustrated'*. Leiper's obituary in the Phnom Penh post stated that 'he knew that in spite of the often times hard to digest, so-called "big picture" it was still worth the effort to avoid wallowing in cynicism and keep at it. He did that every day for the last three-plus decades' (Hayes 2016), suggesting that a steady drip of efforts may have a place, and effects, in the world of policy too.

Another form of scale-making is locating one's own efforts in relation to the wider political situation. I should clarify here that 'political' here does not mean root causes or political economy of poverty, or the dangers of 'rendering technical' (Li 2007), that is, not tackling the political and economic causes of poverty and suffering. As generations of development studies have shown, top-down interventions can also all too often take a technical approach and disregard the political issues to address causes. I explore the aspect of engaging with policy, as a form of interacting with local or national government, in the following section. Typically, though, everyday humanitarians did not raise issues such as corruption, failures of democracy or human rights spontaneously in our conversations. Rather, they reflected as a result of my prompting, loosely framing how they positioned their own efforts in the bigger 'political' picture – meaning, in this instance, the political situation in Cambodia.

When I asked Joshua about the context in which they were operating, and whether he found it frustrating at times, he responded, *'well I guess ... because I'm Asian, I know that corruption is a way of life here. You just have to work with what you have. I feel saddened by the overall political situation but it doesn't detract us from what we're doing.'* Later, he emphasised that *'I'm not an activist.'* Joshua was clearly delimiting their radius of activity: they were investing time in small groups of people, while bracketing the realm of national politics. A similar distinction was evident when I was talking with Leo. He mused that *'we get upset about that every time, don't we? Even about stuff in town like rubbish'*, while his project partner Visal added, '*we* [Cambodians] *are so used to listening to one person, there is always "no question"'*, pointing to the authoritarian nature of their government. Leo thought,

> it can get you down ... how, how, will this country change? The emotional challenge is to not let it get to you. That stuff we see in town every day. But the kids ... the older boys have access to the internet, so once you get them past Facebook and YouTube, they actually get the hang of what's going on – because TV is censored, everything else they hear is so limited. Its emotionally draining ... there is not a lot to gain there. The reward is in the change in the kids.

For Joshua, Leo and Visal, their efforts and rewards were firmly located in small groups of individuals. Leaving the broader situation out of their sights so as not to be distracted or depressed by it, the connection between both was nevertheless manifest through *'the change in the kids'*. I explore the idea of young people as change-makers in Chapter 3.

Finally, I asked Brigitta, the physician working at the private hospital, whether the existence of a corrupt government, a greedy elite and illegitimately gained wealth undermined her commitment to her work. She emphatically countered,

> No. Not at all. It makes me even more compassionate and eager to try and create an environment where people realise that hard work and having a good heart means that you will be rewarded in your professional career. It makes me more committed to create an island here.

She upheld the idea of 'creating an island' where different rules apply, where people are rewarded not for corruption but hard work. In her words, she sketched the geographical scale of 'the island', as something that was apart from wider society, where good things could be done, but they would be limited to a particular place, rather than ripple out. In this sense, her scale-making of 'island' suggested a partial-ness, a small unit within a bigger one, where the former was not affected by, but also did not ripple outward, into the latter.

Policy and the person

This chapter is about making (and linking) ideas of the micro and the macro. One way of joining these is through influencing policy; another is through expanding the time scale, as expressed in 'one at a time'. By virtue of their limited means, or conscious decisions to stay small, many of the projects discussed here did not have ambitions for influencing policy. I wondered why some project founders had policy aspirations, others did not. Maxim for example was the founder-director of a health-oriented project, creating networks of peer educators for diabetes sufferers in rural areas. A trained medical doctor, and with decades of work experience in the refugee camps at the Thai border and in Cambodia's public health sector, he was proud of his innovative model. He had almost singlehandedly established this at a time when being diabetic in Cambodia could amount to a death sentence, owing to lack of basic medical care. When I was talking with Maxim about the future of his project, he was clear: *'I'm interested in effectiveness. To achieve, you need to implement and affect policy. We now have the mass force, the quantity, to be reckoned with.'* With some glee, he recounted discussions he had with Médecins Sans Frontières (MSF), who he had worked with for a time. As he remembered,

> *they didn't like this, my plans for scaling up. They told me that you can't operate on more than one level, implementation and policy. They didn't like the policy level. I believe in both. What we have created here, it would be crazy not to scale this up.*

Maxim's project was perched between the decidedly informal and serious ambitions to impact public health policy. He was keen to connect scales, to be active in villages, recruiting and training peer educators, while at the same time shaping a national policy conversation. In his view, their relatively small size made them a nimble, and thus effective operator. This gave them an advantage over behemoths such as MSF, who struggled with straddling those scales:

> *of course, MSF are also in the policy world. They can't operate on all levels, though. I think you have to connect those worlds. In the world of policy, everybody wants money, they want their per diems, they are too busy for other things, like the work on the ground. It takes so long, training educators, and so many people. You can see our model is going to end up as government policy and that's a huge joke because they have ignored us, and because I make them look like idiots.*

Maxim thought that having policy ambitions was a hallmark of people's commitment to their cause: *'if they are serious about the case, they need to feed into policy. So if Beat Richner is serious about it, what he is doing is immoral.'* Maxim was referring to the (now late) Swiss paediatrician, Dr Beat Richner, who had over three decades set up several children's hospitals in Cambodia, based to a large extent on private donations raised by himself. Richner, in his books and on social media communications, stressed his success as defined in numbers of children treated and lives saved. Maxim viewed this model as 'immoral' in so far as it undermined public health approaches, taking capacity away from rural areas and diverting it to a handful of high-end hospitals. While this warrants further discussion, the tension evident here is between numbers and policy, in the sense that serving even large numbers of children does not equate to impact on a policy level. What counts as success depends on the scales chosen, whether sheer numbers of individuals, or changes in law, health policy or practice.

While Maxim was adamant that policy-level engagement was a hallmark of being serious about one's cause, such an attitude was not shared by all everyday humanitarian practitioners. Some moved in the opposite direction as they began work on a policy level, traversing the formal aid sector, to eventually find themselves in a place where policy did not present an appropriate way of going about things. Stella, mentioned earlier, cared deeply about the people in the final stages of HIV/Aids-related illnesses whom she was supporting. When I asked her how she felt about possibly enlarging her project to reach greater numbers of patients, trying to influence policy, or to reach deeper into affected communities, she explained her journey as follows:

> *I started out very much at the other end of things, doing broad-based human rights information work as a way of changing policy, and so on. And that was after having been active during the Vietnam War, when it was actually possible for ordinary people to have an effect on US policy. I do not believe this is the case any longer.*
>
> *So I went to Palestine with the idea of helping create peace, through policy change and settled into human rights documentation. It was after the first Gulf War that I began working more directly with people. In Palestine that work included political implications. But it was and remains always necessary to differentiate between human rights and politics – I recognise how little that happens in practice.*
>
> *While it is essential to understand the politics, the purpose of that understanding, at least in my work, is to be able to find the interstices where help might actually be accomplished. In Cambodia we do best by staying altogether away from the political arena.*

For Stella, the journey away from the world of policy and institutional politics, ran parallel to her own life course. One reason for her to stay on this trajectory, and limit the size of her project, the hospice, was that,

> *I am too old to be concerned with scaling up my work. If I were Simon's age it might be different. He has done a magnificent job with [a sizeable NGO], beginning by letting homeless children sleep in his apartment to creating organisations which are effective at a broad range of levels in six countries. But I am 70 now.*

As often, many everyday humanitarians' relationship to scale is connected to a stage in their life course, though not always in linear ways.

While Nasrin and Abby brimmed with youthful enthusiasm to grow their projects, there were also those in late middle age, like Sabine, who felt that after raising their own children, taking retirement or divorce, they were finally able to fully devote themselves to a project, with strong ambitions to grow.

Independent of their life stage, uneven trajectories, and zig-zagging between work at the policy level and that of the individual, were common. They were evident also in the case of Nasrin, an experienced researcher, consultant and previous staff member of large aid organisations. She reflected on the enormous amounts of overseas aid money that had poured into Cambodia over the previous twenty years. She had benefited from this, providing her with an interesting job and an income. As she pondered soberly though, as a result of her policy work in Cambodia, *'we* [international aid workers] *made Hun Sen* [Cambodia's prime minister] *who he is today. We helped through the decentralisation agenda; it was a high point of my career. I needed the experience; it was a good time for me.'* At the same time, her comment was laced with regret: she recognised her role in aiding a political regime she was very critical of, while furthering her consultancy career.

She remained deeply ambivalent about the role of policy advice and implementation of change on a national level, in contrast with getting personally involved with women in need of assistance. On the one hand, her training at an internationally renowned programme in development studies had ingrained in her that personal gratification must not be part of one's imperative to act: *'my university training always taught me: "it's not about you". You have to separate yourself from the issues.'* On the other hand, she found that such personal involvement was precisely what drew her to supporting others, a sentiment I explore further in Chapters 5 and 6. Nasrin recounted a situation where,

> *there was a woman getting sewing training in one of our workshops. She was in an abusive relationship, but she was able to leave it, and fled, so I kind of became her godmother. I love that I get to know the story of every individual, that motivates me.*

Such satisfaction at seeing immediate effects was laced with caution about how their policy advice had changed matters – notwithstanding her sense that the influx of overseas aid had helped cement Hun Sen's power status. As she explained,

> *getting the women out of their situation, it's more rewarding than policy work. Our old teacher said that you shouldn't get satisfaction because development is beyond these things, they are suspicious of instant gratification, because the connection we made between us is not changing policy.*

Nasrin became progressively unencumbered by doubts that supporting individuals was not worthwhile. Similar to Stella, she began turning away from policy-level work as a full-time occupation. Initially as a sideline, she organised sewing workshops for women who had been evicted from their homes and forcibly resettled. Through setting up an online shop, she was marketing their products, helping them earn a living. Nasrin emphasised the contrast with her previous way of working, and that now,

> we are taking things into our own hands. ILO, UN – *that* was *the way to do it* – but it's not, that's not the way to do it. You will know, nothing changed because of your policy advice. Now, [with the business model] *I may not be able to change much; but it's sustainable; and it will be* my *politics*.

Expressed in the phrase of '*my* politics', Nasrin relished the sense of ownership over her project, not dissimilar from the joy of a self-made entrepreneur. This parallel is evident in other contexts (Papi 2016; Schnable 2021) and not least echoes the 'DIY-Foreign Aid' ethos highlighted by Kristof (2010). At the time when I talked to her, Nasrin was genuinely hopeful that their approach, helping women to become self-sufficient on the basis of a business model, would change the aid sector: '*We will be a force some day; we will be doing it differently in time … I think* [through taking a business approach] *we are changing the course of the development industry, we are not dependent on the UK government or others*', echoing the neoliberal discourse about self-sustaining business models.

When I received an update from Nasrin, a couple of years later, her business, WhiteJasmin, was still in operation. She had not yet been able to base her income entirely on this model, however, and relied on earning a living through working, as before, as a consultant in the aid sector. This does not mean that Nasrin and others were unrealistic in the expectations they had for their projects. Whenever I followed up with them, I was perhaps unduly surprised at how many were evidently doing well; but they had not necessarily grown. This chimes with one of Nasrin's closing observations,

> *you're not changing the world; you're just creating WhiteJasmin: one village at a time. There is the need to scale down. The issue is complex, we deal with the poorest of the poor, some traumatised. What are the policy implications of that?*

Maxim, Stella and Nasrin exemplify different ways of how everyday humanitarian practices may straddle, combine, reject or tack between supporting individuals and influencing policy. Their efforts are framed by the semiotic labour that makes scales. As I discuss in Chapter 4, exploring how people operate along sliding scales of proximity and distance to those they are supporting, people here simultaneously hold different ideas of which scales exist, how one links to the other, weaving in and out of these realms and weaving them together.

Conclusion

This chapter explores a thorny issue at the heart of everyday humanitarianism: the question, how their efforts relate to what many call the 'bigger picture'. One way of answering this, if not exonerating them from the accusation that they are providing a 'drop in the ocean' without concern for root causes or system change, is that some thought has gone into how their efforts link to the wider problems. This chapter offers a first attempt to answer the question animating this book. In the first instance, one response to the vexing question of where to put your efforts, is to simply concentrate on a part of it, however it is defined. Some everyday humanitarians consciously decide to stay small, and to not 'scale up' and expand their projects. Arguably, some of them are not in a position to do so, being constrained by their financial position. Others have this option, but are careful not to destroy 'what works' and prefer to maintain ways of operating that match their small size. A purposeful focus on the quality of relationships and their work takes precedence over quantity or numbers.

The second part of the chapter explores different ways of how everyday humanitarians link the part with the whole, in what could be described as their theories of change. Key ways are through sequencing or chunking the labour needed to tackle a problem. Echoing a popular motto mentioned earlier, 'changing the world, one person at a time', they negotiate the limits of their agency through 'taking chunks out of a problem', in the knowledge that they are doing this alongside others. This includes a temporal nesting of scales: 'one at a time' is a recurrent mantra, indicating that their focus rests on one instance, one person or one village. Such a serial approach breaks up an overwhelming task into manageable parts. These limited interventions are envisaged to extend along a temporal scale, as well as laterally, as part of a community of people who are addressing the problem simultaneously, in their own ways.

In sum, everyday humanitarians deal with the limited-ness of their actions not by disavowal. They do not simply reject the suggestion that being small is problematic, instead declaring the small beautiful, meaningful or important. They negotiate the limited reach of their actions by making and using multiple and interlinking scales. Some of these connect the part to the whole. Such 'chunking' can be understood as a form of semiotic labour. Through adopting temporal, nesting scales parts are being folded into a whole. The stark division between the mere and the small-scale, and the significant and large-scale emerges as a construct. This chapter illustrates some of the ways in which humanitarians imagine how the part links with the whole. Chapter 3 continues this exploration through Nasrin's invocation – that is, how focusing on an individual links to change in collective futures.

3

Every person counts

A Buddhist monk was on the beach with his apprentice the day after a fierce storm. Thousands of starfish had been washed up and stranded on the shore. Stooping down, the monk carefully lifted a single creature and returned it to the sea. His young apprentice wondered aloud why his master bothered to do this when it made little difference to the mass of helpless creatures. As they walked along, the monk picked up another single starfish and replied, 'It makes a difference to just this one.'

A version of this story (starfish, n.d.) was originally published under the title 'The Starfish Thrower' in a collection by the American anthropologist Loren Eiseley (1969), though most likely not invented by him. Adapted to a Southeast Asian context with a Buddhist monk as protagonist, the parable of the 'Starfish Story' frequently appeared on websites, and was displayed as a motto for a range of everyday humanitarian projects. The starfish lent its name to entire organisations, such as Starfish Cambodia, or the Indochina Starfish Foundation. More than any other single trope, it appealed to the aspirations of founders and imaginations of supporters. It captured the challenge at the heart of their efforts, and provided a rationale for why it made sense to carry on.

Humanitarian endeavours are sometimes described as a 'drop in the ocean' of need. At first sight, the problem of 'scale' might refer to the constant challenge to provide more, or enough, support to those requiring it. As discussed in previous chapters, the response of everyday humanitarians to this situation consists of making and deploying their own scales, in this case, that of the single individual. Adopting a scalar approach to humanitarianism avoids dismissing such efforts as 'small', but makes visible the manifold practices that exist on the margins of the formal, institutionalised sector. In turn, their practices of scale-making demonstrate that their scales are not distinct or oppositional, but interlinked: making 'every person count' also includes those receiving support extending charity to others, into the future, or effecting change in wider society, thus unsettling entrenched notions of what 'small-scale' humanitarianism means.

The problem of not being able to rescue everyone is not unique to small-scale forms, but concerns all humanitarian intervention, no matter how comprehensive (Ticktin 2015, 2019). My argument here concerns scale-making in everyday humanitarianism, though comparable mechanisms are at work and sustain 'large-scale' forms, too, while the scales that they make, differ. One might note that the temporal scales of more established humanitarianisms fit their universal ambitions: the 'Millennium' Development Goals are one case, or the campaign of the year 2005 to 'Make Poverty History'. They express collective or institutional ambitions, while they often subsequently fail to achieve these in their entirety, too. Everyday humanitarian practices are confronted with this in a pronounced fashion, however, rendering them a particularly apposite case for exploring this tension. A key challenge for all forms of humanitarianism is that not all of humanity can be 'saved': whether large institutions or small groups of individuals, their interventions are necessarily limited in scope. They have to decide whom to support. No matter how they are being selected, the challenge of the partial-ness of humanitarianism remains. This chapter explores one response to this situation: the making of the scale of one.

In order to understand how those involved in everyday humanitarianism respond to this situation, I adopt the premise articulated by Carr and Lempert that scales are made not given, and that 'scale is process before it is product', as discussed in Chapter 1. Like their collection, this chapter explores 'how, why, and to what ends people and institutions scale their worlds' (2016:8–9). The framework of making scales, paying attention to what scales are made, how this happens and what use these are put to, is particularly suited to explain a key operating mode of everyday humanitarianism. This is the mode of saving a single life, or the tenet that 'every person counts'. Studying scale means 'to examine how the ideals of social life stand in tension with notions of what is practically achievable' (Carr and Lempert 2016:10). It captures neatly the archetypical tension characteristic of humanitarianism, that is, the tension between certain 'ideals of social life' – such as the wish to save everyone – and the practicality of what one person, or a small group of individuals can achieve. How people respond this situation, is by understanding their response (also) as a form of making scales.

The resulting scales – for example, that 'every person counts', or that the single life is worth saving – are used to justify and frame ensuing interventions. They are a way for everyday humanitarians to guide and make sense of their actions. Carr and Lempert state that scales are useful because 'they help people orient their actions, organize their experience, and make determinations about who and what is valuable' (2016:9). This chapter documents what scales are being made, and how they matter for practices of everyday humanitarianism and what use they are being put to. People deploy multiple scales, sliding between and interlinking them as it suits them. For, as Carr and Lempert remind us, 'scales are ways of seeing and standing in the world, and as such, they are also instruments for political, ritual, professional, and everyday action' (2016:10).

The scales described here stipulate that the individual life and efforts to support it have value in and of itself. In the first instance, I consider examples of the semiotic labour involved in making such scales. It emerges that 'every person counts' contains more than one set of meanings and practices. The first is understanding this focus as single acts of care; the second is, considering the person as a site for change. The question arises whether this tenet is simply born of pragmatism: why is this particular scale being made and valorised? While there are pragmatic limits, I pick up on the view – passionately held by many – that this cannot be reduced to mere necessity. Rather, focusing on the single person, beyond value in itself, is considered as 'the only way to work'. This particular scale comes in different guises. Malkki refers to such framework as the 'logic of the one' (2015:14). This means imagining 'one singular child, one singular benefactor' of their supportive efforts, creating a feeling of responsibility (2015:14). While I would consider this undoubtedly an instance of such making of scale, Malkki herself does not use it explicitly for such purpose in her discussion.

A related case of scale-making in a humanitarian context is provided in China Scherz's work on Franciscan nuns in Uganda (2013). In a charity home, they are providing for abandoned children, which is often in a manner which funding bodies consider unsustainable and unaccountable. This includes not keeping proper records of those they look after or taking more children in than they can reasonably afford. Squarely refuting such criticisms, it becomes clear that for the Sisters, the scales employed by 'professional' charitable bodies lack relevance. Instead, they are living and working with a set of scales which take into account the effects of divine power. As Scherz explains, 'they believe that only God can complete and perfect their imperfect works, which are always broken, always partial, as they believe themselves to be' (Scherz 2013:632; see also Gell 1992 and Watanabe 2015 on the use of temporal scales in development). Scherz notes that while operating within such framework poses constant challenges, such as justifying expenses to donors, it is the only way for the nuns to accommodate the partial-ness of their endeavours. Following from this, I turn to a different form of scale-making, which also offers a way of dealing with the inevitable shortcomings of any form of humanitarianism, and the labour required to enable it.

Semiotic labour

Carr and Lempert argue that the process of making scales is the result of continuous efforts, in the form of 'semiotic labour'. Given their importance for guiding action, 'the scales that social actors rely upon to organize, interpret, orient, and act in their worlds are not given but made – and rather laboriously so' (2016:3). The recognition that people undertake substantial efforts to structure their world linguistically is not necessarily new. Lakoff and Johnson, for example, highlight some of the 'metaphors we live by'. These linguistic forms structure people's realities, are produced and have efficacy in everyday lives (1980 [2003]). While such semiotic approaches are not deployed explicitly in anthropological analysis, Carr and Lempert consider them an 'especially powerful ethnographic strategy' (2016:8). Even though the case of humanitarianism does not appear in their collection, I suggest that such argument is certainly borne out in the context of everyday humanitarianism (see also Brkovic 2016).

A key trope, and indeed the scale that underpins much of everyday humanitarianism, is the value of the single person. It appears as the slogan 'every person counts', which forms the mainstay of the 'Starfish Story'. Many of the outward-facing communications, including projects run by Cambodian humanitarians, are in English, not least to render them accessible to foreign supporters and volunteers. However, the 'humanitarian space' in Cambodia is not clearly demarcated by local religious charity or gifting, although they are important (Feener and Wu 2020). Rather, it is best characterised as a hybrid space, where some manifestations of semiotic labour have origins elsewhere but are being purposed to a local context. A pertinent question is how such 'logics', espousing the value of the individual, point to political or ideological contexts from which they may have travelled. While the 'logic of the one' was invoked by both Cambodians and foreigners, it is possible to read this as yet another manifestation of a neoliberal discourse, which champions the role of the individual over and above other collectively conceived responsibilities and practices. In Cambodia, this takes on particular resonance in the context of the recent debate whether collective action and solidarity have ever been a feature of Cambodian life, at least in its rural areas, as suggested by Trankell, Ovesen and Ojendal (1996). In practice, a more nuanced look reveals differences between everyday humanitarians. While some certainly espoused discourses of neoliberal enterprise, for others, the focus on 'the One' was shorthand for 'a small group', a 'family' or 'a few people'.

The theme of 'the one' was promoted for example by the Indochina Starfish Foundation. They describe themselves as an NGO 'that believes every child has the right to education, healthcare and play', embodied by the motto emblazoned on their website, 'Making a difference, one child at a time'. Another NGO, Starfish Project, also derives its philosophy from the parable. The expression, 'Every Person Counts', was displayed on the walls of a cafe run by a small NGO in a Cambodian provincial town. It featured on its website, merchandise, and on the NGO-branded T-shirts on sale. It summed up their ethos working with and for people with disabilities – who, in the absence of support by the state, are among the most disadvantaged. Such emphatic commitment to the value of the individual is not unique to projects dedicated to those living with a disability. Rather, I argue that the value of the individual, or the belief that 'every person counts', fundamentally motivates and shapes forms of everyday humanitarianism.

The scale that is being made through such semiotic labour is the 'value of the one'. Nothing embodies the spirit of grassroots aid as poignantly as the insistence that every person counts. It finds resonance in earlier forms, such as the belief that 'anyone who saves a life, is as if he saved an entire world' (Talmud, Mishnah Sanhedrin 4:5). Understood as a metonym, saving one symbolically saves everyone. Another prominent form is child sponsorship, popularised in NGO campaigns and documentaries such as 'One Small Act' (2010). This connects one donor to one child, and engages them in a powerful way in personalised relationships (Bornstein 2001; Rabbitts 2012; Watson 2015). This belief can also be central for some large organisations, notably medical NGOs such as Médecins sans Frontières (MSF). These uphold the individual life even in emergencies affecting hundreds or thousands. As Peter Redfield observes, 'MSF humanitarianism operates under the clinical logic of "one patient at a time", seeking to treat "the patient before us" [...] Like a good shepherd, it seeks to secure each and every member of its conceptual flock' (2013:156). This holds that every person is valuable, and every life worth saving, independent of concerns about efficiency or scope. Following Carr and Lempert, we can see how 'people use language to scale the world around them'.

Acts of care

The belief that 'every person counts' belies a more complex reality, in that the proclaimed focus on the individual can mean many things. Here, it encompasses single acts of care; catalysing change in one person; and finally, considering the individual not just valuable in itself, but as the way to bring about change in wider society. Such singular acts of care and relief have been described also in the context of support to migrants (Sandri 2018:74). In the informal refugee camp in Calais, labelled 'the Jungle', the task of a kitchen volunteer, for example, consisted of preparing hot drinks in muddy and cramped conditions, and handing out cups of tea and biscuits to people who had fled, offering a gesture of humanity in a moment of mutual recognition. In addition to support through campaigning, a conversation or a smile are not considered vain gestures, but practices of care that are meaningful in their own right, independent of the broader context.

One such everyday humanitarian engaged in acts of care was Mabel, originally from Malaysia, who ran a volunteer soup kitchen in a residential area of Siem Reap. The kitchen reached a considerable number of people: during the week in the school term, they provided a daily lunch to twenty or more schoolchildren in the area, who would otherwise not have had a cooked meal. At the weekend, with the help of a substantial team of volunteers, they prepared around six hundred lunch packages, consisting of rice parcels and a vegetable curry, to disadvantaged families living on the outskirts of town. Nevertheless, Mabel was very clear that with her whole soup kitchen operation, '*I'm not saving anyone.*' More specifically, she meant that even though the food packages which the families were receiving on a Saturday was '*possibly the most nutritious meal they'll have all week*', the project would not substantially improve their lives. Beyond its nutritional importance, she saw the value of the food packages as an act of care, rather than an act of saving them from starvation.

As the name of her project Reach Out indicated, the ambition was to reach, rather than transform or even save a life. Mabel recalled the case of Sopheap, a woman in her thirties, who was living by herself near Mabel's home. Sopheap liked to attend the soup kitchen and sit down there to have a meal in the company of Mabel's team and the neighbourhood kids. This was not, Mabel assured, because she was not able to feed herself, but rather '*because she wants to be taken care of*'. Sopheap's husband had left her some time ago. She was renting a single room in a house nearby and was earning some money from selling self-made handicrafts. While some of her basic needs were met, Mabel's kitchen provided a place of sociability, mingling with a steady stream of foreign volunteers and providing company.

Such single acts of care were also performed at one of the stops on the food distribution round that Mabel and her team undertook on a Saturday. The stop was a concrete bungalow set in a compound, the building in a state of half-completion, and possibly abandoned by a previous resident. Around the courtyard were a number of rooms, with open doors and empty window frames, each inhabited by one, and sometimes two people. Inside were their sparse belongings, a sleeping mat, a small gas-fired cooker, and a shelf with cooking utensils. As the team approached and were handing out food, Mabel chatted with Srey, one of two sisters who were living here, catching up on the week, enquiring about people's health, whether one of the older residents had been able to get up and walk around at all. Most of the dozen or so people living here had no immediate family to look after them; some had mental health issues, were living with a disability or managing the effects of old age without immediate help. None of them were able to support themselves by earning a living, though some were more mobile and supported others with mundane, daily practical tasks as they were able. The concrete bungalow and its surroundings recalled what João Biehl described as 'zones of abandonment' (2013). And yet, despite the evident absence of care from the state, the people here were not entirely abandoned. In addition to the companionship and support they received from other residents, Mabel and her team were welcomed here. A sign, perhaps, that they were not forgotten, that someone cared enough to visit regularly and bring food with them. Even though most of this may have been remedial, and Mabel's interventions would not substantially improve their lives, they were acts of care which realised the tenet that every person mattered. This is not to gloss over more complex relationships of (in)dependence and care which played out among residents and visitors. These include the possibility that intended acts of care might be perceived as hurtful (Cole 2012). For the present purposes, the fact that students kept returning to pick up their lunch, and village residents queued to receive their family meals, instantiated at least the intention that 'every person mattered'.

A similar scenario was evident in Stella's project, mentioned in Chapter 2. Stella, a US citizen now in her seventies, had turned to Buddhism several years ago, and had set up a hospice supporting Cambodians suffering from HIV/Aids. The main purpose of the project was to provide practical and spiritual support to those in the final stage of life, dispensing medicine and providing palliative care. As Stella described it, *'we are holding their hands and doing* [Buddhist] *chanting with them'*. Her project, House of Hope, was relatively unusual as their interventions, while focused on the single person, were not oriented towards a future. This characteristic set them apart from many other initiatives discussed here. As mentioned, many of the practices documented in the Cambodian context are aimed towards improving the circumstances of young people – activities fundamentally geared towards generating better life chances for them. As becomes visible with those initiatives, the tenet that 'every person counts' can extend beyond singular acts of care, aiming to bring about change in the life of an individual.

Turned-around lives

Initiatives revolving around the person as the site of change abound among everyday humanitarian projects. In its simplest version, an outside intervention turns around the life of a person. Harun for example was a Malaysian national, running an IT business, and living in Cambodia with his wife Nary, who had grown up in a village. As he remarked drily in conversation, '*my wife was rescued by NewHaven*'. As he explained, this NGO that offered young Cambodians training in catering and hospitality, had an enrolment drive in her village, offering her the opportunity to move to the provincial town. Nary had gone on to work in the tourism industry, later being employed by a major hotel and leaving behind what might have been a life of subsistence farming. Having met and married Harun, she earned her own income, and their three children were attending a good school in town. In Nary's case, this life change was brought about gaining a place on a training scheme, being able to support herself, and marrying a middle-class foreigner. In other cases, the change in one person can manifest as gaining dignity, status or social visibility as a person.

Rob, for example, passionate about people living with disabilities, told me what had happened that week with a young woman, Sokanthy. She was living with a disability, the result of an injury caused by a land mine, and was now a wheelchair user. People had brought Sokanthy to his attention. Through his connections and brokerage, he was able to find a collapsible wheelchair previously owned by a fellow American, Mike, a wheelchair user himself. Expensive and difficult to find in Cambodia, a collapsible wheelchair can make a big difference to people's mobility and ability to earn a living. A story of this donation, with a picture of Sokanthy and Mike in their wheelchairs was subsequently featured in the English language newspaper, the *Phnom Penh Post*. Rob thought that this wheelchair made a difference for how Sokanthy was thinking about herself, beyond the mobility she had gained:

> *so there is this land mine victim, Sokanthy, she lives in this haze, I'm poor, there is nothing I can do about it. That's bullshit. It's about helping her build self-esteem, that she does matter in the world. The choice to do that newspaper story was hers – she said, I'm ready, let's go. The piece was in the Phnom Penh Post, with a picture of her. When I had this BBQ at my house, I showed it to her, and a lightbulb went off in her head, you could see it. I'm ready. I matter in the world. She was like, I've been recognised as a human being.*

'Every person counts' can also mean initiating change in a single person; not necessarily in the form of a changed livelihood, though this might follow. In the first instance, it may be about gaining dignity and self-respect, and that being of value in itself. As Rob explained, in the mid-term, '*her idea is to live independently. She's smart, but she has been stuffed inside her head for so long ... they've had such a limited experience.*'

The focus on 'the One', and the sense of self-worth that Rob alluded to, can also be mobilised and transferred to other contexts. In the project that Lynn and Joshua were running in the informal settlement, the women produced handbags from recycled materials. These were sold in local hotels, each bag with a small label attached, with a portrait of the woman who made it. The reverse side displayed the name of the project, 'Women's Worth', together with the maker's name The focus on 'the One' is thus manifest in making the maker visible as an individual, while connecting her with the person buying and using the handbag. The sense of 'worth' can be read in the first instance of the worth of the bag, being handmade with care, by a known person; but also the worth of the person, whom the buyer might boost financially by purchasing the product, thus adding to the maker's sense of self-worth and ability.

For supporters, it was not the numbers, but hoping that they had changed the course of one life that counted. Marco for example, a German engineer whose wife worked for a large NGO, told me about their experiences, and their efforts to support their staff in their home. For a sense of reward, he explained to me, '*you only really need one thing to work out. Like, we saved two souls.*' Marco reasoned that '*even if nothing comes of Ella's work with the aid agency, because progress is just too slow or entirely absent, we will have saved two souls*'. He was talking about Sam, who worked for them as a night guard for their rented house. Marco and Ella paid for him to attend English classes, which he did with such success that he became an assistant at the English school, and later a permanent staff member. While still working part-time for them, he got married and his wife had a baby. In addition, Ella explained that '*our cook who was working for us, we paid her English lessons, and something with cookery, and now she is teaching in a cookery school*'.

A particularly poignant form is effecting change in people who may have faced bleak prospects otherwise. Barbara, for example, a trained social worker, originally from the UK and in her sixties, used to work in the prison probation service in the UK, before moving to Cambodia. She recounted a story of such a life 'turned around' that she witnessed in the UK. I had asked her about her motivation for her job working in the probation sector. She explained that she had a strong impulse that carried her through: '*Michael Howard, he was home secretary at the time, he said that there was an "individual pathology", like people were just individually evil, and I was like, hang on, there are massive social issues.*' As an example she recalled a woman,

> who I am now great friends with. She runs a very successful business in the UK and donates to charity, she's thoughtful and engaged. She was my client when she was on probation. She was hell in a handcart then ... but look at her now!

Stories of turned-around lives were also prominent in my talks with Lynn and Joshua. Though not a social worker, in her voluntary work Lynn had been involved with young Singaporeans who had been released from prison and placed in a rehabilitation programme. As she describes their relationship, *'we don't have children, but in the end, we've got a lot of children'*, with a laugh. *'They give you a lot of joy.'* She showed me some images on her phone, of a group of three smiling young men from Singapore: *'I have seen so many stories, inspiring stories. These three were all criminals, they were gangsters. One has gone to train with Jamie Oliver, he's better than me now, he has his own chain of restaurants.'* They sometimes came over to Cambodia to help with her project in the urban poor community, an example of 'paying it forward'.

'Paying it forward'

It is clear that for these supporters, an act of care had value in itself; and the change effected in a person's life course was all they were looking to achieve. Nevertheless, in the stories told by Barbara, Lynn and Joshua, there was a tangible sense of satisfaction that not only that the lives of their protégés changed, but that the latter, in turn, reached out to support others. Barbara casually mentioned that the reformed character and friend, now 'donates to charity', having found herself in dire straits earlier in life. Lynn's pleasure derives from seeing the Singaporean young men not just achieving professionally, such as opening their own businesses, but especially when they come to Cambodia to join in in her work, having benefited from such projects in the past. These are instances of what Rob describes as 'paying it forward', supporting others after having been recipients of such help previously.

Ralph also talked about his colleague in his small fair trade project, Chantrea, a Cambodian woman in her thirties. Chantrea, who has a disability, grew up in a small place in the provinces. Disadvantaged and excluded from education, she came to the attention of Ralph's project by chance, while spending a few days in town with her aunt. Since then, she moved into the projects' premises on a semi-permanent basis. She has become essential to Ralph's project, first picking up sewing and dressmaking skills, then managing other staff, learning some English, and selling her own and others' designs in the fair-trade artisan shop that she is now centrally involved with. As Ralph put it, *'it's all about quality and dignity. Look at her now, how she has grown. How she is managing everything. She's inspirational.'* What touched him most, though, is a story he keeps coming back to:

> what really got me, after we had put a lot of [resources] her way; she went back to the village where her mum still lives, and where she was bullied when she was little, and neglected. And you know what she did? She went to the

place with the next-poorest family living in it, and said, how can I help you? She was helping them build a new house. She was paying it forward straightaway.

This was echoed by Chantrea herself, who in an interview filmed to support her project, explained:

my wish for the future is to support other disabled people. Because where I come from, disabled people were not allowed to join in, like setting up a market stall. I want to help disabled people find jobs, and realise their value, show the world what they can do.

A similar situation occurred in a small, Cambodian restaurant, whose owners had been friends with Ralph for a several years. A young girl, Phary, a member of the owners' extended family, came to our table, and Rob asked her about her future plans. She replied she wanted to be a doctor. After she disappeared back inside, Rob reflected:

I've invested in the relationship. When I first met them [the family] they were huddled in this hut, she was washing dishes for the family. They had no toilet and no running water. So I paid for them to have a toilet and water ... and then money to get an education. I kept asking questions, what do you want to do? We set up an educational trust fund for her, so she can later take care of the family. She says she's tired of people dying because they are hungry. That's when I get paid ... it's a pay forward. It's about the girl going forward. She's got an intuitive set of values, it's about caring for others. We've got $500 in her trust fund. So my interventions have ceased here.

What impressed Rob was not just her ambition for herself, but for others, and to see the educational support as something that she would pay 'forward' into the future, referencing a temporal scale. Such imagined futures and pay forwards do not, of course, always materialise. When I talked to Rob on a later occasion, no further mention was made of Phary, and when I casually asked about her and her family, all that transpired was that she had not been able to begin her studies yet.

The affective dimension of everyday humanitarianism shines through many such moments. Leslie, for example, was sitting in their office when several of her students came in, having recently graduated from their programme. One of them, Ty, had begun working as an IT teacher in his former village school. Casting her eye over them, Leslie said gleefully, *'they are our results, they are the fruits of our growing. I'm so excited, I squeeze them with love!'* The emotional resonance of working with 'the one' indicates deep personal investments. Speaking as if they were her children, a form of parental pride was apparent, a visceral excitement in investments bearing fruit, as well as pain or denial when such rewards did not materialise.

As Carr and Lempert remind us, 'to 'study scale, then, is to examine how the ideals of social life stand in tension with notions of what is practically achievable' (2016:10). A pertinent question is why people make particular scales. In the case of everyday humanitarianism, one apparent rationale for why people make a particular scale such as the single life, or 'the One', is that by virtue of their size and informal approach, their financial and other resources are limited in comparison to larger, formal organisations. This determines the time they have available, the resources, financial or otherwise; the amount of friends or volunteers they might have at their disposal, or their capacity to fundraise. One might argue that it is hardly surprising that everyday humanitarian initiatives tend to act according to scales that foreground the 'single person'. This may be modesty or humility by design; since, as some occasionally said by way of explanation, *'this is all we can do'*. I mentioned this as a possible reason for focusing on 'the One' in a conversation I had with Ralph. When I suggested that their focus on individuals was born of necessity, he vehemently disagreed: *'Why do we work with individuals? Not out of necessity, no. Because there is no other way. This is the way.'* Reducing the tenet that 'every person counts' to a pragmatist rationale was anathema to him. He fiercely rejected the implicit suggestion that they were operating to this scale because they did not have the means to do anything else. Rather, Ralph insisted regarding their work with people with disabilities, that *'there is nothing efficient about it. You have to work with the person: everyone is different. This is the only way to do it.'*.

Marco, a long-time Australian resident in Cambodia, also vehemently disagreed with the suggestion that staying small was due to their limited financial and organisational capacity. Instead, he insisted, *'I don't sit in a temple of administration. The longer I do this, the more I realise that the best way to do this is one individual at a time … that's the best way to work.'* As Marco went on to explain his community sports project,

> I work with thirty-six women at the moment, and no more. Once they are integrated, then we can take on more. We go to their houses, see their living circumstances, and then nurture them, and they support and network each other.

He gave the following story as an example of how one might take others with them:

> I've got this project manager, Sochan; she gets $200 a month for that work. She used that money to buy a sewing machine, and then she gets contract work – and she brings in the athletes to do sewing work for her as a sideline [along their sports activities]. So she creates a business for themselves. It's about restoring hope in individuals. What they do with that, is up to them. It's about sports steering them towards employment and a better lifestyle.

> We've got a 90 per cent success rate. People who have successfully rebuilt their lives. For example clothes, the new people from Kampong Speu come along, all scruffy. Sochan says to them, 'we're dressing well here', and she gets them to dress well. She shows them how it's done, and they do it for themselves.

The case described by Marco and the others discussed here, allows for the belief that 'every person counts', whether as an act of care, or to effect change in that particular person's life. Beyond this, the objective of 'growing the person' is also an instrument for change in wider society, following Ralph's and Marco's belief that *'there is no other way. This is the way'*. The scale of 'the One' encompasses a range of practices of how and why the individual is a meaningful object for intervention. In addition to the 'Starfish stories' of individual redemption, there is a shift in the making of scale: towards the future, as one person is *'paying it forward'*, and in terms of scope, as this one person, like Sochan, is *'pulling others along with her'*. This underscores how people skilfully operate with several scales, extending one into the other, according to their shifting and expanding objectives and activities.

Considering the debate around necessity or choice being the reason for not expanding, there might be elements of both at play. As discussed in Chapter 2 on 'the part and the whole', there were those, like Lynn or Aiko who would have had the capacity to scale up, but made a conscious decision not to. Some would quite like to expand, but lack the means to do, such as Abby. Yet again others do not have the capacity either, but are quite aware of their limits, and content with keeping their operations at their current level. Finally, and I do not discuss them in detail here, there are projects which started small, but have since grown substantially to become national or even international actors with policy influence, such as Beat Richner's Kantha Bopha Childrens' Hospitals, or the NGO, Friends International.

Investing in people

An orientation towards the future through a focus on individuals sometimes envisaged as a gateway to change in society as a whole. The semiotic labour required to make this particular link between a few and the many, an individual and society was, people reminded me, encapsulated in the dictum to 'never underestimate the power of a small group of people to change the world. Indeed, it is the only thing that ever has.' Commonly attributed to Margaret Mead, the origins of this quote remain somewhat hazy. This was immaterial, though, for the everyday humanitarians for whom it perfectly encapsulated a theory of change. It fitted their endeavours well, in that some saw themselves, everyday humanitarians, as the 'small group of people' who could change the world. At the same time, their efforts were equally channelled into a 'small group of people', those whom they supported and who, they hoped, would emerge as future change makers themselves. The immense popularity of this and similar quotes illustrate the semiotic labour that everyday humanitarians deployed to articulate the scales and scopes within which they were operating.

Such a theory of change was also evident in Sabine's work. She had initiated a creative writing programme, delivered through standardised workshops which could be run by teams of volunteers in different locations across Cambodia. The aim was to give young people skill sets, based on the assumption that *'the combination of conceptual thinking, language skills and self-esteem are some key antidotes to poverty and corruption'* (Salary.com 2023). Despite targeting the individual as the site for change, Sabine was less concerned about maintaining face-to-face contact with her students, and more intent on this model being shared and replicated widely. As she explained,

> *I'm happy to let other people do the teaching, it doesn't need to be me, forty hours a week. As long as I get that connection, as long as they deliver the product as it's meant to be delivered. I like creating things, and connecting with people. I can see this getting bigger.*

When I asked Sabine whether she thought of herself as part of the development sector, she replied: '*I think of myself as a human rights activist; I'm showing these people how to think. I am teaching them the tools to envision change, and ways of changing their country. I'm making use of literature for social change; creating social change ... to me, that is human rights.*' While not commenting directly on Sabine's work, Ralph agreed more broadly that '*what is missing here in the Cambodian NGO sector is local leadership*'. When I enquired how he thought the focus on the individual mattered for the 'bigger picture', he concluded,

> isn't this how it works in the real world? Change comes about through individuals. Hun Sen doesn't spend money on stuff that doesn't fill his bank account. So don't wait for the government. Just think of the Margaret Mead quote, never underestimate the power of a few people.

Ralph was linking leadership skills to the theory of change which allows individuals to affect change. This was also the theory of change evident in an NGO, a small NGO based in Phnom Penh. Their initials stood for 'Empowering Cambodia', with a strong focus on fostering leadership skills, among other objectives. Their newsletter outlined the purpose of the 'Team Leader' strand of their programme:

these young volunteer leaders not only develop their individual leadership styles but also act as role models for the younger students ... Team Leaders become change agents. The Team Leader programme is a powerful tool that helps to foster maturity, accountability, compassion, humanitarianism and confidence, which serves both the individual and the organization.

Several other organisations I was in contact with had incorporated a strand of 'leadership training' into their programmes, albeit not always in a central manner. The Innovation Project, for example, was initially a combined tour-guiding and youth leadership project, whose founder and former director I interviewed. She embodied the 'leadership' aspect, subsequently winning the 'Skoll entrepreneur of the year' award, as did another NGO leader. Other programmes, such as Free to Thrive, put education objectives at their heart, with leadership an integral, but not central, component of it. Leadership training, in the thinking of these everyday humanitarians, was considered as beneficial for the individual, not least to increase their confidence. Their skills contributed to the running of the organisation, as well as to wider society, by becoming change agents.

As these examples show, investing in people, combined with a leadership model, was considered by some as a way to change wider society. While this was borne out in some of the cases I was aware of, such leadership skills were not necessarily evident in those running the programmes. For example, some stated that they were committed to 'handing over' the project to their Cambodian deputy director, often extolling their virtues and readiness to 'take over' at a near point in the future. However, when I visited, talked with or caught up on the projects a year or sometimes two years later, some of the then-directors remained in place. This was the case for a range of reasons, such as the sense that the project needed a 'foreign' outside facing director for the sake of fundraising in the Global North; the feeling that the deputy was not quite ready to take over; or the desire by the founder to carry on what they were doing, since what they enjoyed most was their central, hands-on role. While I have some longitudinal data, there is a range of outcomes. Some founders left, and their Cambodian partners were successfully running the project, especially if they had been equally involved beforehand. Some projects ended, with the founder ceasing to be active; in a couple of cases, a handover had taken place, and later been reversed. While some founders placed emphasis on leadership training within their team, this did not necessarily translate in letting their Cambodian deputies actually take over the overall direction of the projects.

The distinction of the micro and the macro, with the formal aid sector being aligned with the 'macro', persisted in conversations I had with people who had experience of working for large aid organisations, or were still doing so. Often, those in larger organisations were involved in private aid projects precisely because their daytime work operated on a level of policy, and the impacts of this work were not always evident to them. Their engagement in such everyday humanitarianism offered rewards and a sense of accomplishment, as well as personal connections, which were not easily available to them in their daytime occupation. I have explored in more depth how and why professional aid workers pursue their own projects elsewhere (Fechter 2020; see also Polman 2008 on 'MONGOs', and Eltringham 2019).

A recurring sentiment concerned much frustration with the work and its failure to effect the desired change, Richard, one long-term development consultant, who spent around two decades on community development projects and as a consultant in the UK, Cambodia and in other parts of Asia, told me that, *'the only thing I've ever achieved is investment in people'*. This sentiment was echoed by Philip, an economics graduate who had been working for a UN organisation in Cambodia for several years, and had more than twenty years' experience. His conclusion was that *'when I look at all the things that we've done, all the projects, the only thing that I know has made a difference is the* [Cambodian] *people we have trained up in the office'*. Karen, a researcher with a youth-focused local NGO, shared these insights. She returned to Cambodia nearly a decade after having worked there, and had caught up with former staff and volunteers of the NGO which had by then disbanded. It became clear that most of them had found jobs, a couple had moved abroad for further education and one was on a diplomatic career trajectory. Reflecting on her time with them, she found that *'basically, what we have done was capacity building. Allowing them to get better jobs, go into business or in the NGO sector, or maybe just become better voters in a struggling democracy'*. One might wonder how this relates to the current socio-economic situation in Cambodia, where intimidation of vulnerable populations and forced resettlement in contested areas function as power mechanisms of the ruling elites. These practices often prevent residents from enacting effective opposition to instances of land-grabbing and deforestation. Placing faith in educating young voters may thus be an unreliable strategy.

Conclusion

The problem animating this chapter is the inevitable partial-ness intrinsic to humanitarianism, namely that 'you can't save everyone'. Heeding Carr and Lempert's proposition (2016) to pay attention to scales includes examining which ones are being made, how, and what consequences that has. In the case of everyday humanitarianism, one tentative answer is that making a scale such as of the individual, or 'every person counts', allows practitioners to deal with the challenge of the limits of everyday humanitarianism. Considering the semiotics of scale-making, the apparently simple scale of 'every person counts' is associated with a range of practices, and different ways of meaning-making. In the first instance, the semiotics of the single starfish being rescued suggested that the meaning of everyday humanitarian acts is found in saving a single soul. This may consist of a singular act of care, such as being given a weekly portion of curry and rice. The scale prefigured in the 'Starfish Story', however, also allows for acts of 'saving' and redemption, such as the life chances of a person being turned around. If one were looking for a way to conceptually accommodate one's practical limits as an everyday humanitarian, then intervening under the auspices of the 'starfish' paradigm provides such conciliation.

In a twist of sliding scales, it turns out that practices carried out under the mantra of 'every person counts' can be read not only as giving meaning to a single act, but also orient action beyond the individual. This was expressed in semiotics such as 'paying it forward'. This manifested when a change in an individual's life course became part of a process as that person, newly enabled, enacted charity of their own, thus effecting life changes in others. Carr and Lempert warn that 'tropes like scalar "leaps" or "jumps," or the often-used idea of scaling "up" or "down" do not mean any one thing across cases and should not be treated as stable analytic terms' (2016:7). Taking this into account, what is taking place is a scalar 'slide', rather than a jump or leap. Further, the firm focus on the present associated with the mantra of 'every person counts', is infused with orientation towards the future: 'paying it forward', and 'investing in people' who then look after those who are less fortunate than themselves.

More accurately than jumping or leaping, which suggest scales as distinct from each other, everyday humanitarians constantly operate with one, two or several scales at the same time, nimbly interlinking them. One such manifestation consists of shifting from 'every person counts' to individuals as agents of change. Furnishing the numerical scale of 'every single person counts' with a temporal horizon – that is, becoming change-makers and 'paying it forward', as well as envisaging greater numbers than 'the one' through 'taking others with them', shows how everyday humanitarians creatively extend and fuse temporal and numerical scales. They are thus producing a more comprehensive answer to the problem of the limited scope, and partial-ness of their endeavours. In addition to contributing to our understanding of scale-making, this approach renders a better understanding of humanitarianisms. Specifically, it unsettles notions of humanitarian practices as being either 'small' or 'large-scale', 'local' in contradistinction to 'international' and 'global'. Instead, a scalar approach allows us to see how humanitarians themselves conceive of their activities, where such binaries are replaced by interrelating humanitarian practices, and predefined sets of scales are exchanged for a set of self-made, interlinking ones to guide their actions.

4

Distance and proximity

What is wrong with Cambodia that these people need to come here to fix it? And what is wrong with all these people that they need to come to Cambodia to help?

This exasperated sigh by Sovann, a Cambodian researcher and consultant, spoke of his incomprehension and dismay at the flow of both international aid workers and everyday humanitarians to Cambodia. As if to reinforce his point, when I asked a class of first-year students in development studies in the UK which one of them was hoping to work overseas, almost all raised their hand. There is indeed 'potency to the idea of distance in humanitarian practice' (Pallister-Wilkins 2018:998). This is prominently embodied in the figure of the distant stranger, a trope as ubiquitous as it is simplistic, but nevertheless a 'key component of a dominant humanitarian imaginary' (Barnett 2011). Craig Calhoun similarly finds that 'humanitarian response to emergencies is quintessentially cosmopolitan. It is an effort to mitigate the suffering of strangers' (2012:3–2), espousing the globally minded and border-crossing nature of such endeavours.

The notion of distance, including its physical and social dimensions, has loomed large in how philosophers and ordinary people construct responsibilities towards others. A key question is, 'what difference does distance make to our concern for others? Should it matter at all?' (Silk 2000:303). Others have aimed to 'flesh out the role that distance […] plays in both our moral and political relationships, as well as our theories about those relationships' (Ghandeharian 2014:4). The tentative answer offered here is that a scalar lens recognises the fluidity of geographical scales, acknowledging that distance is 'multi-scalar in the extreme' (Pallister-Wilkins 2018:997). Rather than considering distance in the modus of 'saving distant strangers', it is also a distance marked by self and other (Pallister-Wilkins 2018). Efforts are made to overcome this through the practice of supporting others, or indeed accepting support from them. I turn to this in Chapter 5, which highlights the desire to connect with others across such distances.

The term 'humanitarian distance' emerges from studies of long-distance humanitarianism arising from the empire-charity nexus in the context of colonial expansion (Stamatov 2010; Barnett 2011). Historian Michael Barnett centrally aligns the 'the relationship between the extension of western concern for distant strangers and the expansion of western empires' (Barnett 2011). As 'colonial relationships were the means by which the distance and difference that lay at the heart of humanitarianism came into Europeans' view' (Skinner and Lester 2012:732), this has given the distant stranger a more canonical role than is borne out in practice. Such focus has been cemented by a concern in media studies with 'humanitarian spectators'. These watch suffering from afar, while those in need remain physically remote from them, raising questions about the ethics of this engagement (Boltanski 1999; Chouliaraki 2012). While historians have often foregrounded the centrality of geographical distance for notions and histories of humanitarianism, this misrecognises that humanitarian activities and geographical distance mutually constitute each other in a more complex and dynamic way. Studies of humanitarian space – a concept related to, but different from, humanitarian distance – allow for a more flexible conceptualisation of this relationship. This is because space is more obviously being made, and shapes people's practice in turn. This has led to rich debates about how space matters for aid work; how close practitioners are to the communities they are working with (Hilhorst and Jansen 2010; Smirl 2015), and how increasing distance to these communities can diminish the kind of aid being delivered (Collinson and Elhawary 2012). The humanitarian arena has been characterised as a country in itself, as 'Aidland' suggests a distinctive space with its own inhabitants, history, time and culture (Apthorpe 2011).

In contrast to the foregrounding of humanitarian distance as central yet fixed, this chapter argues in the first instance, that the distance between people extending support and those that it is aimed at is dynamic. The geographical scale of 'distance' is being shrunk and expanded; everyday humanitarians move between seeking proximity, and then distance. The manifestations of this making and unmaking of proximity and distance are illustrated here. Second, it becomes clear that these intersections between the production of proximity and distance are characterised by fundamental tensions. On the one hand, geographical distance, and what it entails or promises, can offer an incentive for humanitarian action. Subsequently though, proximity may produce demands and posit responsibilities that some find troubling and overwhelming, and can eventually lead to people extracting themselves from such proximity to poverty altogether. While physical nearness is sought initially, its consequences are then sometimes feared or avoided. This chapter examines some of these movements between proximity and distance, the tensions arising and people's responses to them.

One of the intellectual implications of acknowledging this dynamism is unsettling the figure of the 'distant' stranger as the archetypal object of humanitarianism. We need to recognise that humanitarian activity is not predicated on someone who is both faraway and alien.

The interrelation between geographical distance and humanitarian practice is multi-faceted. This section highlights an aspect of this relation which is in many ways fundamental, but not often discussed systematically. This is the role of geographical distance, and the attendant differences embedded in it, in attracting people to undertake humanitarian practices across borders and outside their countries of origin. The very notion of distance and all that it entails can be a key factor drawing people into aid work in the first place. Owing, perhaps, to a paradoxical logic, the fact that these needy populations are both geographically far away, as well as different socially, culturally and economically, act as an incentive to assist, rather than being a drawback, due to what some moral philosophers posit as a reduced obligation caused by greater geographical and social distance. The fact that helping needy strangers can be as attractive, if not more so, than helping one's 'nearest and dearest' at home, is nevertheless consistent with a moral intuition which holds that people are more likely to assist those who are socially close and geographically near. Precisely because helping those nearby is considered the norm, it becomes more visible, and perhaps more valuable, to help those who are unrelated and far away. This may mean that it becomes more attractive to those who want to make their humanitarian work visible to themselves and others.

This chapter explains the role of distance for everyday humanitarian intervention, and how these practices, in turn, shape the kinds of spaces and distances that are created in the process. It also makes visible how constructing responsibility and distance are entwined processes. The chapter provides tentative empirical answers to the question how distance matters for our concerns towards others. This means understanding distance not as geographical and fixed, but as dynamic, flexible and made or scaled. The ethnographic material considered here suggest that geographical distance is not given and fixed, but is being scaled by everyday humanitarians according to their purpose, shaping them and their activities in return. In the first instance, distance invites humanitarian action, by promising quicker and greater gains across transnational borders. Once being in proximity to poverty however, this forces deliberation, and deploys formal scripts to facilitate moral reasoning. Physical closeness to poverty is valorised as morally good; at the same time, distance is being continuously re-created and retained when it becomes too uncomfortable.

Finally, saturation with such proximity can lead overseas humanitarians to extract themselves altogether, not wanting to participate in what they perceive as a direct complicity in the inequalities they witness. Some take over social responsibilities in their home countries instead, eliminating physical distance as a condition for everyday humanitarian practice. While broadly speaking, everyday humanitarians comprise Cambodian nationals and those from abroad, the arguments considered in this chapter mainly emerge from, and apply to, international humanitarians and aid workers. They matter for Cambodians, too, in so far as distance between urban and rural areas come into play, or relative nearness or distance to poverty. The chapter concludes that humanitarians with mobility privileges, whether Cambodian or foreign, can scale and modulate distances to suit their purpose.

The value of distance: making a bigger difference

One example of the potency of 'distance' for humanitarian interventions can be found in a poster seeking recruits for the North American Peace Corps. This boldly claims that *'The difference between a career and a purpose is about 8,000 miles'*, with an addition in smaller print, *'Life is calling. How far will you go?'* (The Borgen Project 2013). Geographical distance is presented here as inviting support to others that is more noble and meaningful than what could be achieved in an ordinary career at home: a frequent slogan on similar advertisements asks, 'Life is calling: how far will you go?' A similar exhortation is visible in memoirs entitled, 'When the world calls' (Mathers 2010; Meisler 2012). References to distance are threaded throughout such discourses, such as 'where do you go when your desire to help is larger than your zip code?'

Geographical distance offers rewards to those who traverse it, whether as spiritual merit, a sense of purpose or in more material forms. This is not specific to humanitarian practices. Matthew Hayes has described this dynamics in the context of socio-economically privileged migrants, US retirees who move to countries such as Ecuador. They capitalise on their economic and social assets to enable them to live in more luxurious and comfortable conditions abroad than they would have enjoyed in their home country, a condition which Hayes describes as based on geoarbitrage (Hayes 2018). This refers to differentials in earning power, income and living costs between countries of origin and, in Hayes's case, in the destination countries of these lifestyle migrants. A similar dynamics is arguably at work among business expatriates who are posted by their companies with generous pay and benefits packages to countries in the Global South (Fechter 2009). Such geoarbitrage is also at play in forms of transnational everyday humanitarianism, and partly explains its attractiveness to overseas humanitarians. The concept of rewards in Hayes' example, and in the context of everyday humanitarianism, means that more can be gained or achieved with comparatively modest means. The relevant assets in the Cambodian context mean that people's efforts to 'make a difference' can yield much greater rewards in a low-income country context than they might do at home.

A case in point was Jan, a German researcher and development consultant, who had been working intermittently in Cambodia for three years. One reason he was attracted to living there was the 'sense of possibility' that Cambodia offered him. In particular, he was taken by the extent and speed of personal development it afforded him, alongside a much higher efficacy of his work. He explained this by the fact that, *'the stakes are so much higher here. Everything is so tragic that that you have a much better chance of making a difference.'* What Jan meant by 'tragic' was Cambodia's history of recent civil war; the loss and trauma that many families experienced, and indeed the still widespread poverty among the population. In in his view, the stakes were higher due to the severity of their experiences, which meant that the possibilities for improvement in their lives were greater, especially with the means afforded a foreigner with spare time, expertise, financial means and good intentions. Jan, specialising in anti-corruption and good governance programmes in his paid work, felt that need for political reform in Cambodia was more urgent, and he was able to help address this more effectively than he would have been in Germany.

Magnus, a Dutch engineer, illustrated a further facet of this situation. He had been setting up his own aid project alongside his work for an international organisation. What excited him most about doing this in Cambodia was, as he explained, *'that so much is possible. Something always comes up, there are so many contacts and opportunities.'* Cambodia's relative lack of regulation of the NGO sector, the comparative flexible and fluid conditions that were non-existent in the Netherlands, were crucial for his decision to become active in Cambodia. For other people such as Hilde, Cambodia represented a space to grow professionally for similar reasons. Working in a small social enterprise in the arts, she recounted how she had set up 'a huge festival' when she first started in Cambodia, *'with very little experience – I don't know how I thought I could do it, it was huge'*, not only initiating it, but also subsequently growing it. For Hilde, the benefit was to try things out and in her words, 'make mistakes' without severe repercussions. Making mistakes here referred to having the leeway for trial and error, and that the consequences of making wrong decisions, Hilde felt, could be righted more easily, in a context where people were not held to the standards she might have expected at home. Such leeway to 'make mistakes' is undeniably tied to people's status as foreign, and often white, experts, and can have lethal consequences. A case in point is the American missionary Renee Bach, who was accused of killing more than one hundred children through treating them in a 'clinic' she ran in Uganda without any medical knowledge or qualification (Levy 2020). Others, such as the late medical doctor Beat Richner, a founder of childrens' hospitals, keenly emphasised that only the highest standards of medicine were acceptable in the hospitals he oversaw, and that there would be no tolerance of 'third world medicine' that meant being of a lower standard (Richner 2010).

Rita, a German trained nurse and long-time development worker, had begun her professional trajectory in a refugee camp in Djibouti, followed by a post in rural Afghanistan in the early 1970s. She was drawn to international aid work because she felt that as a nurse in post-war Germany, her ambitions at work were continuously thwarted. In this sense, there are parallels with colonialism and other forms of migration for career advancement, especially for women, which were not possible in the metropole, but in the reaches of empire (Cooper and Stoler 1997). Rita remembered how she had repeatedly asked her supervisor to take on a more senior nursing role, only to be told that 'she would be starting a family soon anyway', and that her ambition was misplaced because of her being female. Rita had remained single throughout her life, but was keen for adventure and to see the world beyond her hospital in the south of Germany, as well as escaping its gendered hierarchies. Choosing to work overseas, without having familial responsibilities to consider, she left her nursing job and joined a branch of the German overseas development service. For the duration of her career, until her retirement in her early sixties, she was working in the health sector, training nursing practitioners. This ranged from time spent in male-dominated missions in Afghanistan, and a series of postings in sub-Saharan Africa, including Ghana and Rwanda. The last years of her career were spent training nurses at a provincial government hospital in Cambodia. The opportunities available for someone in her situation at that time to grow professionally and personally were found in places distant from home. The bigger difference invoked here related to her professional work, as well as to her own life. Rita had been able to travel, to work in circumstances which were both precarious and exciting, and to gain responsibility in a way that she had desired. In her free time, she was actively engaged in everyday humanitarian projects, which she found particularly rewarding. All of this was made possible by geoarbitrage, benefiting from differentials borne out of geographical distance.

'Helping plus': the colour and the chaos

In his novel, *Bleak House* (1996), Charles Dickens satirised the 'telescopic philanthropy' he saw among well-off Victorian families who were more interested in the distant poor in Africa than the urban poor on their doorstep. A group who are, by definition, engaged in telescopic philanthropy, are everyday humanitarians who set up projects outside their countries of origin, whether in Asia or in the Global North. The figure of the overseas humanitarian is apposite to draw out some of the complexities of relations between proximity and distance. This is partly because the debates on the moral relevance of distance are marked by oppositions of 'near' and 'distant', which are usually equated with 'the well-off' and 'the needy' respectively. International aid workers offer insights on this matter because they traverse geographical distances for professional purposes, between the 'well-off' in their home countries, and 'needy strangers' overseas. This distance, and all it entails, is an incentive to become involved in the assistance of others in the first place. One of the assumptions underpinning the debate on the relevance of distance is that people are more inclined to assist those who are geographically and socially close to them, rather than those who are far away and unrelated, an assumption that does not withstand empirical scrutiny. Dickens' dismissive portrait of long-distance charity suggests some of the motives that attract people, including the romance of exoticism. The snapshot that follows offers a starting point.

One afternoon in Phnom Penh, I was wandering along the local riverfront with a couple, Matt and Anya, both working for international aid agencies. In the early evening light, families had spread their mats on grass patches; vendors with wide-brimmed straw hats were assembling flower garlands and lotus flowers to sell; roast sweetcorn and plastic pouches of popcorn were strung across food carts, honking cars and motorbikes were passing by, tourists trying to cross the busy thoroughfare, new coffee shop outlets flashing their signs alongside the murky river down the slope below. Taking in the scenario, Matt gestured, '*I just love this – the colour and the chaos.*' This remark was intriguing: what difference did distance make? Why was it more appealing to improve other people's lives in a place far away from one's home? What did the shorthand, 'the colour and the chaos', stand for?

Such questions were raised by several of my informants, both Cambodian and foreigners. Sovann, the political science researcher and consultant quoted at the beginning of this chapter, frequently worked with foreign NGO staff. He wondered aloud, '*why do they come here to help? They can do that at home. It's just more sunny and adventurous here.*' Other Cambodian NGO workers used similar references, describing international aid workers as '*looking for heat and adventures*'. Another phrase summed up the desire for such long-distance work as '*helping plus sunshine and adventure*', casting international aid work as a desirable lifestyle (see also Fechter 2011). This resonates with motives for privileged labour migrants such as corporate expatriates, who describe their motivation for seeking employment in Dubai or Singapore as looking for 'tax-free sunshine' (Walsh 2018).

Matt, the Canadian civil servant who first put this to me, described this as having similar responsibilities as working for a government at home, but in 'more colourful' circumstances, such as having a diverse set of colleagues, 'mango parties' to celebrate a bumper harvest in a friends' backyard garden, trips to other countries in the region, a variety of foods to sample, and enjoying the hustle and bustle, or 'chaos' that the Phnom Penh riverfront presented to a casual spectator. Sandra, a Swiss national working for a UN agency, felt similarly that, *'it's a great lifestyle; better than at home!'* For younger people, such as Jan, working overseas and specifically in Cambodia embodied the *'essence of freedom'*. As an enthusiastic dirt biker, he headed out most weekends with friends on trips through rugged countryside terrain. As he explained, such activities went beyond exciting leisure pastimes; rather, Cambodia offered the chance *'to completely re-invent yourself'*.

Geographical distance offers incentives to engage in humanitarian practices across borders, at some remove to international aid workers' home countries. This is partly due to the personal and lifestyle benefits than can be derived through working abroad, captured in the formula used by Jan, *'helping plus'*. One might pick up here a tension between self-interested activities, such as an adventurous lifestyle, and the overall purpose of their activities to assist others. As demonstrated by Malkki (2015), those who help others are often driven by their own needs, such as finding a purpose or battling loneliness. I take the neediness of the helpers as a given here, rather than a contentious issue. Not only has this been widely recognised in the literature (Vaux 2001; de Jong 2011; Fechter 2011), but overseas everyday humanitarians often pointedly remarked to me that 'all their needs were being met' in Cambodia, rejecting a mantle of saintliness that they feared might be bestowed on them. The effects of geoarbitrage, capitalising on differentials in power, expertise and not least privilege, mean that the stakes and rewards of doing humanitarian work abroad can appear higher than in charity work carried out in the Global North.

Incidentally, this holds for researchers too. Going to parts of the world which may be considered 'remote' in relation to academic institutions in the Global North offers advantages in terms of how original or valuable one's research might be considered. As such, even while the kinds of rewards may be different, anthropologists such as myself, benefited from geoarbitrage just the same. Having traversed geographical distances to engage in humanitarian practices, however, the resulting proximity to poverty can be more problematic than expected. The following section explores what happens when people come face to face with hitherto abstract distant strangers.

What are the consequences of their proximity to poverty, and how are they being negotiated?

Troubling proximity

Geographical distance, and the myriad differences engendered by it, incentivise involvement in humanitarianism in the first place. At the same time, physical proximity to those in need, desired as a space for intervention, also necessitates decision-making about how to respond to poverty and suffering, which international aid workers are now facing on a daily basis, in a way that was not the case in their home countries. I have argued that their efforts constitute a form of moral labour (Fechter 2016). This means negotiating moral quandaries that emerge out of physical proximity to poverty. Such situations are not unique to aid workers; but those who travel to Cambodia for the purpose of supporting others, may perceive this as a challenge they must respond to. Among those who do, some prepare a 'script' that provides a course of action. Such scripts exist also for people's encounters with poverty in the Global North (Dean 1999; Lynch and Hilton 2006). What makes them significant and analytically relevant here is that they are a consequence of having crossed distances to support others. Having sought out Cambodia as a country with poor populations where their interventions would be impactful, encountering extreme poverty on the streets is par for the course. Since they were seeking out poverty as a rationale for their journey, an appropriate response to the resulting dilemmas is required. The stakes are indeed higher or, in Jan's words, the situation in Cambodia was 'so tragic anyway'. This extends not just to the possible rewards, but also to being troubled by proximity to poverty. An archetypical situation is the 'beggar's dilemma'. It involves asking, 'What is my personal rule I follow when I encounter a beggar? Do I even have a rule, or do I struggle every time over what I should do?' (Finn 2016). This dilemma is not particular to Cambodia, or encounters in low-income countries, and subject to debates as much in countries of the Global North. Numerous blogs engage in such deliberations, because, authors reckon, it is 'important that we face the moral dilemma' (Nemiroff 2018).

Having such a script or a rule means that people do not re-trace their moral reasoning every time they encounter a similar situation, but they will know what to do, and why this is the right course of action. One might argue that the situation encountered in Cambodia is no different in principle from the homelessness and destitution evident in countries of the Global North. In conversations, however, it emerged that many overseas humanitarians found instances of poverty in Cambodia more intense and challenging than in their countries of origin. They were faced with such troubling intensity when coming face to face with a disabled person begging at the roadside, just metres away from their doorstep; ragged children knocking on their car window at traffic lights; or being approached while having dinner at an outdoor restaurant. Such occurrences were so common that Emma, a former country director of an NGO commented,

> *you must have come across the baby beggar mums. I call them zombie mums – you know, they're holding out their babies in front of them, at night on the Riverfront. You have to work out what to do about them.*

Another aid worker, Linda, who was based in Europe with frequent travel to Cambodia, explained, *'when I see the baby lying on the blanket on the pavement, it reminds me of my own daughters ... it makes me think of the similarities between us'*, and as a result, she normally gave money to the mothers in these situations. These are the consequences of face-to-face proximity which establish a sense of shared experience, such as being a mother of young children, which is not necessarily activated unless faced directly with these situations. This physical proximity triggers a sense of sharedness and gives rise to a moral obligation she then often fulfils by giving them money. Other possibilities were illustrated by one long-term international aid worker, Tony, a highly conscientious and reflective person, who had worked in humanitarian relief for decades. He described this to me as follows:

> *I've spent a long time trying to figure out what to do, and I've come to the view, do whatever I feel like in the moment. When I feel like giving them something, I do, or if I don't, then not. Just be spontaneous.*

While this signals an impulsiveness of self-action, it may come across as dismissive, rather than navigating something more transformative – quite possibly the result of being an 'old hand' in the development world. Such an approach merges the advantages of having a 'script' – a pre-prepared response – with the flexibility of following one's mood. Such spontaneity, however, also means that there is no single right course of action. Rather than going through a laborious reasoning process, Tony found that this satisfied his moral intuition that he ought to do something, though not necessarily all of the time. Such an approach also resonates with what Erica Bornstein termed the 'impulse of philanthropy' (2009), animating acts of spontaneous giving.

Hilde, in contrast, was in her late twenties and had been working for a local NGO involved in arts education for children with disabilities in Cambodia for several years. She was fluent in Khmer language and credited her time in Cambodia as an amazing opportunity for personal and professional growth. She mentioned that her parents were currently visiting her from the UK, but mentioned that her mother 'was not doing so well'. The reason was, she explained, that her mother found it difficult to cope with seeing the poverty around her. '*She doesn't understand how I can face this every day, how I can cope with it without going mad.*' Hilde explained how she found a way of being in Cambodia without the feeling of constantly falling short in responding to moral obligations caused by nearness:

> *First of all, I'm committing a lot of time and energy to my job – which is to support disabled kids, so I feel I'm already doing my bit there. Then, I don't have a guilty hang-up every time I have a can of soda* [pointing to the drink in front of her]. *I'm earning money and that's fine. You have to get over that, otherwise you won't last.*

Hilde thus rejected a particular obligation caused by nearness through a recourse to her paid work, which addressed discrimination and inequalities more broadly already. However, she also told me that she had adopted a particular attitude with regard to people begging:

> *I don't give them money – I smile at them. I used to work a lot with the homeless in the UK before I came here, and I've learnt that it is important to acknowledge them. Even if I don't buy a magazine from them or something, it matters whether I turn away, or if I look at them. They said that this is what makes them feel human.*

While this differed markedly from Tony's response, emphasising the other, it also strategically focused on the other 'feeling' human, rather than engaging with them as human and equal. A distance being emphasised here was still one of inequality.

There was an acknowledgement of a parallel between proximity encounters at home, and in Cambodia. In a different scenario, people who had experienced children begging at their car windows on their way to work explained to me that they thought giving beggars money was generally not advisable. Their response to this particular dilemma was to establish a relationship with the family and give them money, with the obligation that this be used for the children's school fees only. While this appears as a different kind of response to the impulse, as a form of 'diverted giving' (Pérez-Muñoz 2018), it nevertheless involves having a script to counteract the effects of proximity with poverty. Finally, when I joined a group of young volunteers during a discussion at a workshop, several explained to me that they never gave anything to people who were begging, especially not to children. This was partly because they had been told of instances where street children were exploited by a 'handler', who would send them out to beg, in order to collect the money from them afterwards.

The implications from such face-to-face encounters are how distance, as desired by everyday humanitarians, also brings consequences that can be experienced as troubling, such as proximity to extreme poverty. In outlining how people respond to those dilemmas, I show how the 'potency of distance' (Pallister-Wilkins 2018) becomes a potency of proximity. This reveals how rather than distance being central to humanitarianism, it involves handling proximity. It poses potentially more challenging consequences which require deliberation, the production of scripts, and in short, forms of moral labour. The following section examines other instances of the potency of proximity, such as closeness being morally valuable, and as a motivator for everyday humanitarian action.

Closeness as moral good

The country brochure of the then German Development Service for Cambodia one year featured on its front page the caption, 'Nahe dran' (meaning 'nearby' or 'close by'). This signalled the physical proximity, and by extension symbolic closeness, of this voluntary service agency to the people and places they were supporting, Cambodians and rural communities. Such validation of 'closeness' is not uncommon among certain segments of formal aid sector. Indeed, having engaged in 'telescopic philanthropy' as described in this chapter, and taking heed of the Peace Corps' motto that 'the difference between a career and a purpose is 8,000 miles', those agencies and individuals that traverse substantial geographical distances in order to support others find themselves in a situation where they feel compelled to declare how closely engaged they are with the communities they seek to support.

Noticeably, one can observe that such 'closeness' – physical proximity and placing oneself in living conditions that are similar to those of the people who one works with – is more prominent, and more highly valued among volunteers or voluntary service staff, such as the British Voluntary Service Overseas, and those aid workers who are at the start of their careers. Susanne, for example, who worked in private sector development with women pottery makers, remembered how she and her colleagues had been prepared for their two-year stint in Cambodia. Following a month's residential training in Germany, they were transferred on arrival to a guesthouse in a rural area for their in-country preparation and language training, rented by the agency for this purpose. Susanne recounted how, without air conditioning and with only basic facilities, they experienced a sensory immersion: *'you could hear all the sounds at night, see the stars, eat the local food from the market ... and get really sweaty!'* While one might question how much actual similarity there was, unlike other foreigners living in the capital, Susanne was was keen to approximate local living conditions, even though she was cognisant of the fact that she occupied a fundamentally privileged position by voluntarily inserting herself into such circumstances (Osner 2007).

Similarly, when I observed a training session for a group of young German volunteers, part of a government programme, it emerged how living 'close to the people' was not just a consequence of their limited budgets, but also symbolically valued. Comparing notes on their placements in small NGOs across different provinces, the standard way of living for these 19-year-olds included, for example, their accommodation being on the site of the NGO's office; sourcing their main meals from market stalls; and cycling, or riding on the back of pick-up trucks for transport. Even so, one of their training units consisted of an 'immersion weekend' in a local village, where they stayed with a family and took part in farm work, such as rice planting. The aim was to gain as insight into the living conditions in a rural village. This, perhaps unsurprisingly, involved some unwanted consequences, as one female volunteer injured herself handling the tool for cutting rice stalks, while participating in harvesting; a second was bitten by a village dog and had to travel to the nearest town to obtain a preventative does of anti-rabies vaccine. A third contracted typhoid afterwards and was bedridden for some time after, while another volunteer I spoke to explained that they could not handle the manual labour in the fields in the heat, and returned to the village huts to rest and recover. One might argue that such experiential knowledge may be particularly validated in the context of volunteering, in that such programmes are often orientated as much, if not more, towards the personal transformation of the volunteer, rather than the people they are aiming to work with (Irvine, Chambers and Eyben, 2004; Chambers 2007; Fechter 2011).

Some people explained to me that they purposely created some form of physical proximity, or living conditions that did not place them at a remove. Pierre, who worked for the UN, consciously did not switch on the air-conditioning units in his flat, a habit echoed by others. Thomas told me that his way to 'stay close' was to do the grocery shopping himself, in the open market and without someone accompanying him, so he would be forced to negotiate, struggle to communicate, be looked at and occasionally made fun of. '*Look at me*', he said, '*I'm 1.90 tall, white and blonde: of course I totally look out of place, and they'll make fun of me. But I think it's important to put myself out there.*' In Thomas's view, it was important to reduce any semblance of white arrogance or superiority, enacted through creating such physical proximity, rendering himself visible, an object of attention and possible ridicule. Even Callum, a retired school caretaker who lived in modest accommodation in a provincial town, told me that he did not mind that the water supply to his lodgings could be scarce, and was occasionally turned off, along with the rest of the residential area: '*I kind of like the fact that we can't get things, the scarcity. It makes me feel more alive.*'

The physical proximity sought out here is not necessarily equivalent to that advertised in voluntourism experiences (Pedwell 2012). The aims of Thomas, Pierre or Callum, though driven by a range of desires, are not to generate empathy with the poor. Pierre was a battle-hardened, dispassionate international civil servant with little delusions about the role he might play in development. Nevertheless, they all preferred to live in ways that resembled some of those among Cambodians more closely, and perhaps consciously not make use of the privileges afforded to them, such as shopping in supermarkets, switching on air-conditioners, or renting accommodation with a reliable water supply. Physical proximity also generated moral value, a symbolic refusal to take advantage of the privilege available.

Motivating action

Such 'closeness to the people' or maintaining physical proximity is not limited to young volunteers, or those in the early stages of their careers as aid workers. Some professional aid workers may skip such stages altogether, while others take care to maintain such closeness throughout. They need close contact to the base, or the 'coalface', to maintain the motivation and drive for their work. Scott, for example, was an American who ran an educational after-school club in one of the poorer communities on the outskirts of Phnom Penh. One day, I was accompanying him on some errands for the project around the city, when we stopped in a dilapidated area, where he had set up his first English class several years earlier and where he still knew some of the families living there. As we were walking along the streets, and finding our way to one of the classrooms, he was exchanging greetings and talking to a couple of motorcycle taxi drivers, a girl working at a roadside beauty parlour, and stopped to chat with a middle-aged woman selling vegetables. He was recognised, people called out to him, exchanged greetings and nods. '*I'm not doing this often enough*', he explained, '*this is the area where set up our first English classes ... the girl with the beauty parlour, I am glad that she has come off the street ... her sister is a very good singer, they both are actually. They were both part of our first programme.*' A few metres on, he stopped to chat to an older boy, asking him casually, '*Hey, why are you not in school?*'

Scott said that even though this area was only a short *tuktuk* ride from their office building, '*I don't get out enough from the office.*' For him, even these occasional forays, and moments of proximity to the communities their project was seeking to support, checking in on people, were valuable. This may have been partly for symbolic reasons; it was good to see and being seen to be close, as an expression of care and commitment to their endeavour. It was also for pragmatic reasons. In the first instance, it helped Scott get a sense of how people, families who had been or may be part of their programmes were doing; to what extent their work was having any effect, and where possible gaps lay, as in his attention being drawn to the young boy whom Scott thought needed to be in school, not wandering about. As he explained, such proximity motivated his efforts, both through seeing their impact, such as the girl who had 'come off the street' and was selling beauty treatments; and flagging all the people and things that needed tending to further.

This mattered especially since after the initial stage of setting up their schools, Scott found himself spending increasing amounts of time doing management and organisational work in the offices of his organisation. Even though they were still modest, they were located within a music school, dealing with parents, in a central and relatively middle-class location. As an antidote to what he perceived as a comparatively removed position, he made a conscious effort to regularly get out and spend time in the social housing complexes, walking through the narrow alleyways, greeting people, asking after students and their families. Many there made their livelihoods as sex-workers, night-workers, petty traders or offering beauty treatments. While Scott's friendly exchanges took place in a setting marked by poverty, this was not necessarily a source of distress, but a crucial reminder of why he worked there, providing renewed motivation for his, and his team's, efforts to improve opportunities for the young people growing up there. The proximity he sought was here for a functional purpose, in addition to the broader 'closeness' being generated. Scott kept walking through the area not just for a sensory immersion, but also as a reminder why he set up their project in the first place and why it was still very much needed, as the basic living conditions of people inhabiting the area had not really changed.

A similar strategy of seeking proximity to their clients was adopted by Maxim, who had set up a pioneering peer-to-peer diabetes support programme. As he explained, he took care to regularly go out into their project areas, as well as bringing clients or peer educators into the head office in Phnom Penh. In particular, he was keen that the Cambodian staff members '*don't forget what it's like in the village*'. Similarly, Justin, who had been deeply involved in primary school educational programmes for more than twenty years, had always insisted on working out of an office in a provincial town, and travelled to Phnom Penh only when necessary, for meetings. As he told me emphatically, '*I couldn't do this if I wasn't close to the project and the people. I could never work on government level.*' This matters, as it shows that such 'closeness' is not merely a stage which people move through before they establish themselves in a capital city or wealthy part of town, at a remove from those they want to support. Rather, it can be a choice of a mode of being, and how to carry out their activities. This resonates with findings of professionals in the Global North preferring the 'coalface', such as teachers who choose the classroom over managerial roles; social workers who aim to remain in close contact with clients rather than working in policy areas, or industry managers who aim, at least periodically, to remain in touch with the 'factory floor'. To sum up, proximity to poverty can precipitate a range of responses: sought-after in the first instance, it can become troubling as a feature of the everyday, requiring a search for adequate responses. At the same time, it is experienced as morally good, with physical closeness signalling empathy, displaying and generating an ongoing desire to support others. These moments of interaction emphasise their equality more than structural inequalities, even though such interactions remain symbolic rather than transformative.

Reducing and retaining distance

In a movement of 'bringing things back in' or 'keeping them close', some purposefully reminded themselves of the circumstances out of which their own projects had been borne. The usefulness of 'bringing things back in' not just for those mainly running their own projects but also, and perhaps especially, for those employed by large agencies (and thus more likely to be alienated from the realities 'on the ground') was highlighted by Emma. As a former country director of a large INGO, she was particularly passionate about women's rights. She used to run training workshops on maternal health, including a segment to remind participants of the urgency and violent consequences of a lack of healthcare. As she described, '*I opened the workshop with a tape recording of women screaming. And I said, dying in childbirth is dying under torture. To remind them, to bring it home to them what our work is about.*' As in Scott's case, experiential proximity was not considered as unavoidable, yet unpleasant, which had to be managed. Here, it was actively (re)created in order to generate a sense of urgency, stimulating a moral obligation for providing better reproductive health care.

Intentional forays into situations of poverty may thus be instrumental for reinvigorating those who are working to support others, and their sense

Distance and proximity 97

of purpose. At the same time, 'keeping things at bay', in the words of one informant, creating and maintaining distance between oneself and situations of poverty or injustice, may constitute a key condition which enables them to live in a low-income country on a long-term basis. This was articulated by Karen, a Danish graphic designer who had travelled with her partner to Cambodia for his job in an NGO focused on town planning and informal settlements. Having established a reasonably comfortable existence in the capital, she was well aware of social injustices she encountered there in everyday life. Her own work, a teaching job at a local university, did not necessarily put her in a position to address these injustices in a straightforward way. Her way of balancing this, or 'keeping things at bay', was through distancing and reflection. As she explained: '*I think you cannot let this get to you ... when you look at the injustices with land distribution here* [in Cambodia], *if you keep looking at it and thinking about it, then you have to leave the country.*' For her, the response was to consciously '*check yourself, step back. I don't always manage that myself. Put some distance between yourself and the issue. Trying to reflect, why are things the way they are?*' She was thinking in particular, as she listed, of

> the overall political situation in Cambodia, the nepotism, the corruption; the acid attacks on women on their way home. All the social problems; the violent attacks committed because of jealousy in relationships; and especially the fact that all of these issues are unresolved, no one is brought to justice. The murdering of trade union activists. And nothing is done about it.

When I asked her what strategies she might use to deal with this, she did not see many avenues, apart from '*getting involved with an NGO*', and her ongoing efforts to have conversations about such issues with the university students she was teaching in design classes. Karen's struggle being faced with a politically hostile environment echoes the quandaries discussed in Chapter 2, and the efforts of everyday humanitarians to scale their efforts: that means devising and working with scales that render their work meaningful, while maintaining awareness of the broader context in which they found themselves.

For others, being able to 'keep things at bay' did not require ongoing efforts to create reflective distance. Rather, especially being and becoming a 'professional', a full-time, paid aid worker may be predicated on such reasoning being built into a professional habitus. During weekdays, for example, a French-themed open-air restaurant in one of the central districts in Phnom Penh, was a favoured lunchtime meeting place for international agency staff. Staff in formal business attire would hold meetings over three-course meals. As they were rounding off such a lunch with an espresso, on the other side of the brick wall separating the courtyard from the road, an emaciated woman would pass by, under a wide-brimmed hat and wearing textile gloves, pulling a cart behind her loaded with recyclables, cardboard, plastic bottles and cans. Having being part of, or witnessed such meetings, there seemed no effort necessary to 'keep things at bay'. The woman's passing presence was unrelated to the staff's meeting, concerned with how to implement good governance in Cambodia. As Katharina, a senior manager with an international aid agency explained to me, *'we are experts, and we deserve our salaries'*.

Having adopted and grown into such reasoning, made it possible to live in close proximity to poverty, without having to negotiate one's own position vis-à-vis this situation on an ongoing basis. At this stage, it is worth noting that being able to scale distance is predicated on certain privileges: such as being able to manoeuvre oneself closer, or further away, from the sights of poverty. More broadly speaking, this applies in a different way to humanitarians from abroad than to Cambodians, even though more affluent, urban residents have choices as to what extent they engage with urban poor communities, or the rural poor. How they create distance or proximity is an important dimension which is not sufficiently explored (Kent and Chandler 2008).

Leaving the 'parallel society'

At the far end of the spectrum of scaling proximity and distance are those who perceive moral obligations or responsibilities arising from physical proximity and find these difficult to fulfil. Some prefer to be in a situation where they are not constantly faced with them. One possible response is to extract themselves entirely by returning to their relatively affluent home countries (or indeed not leaving them in the first place). This move does not reduce the poverty they witnessed in Cambodia; but not being faced with it seemed to make life more manageable, perhaps because sufficient distance had been created to lessen these moral obligations. Some of these responses occur, perhaps unsurprisingly, among shorter-term visitors. Such sentiments can also bring long-term residents to the point of leaving Cambodia, and are sometimes mentioned as a key reason for deciding to go home. In some cases, this is being framed as a moral choice, expressed as not wanting to live in a 'parallel society'.

Thorsten, for example, who had been visiting an old school friend now working for an NGO, had spent several weeks in Cambodia, accompanying his friend on her work trips. A primary school teacher by training, during his last days, on the fringes of a salsa dance party, he explained to me why he was happy to leave, and why he would not consider swapping his life in Europe for his friend's in Cambodia:

> I don't want to witness this any more, I want to go home and do my normal teaching job in Europe. That way, I am less complicit in the injustice that's everywhere here. If you live here, even if your work tries to improve the situation, you are complicit. Because living here suits your needs.

For Thorsten, physically extracting himself, and thus creating distance, was an ethical choice, and reduced his complicity (see also Chouliaraki 2010:6 on banal and historic complicity). A similar sentiment was voiced by Katrin and her boyfriend Max. Katrin, a lawyer by training, had been working for a human rights organisation for two years, but was very clear she did not want to extend her contract beyond that. Her boyfriend, who had interned at a research institute during this time, held similar views. Self-identifying as politically left-wing and socially engaged, they would not countenance living in what they called a *Parallelgesellschaft*. This term was used in Germany originally to critically describe the lack of interaction between minority ethnic groups and 'mainstream' society. In the Cambodian case, the 'parallel society' they did not want to be part of consisted of the wealthy middle classes, local elites and the segment of foreign aid workers that had few social relations with Cambodians, and was not 'integrated' into the fabric of Khmer society. Such sentiments were also echoed by Fred and Miriam from the Netherlands, a couple in their early thirties. A researcher and photographer respectively, they had spent several years in Phnom Penh, working to set up a social enterprise focused on offering media training opportunities for young people. Eventually though, they reluctantly dissolved their household, which included a dog, and said farewell to their social circle which included Cambodian as well as foreign friends. Fred summed up their unease, '*we just don't want to be part of this any more*', as they were preparing to relocate to Europe and settle there.

The decision to extract themselves meant creating physical distance between them and what they saw as the desolate state of Cambodian politics and society, and their own role, and perhaps complicity, in it. Clearly, for Thorsten as well as for Katrin and Max, and Fred and Miriam, geographical distance reduced their responsibility in, or for, this scenario. One might consider their attitude in several ways. In the first instance, one might ask whether refusing to continue to witness injustices might be equivalent to a child hiding their face behind their hands: not being able to see it, means that it ceases to exist. Timothy Pachirat (2013) has argued in relation to the animal slaughter industry in the USA, that such a 'politics of sight', which reduces and minimises the visibility of contentious practices, exonerates the wider public from acknowledging their own role in, and responsibility for, these practices. Following such a logic, simply extracting oneself and creating distance is disingenuous, as it does not alleviate poverty; one just is not around to witness it face to face, in close physical proximity. Another perspective draws on mobility (in)justice between international and national aid workers, which Peter Redfield has drawn our attention to (2012). For the staff of MSF, the facility to extract oneself from a situation that is not only uncomfortable, but dangerous, is unevenly provided to staff members. International passport holders enjoy privileges of mobility unattainable to nationals of the country in question. Extracting oneself from Cambodian society for ethical reasons, as Thorsten did, is based on mobility privilege. It arguably undermines 'creating distance' as way of dealing with the physical proximity of inequality. One might also read it as a form of integrity; however, simply not facing poverty, while not enacting other changes, does not challenge the status quo, but merely reduces one's direct exposure to it.

Taking responsibility at home

Creating this particular distance – that is, leaving Cambodia – does not need to entail a disavowal of obligations altogether. Instead, for some of my respondents, the most meaningful engagement consisted of taking responsibility, and dealing with people 'near' to them, in their home country setting. Bella, an Australian development worker in her late fifties, had been with a multilateral agency in Cambodia for several years, but had become increasingly disillusioned with the practice of overseas aid. After returning to Australia, at a time when her daughter was expecting her first child, she began working with the Refugee Council of Australia. As she explained later, this was work where she felt she had greater efficacy, and her presence was more meaningful; an example of how disillusionment with international aid, and the draw of the 'distant' and thus exotic can turn into a situation where it feels more meaningful, for a range of reasons, to constructing and responding to 'domestic' or nearby support work. One might raise the question, however, if both the decision to come to Cambodia and stay, and the eventual move back home that many undertake, tend to be framed as moral rather than personal choices.

In a related, if somewhat different situation, Petra and Klaus had worked in Cambodia for an NGO for more than two years. After their initial contract finished, they opted, unlike others in their position, not to extend it but return to Germany. Instead, or perhaps as an extension of their humanitarian engagement in Cambodia, they resolved to adopt a child at home. Petra was a trained social worker, and had been director of a children's care home in Germany before they left for Cambodia. As she explained their decision-making, '*When we discussed it, we valued our time there, but we wanted to go back. For us, it makes most sense doing something closer to home, so it was a logical step to see if we could adopt.*' When I spoke to them a couple of years after their return, Petra had gone back to being a social worker, albeit part time. They were living with their 7-year-old adoptive son, who had been looked after in a care home beforehand, in a village near Petra's extended family in Germany. Klaus was working from home as an IT consultant. Making a difference to someone's life closer to home had, for them, been the appropriate choice.

Deciding that their efforts for social change were not necessarily best placed in low-income countries was not unique to those who had spent at least some of their working lives overseas. Bella's older son, for example, was in his mid-twenties, and had visited his mother on her postings in Asia several times in the years after Bella and her husband had separated. Eventually, her son had decided that setting up an organic farm in Australia was, for him, the right way forward. Emma's two sons, also in their twenties, had lived during their school years in several cities in East Africa and Asia before deciding to return to the UK, their passport country. At the time I spoke with Emma, both sons had settled in Wales where they were setting up an eco-lodge. Rosie's daughter, who had also spent her formative years on the development circuit with her parents, now lived in Northern Ireland with her own family, and was committed to local community development in a rural area there.

Many factors are at play when someone decides whether to engage in pro-social activities in their more affluent home countries or in a low-income one. Returning to the opening theme of the chapter, decisions such as these speak to the role of geographical distance in everyday humanitarianism. In the cases of these adults, or their grown-up children, the lure of distance and thus difference, is neither necessary nor sufficient to attract someone to a life of supporting others abroad.

Conclusion

The question driving this chapter was what difference distance makes for our concern towards others, and identifying answers emerging from everyday humanitarian practice. Adopting a scalar approach, I argue that humanitarian distance is not fixed, but fluid. Everyday humanitarians scale distance to benefit from geoarbitrage, both to achieve greater efficacy in their humanitarian projects, and to enjoy adventures or amenities in their personal lives. At the same time, the proximity to poverty that results from their mobility poses other challenges. These include making moral decisions about how to act when facing poverty. While it is no different in principle from their countries of origin, the poverty they encounter is perceived as more intense and severe. One of their responses is developing scripts that allow them to not constantly consider its implications and appropriate responses. One empirical answer to the question about how distance matters is that everyday humanitarians traverse geographical distances in order to bring themselves close to poverty, while benefiting from differentials in power and income – partly answering Sovann's lament at the beginning of this chapter. Proximity to poverty can be experienced as challenging, raising notions of complicity, guilt and reflections on privilege. One response to this is the use of scripts, short-circuiting what might otherwise be frequently arising ethical dilemmas.

Distance, or rather lack of it, comes into play for (everyday) humanitarians in the form of desired closeness, or the valorising of proximity to poverty – or approximation of one's own living conditions, geographically and physically, to those they aim to support. This can hold both for those working for aid agencies, as well as those engaged in their own projects. The purposes of such proximity vary: it can be a symbolical good, such as expressed in official aid agency booklets; or it can be a continued motivator for one's humanitarian practice. Proximity can include sensorial approximations, such as temporarily adopting 'local' living conditions. While they do not mirror structural poverty conditions, they may be a conscious effort to counteract accusations of foreign or white arrogance. They are not generally meant to induce empathy, but can be used to that effect in professional contexts, such as reminding oneself of the relevance and urgency of their work. There can be an uneasy balance between such reminders, and retaining a distance, such as not being constantly mindful of the overall political situation in Cambodia, as discussed in Chapter 2. Finally, some people consciously 'scale back', that is, physically extract themselves from the situation, as they find their immediate complicity unethical. A subsequent move is to increase the distance from humanitarian need in Cambodia, and instead decide to intervene in their countries of origin.

The implications from this are twofold: the foregrounding of the geographical as constitutive of humanitarianism distance in the context of empire obscures much more dynamic processes of scaling distance. Movement between proximity and distance characterises everyday humanitarianism. Following from this, it becomes clear that the humanitarian object, the distant stranger, is not at all that distant. In fact, as the following chapter shows, neither are they strange, as humanitarian efforts can be understood as efforts to render them familiar.

5

Desire to connect

Cycling on a dirt track towards Munny's place, for a while I followed a motorcycle taxi ahead of me, with children seated on its two benches inside. Its sides were emblazoned with the sign 'Sofia's Children of the World'. It pulled away, but when I arrived at Munny's house, I found it parked at the entrance. Munny explained that it was a gift from Steve in Manchester, who came to visit twice a year. A Cambodian teacher friend had made the connection. Inside Munny's compound was a wooden shack, with multiple images tacked to the walls: a hand-drawn sketch of Munny himself; fading Christmas decorations; a selection of Australian, Japanese and other flags; and many photos, showing the children who attend Munny's school sitting down for a meal of rice and vegetables with visitors from Ghana and Japan, and having a party with visitors from China.

This lively gallery spoke of the importance of connections – between visitors, supporters, Munny and the children in his project. These connections matter most obviously for the purposes of fundraising, as well as beyond. Ilan Kapoor has pointed to the role of desire in the development process, even though it has often been ignored, betraying a 'a suspicion of human/social passions, which threaten to destabilize and alienate the subject, divide social identity, and thus endanger development's projects, intentions, aspirations' (Kapoor 2020:4). Similarly, Arturo Escobar admits that 'development is a desiring machine … not only an apparatus of governmentality' (Escobar and Rocheleau 2008:175). The desire described by Kapoor has often been analysed as being on the side of the (overseas) supporters, but Munny's wall tells a more nuanced story. Munny and the students also appreciate connections, for a range of reasons. This chapter considers what kind of connections are desired, by whom, why, and with what consequences. In so doing, it transitions into the second part of the book. While Chapters 2, 3 and 4 examine the making of scales, Chapters 5, 6 and 7 are about creating relations. They pick up the argument of the previous chapter that the objects of humanitarian intervention are not necessarily distant; this chapter shows that they are not necessarily strangers, either. While the majority of material revolves around the desires of foreign humanitarians, it also brings into view Cambodians who are involved in or leading humanitarian projects.

The endeavour of development has, at its core, been characterised by the motivation to 'help', that is, to intervene in the lives of others in supportive ways. This chapter argues that this perspective has obscured how development activities are also animated by its twin desire to 'connect'. While this holds significance for development more broadly, it becomes particularly evident in everyday humanitarianism. The chapter argues that the relevance of 'connecting' has been insufficiently recognised so far. It explores different aspects of what practitioners mean by 'making a connection', including face-to-face contact, direct experience of aid activities, and their tangible efficacy. It also finds that establishing interpersonal relationships across national, ethnic and cultural differences, while potentially challenging, is a key motivation for those involved. Finally, the chapter argues that acknowledging the desire to connect undermines the notion of the distant stranger as the archetypical humanitarian object, highlighting the wish for familiarity and closeness as potentially just as important for motivating and directing assistance to others.

The term 'connections' is appropriate for the arguments proposed here, and is frequently invoked by participants themselves. In a broader context, the notion of 'connections' refers to establishing personal social relations. The debate to which this chapter contributes concerns how the role of social relations has been conceptualised with regard to how they matter for aid and development. Even though one might assume that development, a profoundly humane project at its core, is necessarily underpinned by relations between people, relevant debates are dispersed. The uneven theoretical visibility of social relations in aid is all the more noteworthy because the link between 'helping' and 'relating' clearly emerges from readings of development as a gift (Stirrat and Henkel 1997; Mawdsley 2012a, b). Drawing on Marcel Mauss's classic essay, 'The Gift' (1954), the act of giving produces, and is reliant on, relationships. In this paradigm, an important if not the main reason for the giving and receiving of gifts is the maintenance of relationships. If development can be considered as a gift, then the making of relationships is a central part of delivering and receiving development assistance.

From this interpretation follows an imperative to understand the implications of social relations in aid. One way in which this has been acknowledged is in how relationships matter for the implementation of aid (Eyben 2006). This perspective draws attention to the instrumental value that relationships have for aid policy and delivery. Eyben argues that, 'the quality of relations within and between organizations in the web of aid is crucial for organizational performance' (2006:2). This concerns relations between practitioners within the 'aid bureaucracy' in both formal and informal capacities (2006: 43). Further contributions include how friendships between differently situated aid workers, such as local and international staff, matter for capacity building (Girgis 2007). Mawdsley, Townsend and Porter (2005) emphasise the importance of face-to-face encounters to improve mutual understanding and trust between northern and southern NGO partners. These accounts examine social relations among aid practitioners themselves, and their role in enhancing aid effectiveness. While this highlights an important dimension, the relationships at the heart of aid, following Mauss, are those between gift-givers – that is, donors or supporters – on the one hand, and the gift recipients, that is, recipients or beneficiaries of aid on the other.

The contribution to the discussion here is to take seriously implications arising from aid as a gift, specifically the fact that relationships are inevitably part of processes, not merely for operational purposes, but as a key motivating factor. This chapter explores how the desire for development and the search for connection are linked in the informal, privately funded modes of assistance that constitute everyday humanitarianism, and what these insights contribute to how relationships in aid are being theorised. There is broad acknowledgement in the literature that relationships matter for aid. Erica Bornstein, in her account of charity practices in urban India, finds that 'only [...] through a relational prism, does humanitarian activity make social sense' (Bornstein 2012: 170). The acts of charity she explores are, at least partly, driven by the 'impulse of philanthropy' (Bornstein 2009). Malkki (2015) provides a different reading by foregrounding the 'need to help' rather than the 'desire for development' (Heron 2007). This means recognising the helpers – in Malkki's case, Finnish staff or volunteers for the Red Cross – as those who are in need, searching for purpose, companionship or ways out of the mundane realities of their lives in Finland.

The relevance of relations is acknowledged in both Bornstein's and Malkki's works. In Bornstein's account of charity in Delhi, she identifies a 'relational empathy' that is at stake (2012:149). More specifically, this means that in contrast to forms of liberal altruism based on individual autonomy, what matters in the Indian context is the forging of kin relations, a theme I turn to in Chapter 6 (Bornstein 2012: 143). In a more tangential manner, Malkki emphasises that connections are an important – if not the most important – aspect of helping others. For many of the elderly volunteers for the Finnish Red Cross for example, the making of connections was of vital concern (2015:43). Such connection could be with a child for whom they had knitted a soft toy, even if this was an imagined connection across a geographical distance.

A more comprehensive proposal of how the desires of helping and connecting are intertwined is found in Heron's work on Canadian women development workers in sub-Saharan Africa (2007). Her analysis is grounded in the assumption that development is a relational experience (Heron 2007:55; see also Schech, Skelton and Mundkur 2016, on voluntourism). In fact, she observes a 'disappearance of altruism' from participants' narratives once in situ, and instead a focus on establishing relationships with local people. A key question is thus how the two desires are linked (Heron 2007:88). In Heron's reading, central to the desire for development is that it offers 'new dimensions of identity formation for Canadian women development workers' (Heron 2007:123). Drawing on Ann Stoler's (1997) work on the making of bourgeois identities through the colonial project, Heron argues that the development encounter is instrumental in constituting white identities. There is, however, 'a constant tension for us in these connections born of our need for African people to be "different" and our simultaneous desire for the kind of pure meeting across and beyond difference' (Heron 2007). The wish for relations is further complicated by the fact that 'seeing African people as fully equal, that is, "just like us", however, is risky because it erodes the ethical basis for our presence "there"' (Heron 2007:89).

Relationships with aid beneficiaries are imagined and practised in particular ways to justify development interventions. All these accounts articulate, more or less explicitly, the importance of relationships in aid. The search for connection among some actors thus warrants a more comprehensive discussion than has been conducted so far. As everyday humanitarianism fundamentally revolves around a person-to-person connection, this chapter aims to provide a fuller, more nuanced exploration of what participants mean by 'connection', and how it matters for everyday humanitarianism, where having a personal connection with those supported matters greatly for individual project founders, supporters and donors.

What does it mean to 'make a connection'?

Establishing the sense of a personal connection between donors and a cause, or a group of beneficiaries, is a well-recognised challenge for large international NGOs. Specifically, individual donors may feel that the promise of connection, as presented through campaign materials, is tenuous and often not realised to an extent that they find meaningful or rewarding. This apparent disconnect between donor and beneficiary in large-scale, state-funded or formalised modes of aid is one reason why small aid initiatives appeal to potential supporters, and even motivate people to found their own projects. Going further, I propose that the significance of connection is not limited to an instrumentalist incentive for fundraising, or a tool for aid effectiveness, but a desire which needs to be fulfilled through acts of assisting others. This does not mean that one excludes the other but offers an expanded perspective on how connections or relationships, and acts of giving, are interrelated. A fundamental question is what people mean when they invoke their desire for connection. The following sections unpack some of these meanings.

In the first instance, a key element that emerged was being physically present in a place, at events, and having face-to-face contact with those involved. The desire for 'being there' resonates with its perceived lack in formalised aid work (Irvine, Chambers and Eyben 2004). As Adam, an Australian in his late twenties, described supporters of his educational project,

> *in fact most of our supporters are looking for small organisations* [to sponsor]: *they say they used to give money to the Red Cross, but they have such big operations, big cars, they don't want that. People really want to do the work themselves, in a hands-on environment. They want to be part of it, to build that house; to know the students who are benefitting.*

Variously described as 'being there' or 'being part of the process', physical presence and participation were cited by many as essential to 'making it real', and to bring about a connection – with the people, a place or a process, that they were looking for. This wish was for a connection that was as little mediated as possible. As Laura, who ran a small education project says, *'what our supporters are looking for is direct, first-hand experience of the situation'*. In this sense, people who are engaged in everyday humanitarianism as founders, supporters or volunteers are looking for relationships built on physicality and promising authenticity. Such a quest resonates with what fellows of the microlending platform, Kiva, seek in their personal visits to borrowers in the field (Schwittay 2015).

'Making a connection' thus indicates a desire for being directly and effectively involved in acts of supporting others. This was also illustrated by Patrick, who runs an after-school club in a disadvantaged community on the outskirts of a provincial town, which he co-founded with his Cambodian project partner, Khean. Patrick talked about one of their supporters from Northern Europe, who raised funds among his work colleagues for a number of bicycles, to be distributed among families in their community. As Patrick pointed out, it was not sufficient for him to send over the money, but

> *he came over* [to Cambodia] *because he wanted to meet the people and learn about the culture. He bought and delivered the bicycles himself, he wanted to be part of the process. So he knows, this mum doesn't have to walk far any more to the market – it's very concrete.*

In this case, Patrick attributed their supporter's decision to travel and organise the delivery of the bikes in person, to their wish for connection. On another occasion, Patrick and Khean were supporting the construction of basic houses for families in Khean's home village. In a similar fashion, some of their overseas supporters chose to come along and help because, as Patrick put it, *'they wanted to be part of it, to build that house; to know the students who are benefiting'*. Being physically present and immersed, combined with a sense of their tangible efficacy, was a significant incentive.

This was also evident in a related project, aptly named Reach Out. Its main activity consisted of distributing hot meals on a weekly basis to marginalised families, and elderly Cambodians without recourse to other assistance. Their meal preparation sessions were often well attended by a mixture of tourists, resident foreigners and some young Cambodian volunteers. Asked about what attracted them to this initiative in particular, Rob, an older Australian who frequently helped out, explained that he and his wife *'want to do the work ourselves – this is a hands-on environment. The best bit is at the end, when we get to distribute them to the families who are waiting for us.'* The name of the organisation encapsulated aspects of 'connection' mentioned earlier, that is, reaching out – a tactile experience – to others and establishing contact with fellow human beings in a supportive manner.

Borey, a young Cambodian working in the hotel sector, had had similar experiences. He explained that he often encountered hotel guests who wanted to make a donation, so Borey took them to a rural area he was familiar with for this purpose:

> *they want to do something to help; so they bought school uniforms, fish, rice, and took it out to the village. They are back in the States with their careers now, but they told me that that was a special moment for them.*

Through taking them to the village, they said, Borey had *'made it real'* for the tourists. Such quests for 'realness' or authenticity have been widely documented and critiqued within tourism studies (Kuon 2011). It is nevertheless worth noting that in the context of aid and development, this desire plays a more substantial role for drawing in, retaining and enlarging networks of supporters than is often acknowledged, or achieved.

As discussed by Schwittay (2019), the appeal of a unique person-to-person connection for aid donations has long been recognised by NGOs. While early forms of child sponsorship are a typical example, it has more recently been extended to microlending through crowdsourcing platforms (Banerjee 2020). It is also reflected in campaign materials produced by large NGOs, which seek to present possible beneficiaries in a personal, intimate style, often with curated quotes and biographies. These can be perceived as 'thin' connections, in that supporters are aware that, for administrative reasons, their donation or loan may not be received exactly by the person they viewed on the platform or campaign website. As Schwittay suggests, one way of addressing this relative distance is to become a 'Kiva Fellow', in order to establish face-to-face contact with some loan recipients (2015). I suggest that when those involved in everyday humanitarianism speak of 'making a connection', they aspire not to managed, distanced and to some extent fictive connections, but rather those of a 'thick' quality, that is, holistic and immersive.

Such desire for 'thick' connections was illustrated by Patrick's and Khean's experiences in their after-school club for marginalised young people. As an initial fundraising strategy, they set up scholarships for named children, but realised that they were not particularly popular among supporters, compared to other forms of fundraising. As Patrick explained, the most effective modus was indeed for supporters to have personal knowledge, either of particular young people through visiting, or through personal acquaintance with Patrick or Khean as the founders; or through following regular updates on particular children's progress posted on the project's website. The person-to-person approach in itself was therefore not sufficient to get people involved – it had to be someone known to the supporter or donor, even if that extended to just the project founders. The following examples illustrate some of the ways in which such 'thick' connections are pursued and made.

Ronan for example, an American in his early sixties, ran a small project for students with impaired hearing. Alongside this, he facilitated contacts between visitors in a Cambodian provincial town and local communities, schools or groups of potential beneficiaries. In this role he was sometimes asked by local friends, both Cambodian and foreign, to take hotel guests or personal visitors to projects or communities that he considers worthwhile recipients of donations. He reflects that it is the 'personal connections' that are sometimes made during these trips which prompt visitors to make financial contributions, often towards the end of their stay, as they feel they have caught a glimpse of the 'real Cambodia', as Ronan says, as opposed to what they consider a façade presented to tourists. Making these kind of connections begins, and sometimes ends, with a single donation. Occasionally, they set in a motion a chain of events where acts of helping and establishing relationships are interlinked.

Such emphasis on experiential immersion surfaced in participants' accounts, as reflected in phrases such as the enjoyment they derived from *'seeing the smiles on the kids' faces'*. This was frequently cited as a key reward when visiting communities or interacting with those they were supporting. This desire for face-to-face contact for a sense of reward, and evidence of one's impact, was also mentioned by those involved in educational activities. Aiko for example, a teacher from Japan, had set up a creative education project. Together with an assistant, she ran workshops and weekly classes for young people on the outskirts of a provincial town. As she explained to me, she had made a conscious decision not to 'grow' her project, even though that would have been possible for her financially. It would have meant, however, having less time available to in direct interaction with her students, which was what really mattered to her, as explained in Chapter 2. Such sentiments are well documented in other human service professions such as in teaching or health care, and in this respect not unique to everyday humanitarianism. They do, however, illustrate the centrality of unmediated interaction for those engaged in everyday humanitarianism.

These aid relations cannot be considered, by default, as less mediated and more holistic or authentic than other forms of development. Rather, they are mediated to a different extent and in other ways. For example, much of everyday humanitarianism is facilitated by local and foreign brokers or facilitators (McKay and Perez 2019; Fechter 2020). What matters to supporters is that they often know these brokers personally, and feel that the information related through them gives them a more trustworthy connection than if they received letters from a sponsored child, sent via a large NGO. With regard to relationships being direct, it is important to recognise that everyday humanitarianism also depends, to some degree, on mediated forms of contact.

It also becomes clear that the 'personal connection' is considered central by supporters as an idiom for personal knowledge and trust. Time and again, those involved in these everyday aid projects reiterate how for themselves and their supporters, the sense of *'knowing where the money is going'* matters hugely. George, for example, ran a project for children affected by HIV/Aids in the capital, Phnom Penh. Talking about how they recruited donations and volunteers, he explained that after people have visited their project, *'they've been touched, they can tell a story about kids and HIV to the people at home – and they tell the others where the money is going to'*. While their personal knowledge of the project makes them credible witnesses in the eyes of others, their own lives have been 'touched' by these visits, too. They can 'tell a story' to widen the fundraising circle, and have become part of the story themselves.

An example of how this works is provided by Kevin, a British man in his sixties, who took early retirement after becoming disillusioned with his job in the UK. Having relocated to Cambodia, after a while he became friendly with families living in the residential area near the Angkor temple complex. He subsequently decided to fundraise to enable one of the children to attend school. To this end, he regularly organised quiz evenings in a pub in his home town in the UK, with the proceeds going towards the Cambodian family. These quiz nights tended to go well, and his friends were happy to participate because,

> with my mates in the UK, they know me personally, it's a personal connection. They know that I know the places that I am fundraising for. Of course you have to have a certain amount of trust, of faith. They know me, and this is for Mai – you know the person it goes to. It makes it more real. It's going to be for Mai's education. I take photos and bring them back to them. They are always only one step away from what is happening, and where it goes to.

This, he explained, constituted the key difference compared to other, large organisations, which would be unable to provide that level of assurance where and how the money was spent, and who exactly it is supporting. Samantha, who ran a small food security project, had similar experiences. A personal connection for her meant accountability not just to one's supporters, but to the community her project was serving:

> in my project, I know these kids ... I know what they need, and that they deserve it. You need a business mindset; but it's the personal connection that matters. You don't want to have a disconnect; you come in with these awards ... but these awards begin with the community, and the big organisations, they've lost sight of it.

Chhay, a Cambodian graduate in his late twenties, had been working in a small, privately funded project as the 'second in command', as he put it, to the Australian founder for several years. As he explained,

> why we have foreigners: because of the social connections, the funding connections. When it comes to funding, you need a combination of Cambodians and foreigners. It's not easy for me to look after the donor. They need trust. We need Ben [the Australian founder] to help us with that.

However, Chhay found that he, like others, 'needs to go to the communities as well. For motivation, but also so I know what has happened there. So I can be a better storyteller for them, so I know the story to tell to the donors.' Chhay became a mediator between the people receiving support, and the private donors to whom he relates the stories of what was happening at ground level, increasing trust and sense of accountability that the project aspires to. This is often cited by donors as a key reason that draws them to private aid, rather than to formal organisations. For development practice more broadly, it is worth noting that it was not the well-established monitoring and evaluation practices of large aid agencies, but the small-scale, individual relationships enabled by private aid that functioned as a basis of trust and loyalty for supporters.

Connections across similarity and difference

An immersive presence, 'thick' relationships and personal knowledge of founders and beneficiaries can all be part of what it means to make a connection. In order to understand how this matters to everyday humanitarianism and development more broadly I consider connections in the sense of establishing personal relationships, an aspect that emerges most prominently in the academic discussion of development. How central this is for everyday humanitarians is illustrated in an exchange I had with James, from New Zealand, who set up a community development project in a Cambodian village. When I asked him why he had done this here, rather than in his home country, he responded emphatically, *'because it's so fulfilling here! It is about making a connection with the people.'* This is less so because he did not connect with people at home; he spoke warmly of his grown-up children and the local community where they lived. Even so, James wished for connection with people who were very different from him – villagers in a country of the Global South – yet whose acquaintance afforded similarities, such as the fact that they were both farmers, 'working the land', albeit under very different circumstances.

Arguably, for some, it is easier to form a connection with a more distant, and different Other, than with those in need at home. The greater social distance created through multiple structural inequalities does make it easier for a donor make a connection with someone for whom this makes a large difference to their life, compared with bridging the shorter distance with those in need at home, who have a greater capacity to resist such a personal connection.

One argument animating this chapter was that the desire to give and to connect with others are closely related, and might represent two sides of the same coin. This holds to the extent that wanting to 'make a connection' can be a motivation for 'making a contribution', as much as the other way round. The previous sections have differentiated what people mean when they speak of such connection. Further, a vital component of 'making a connection' is, in a more literal sense, to establish a meaningful, personal relationship with someone who is very different from oneself – but also offers similarities, shared experiences and perhaps mutual recognition. Such relationships can be highly valued in spite, or perhaps because, of their possible tensions and the challenges they pose. Among many everyday humanitarians, there is a desire for connection across national, ethnic, or cultural difference engendered by geographical distance, as discussed in Chapter 4. This difference may be part of what makes them appealing in the first place. Everyday humanitarianism constitutes a prime example of the significance of such personal connections in development, partly because they are actively encouraged, rather than frowned on, and because the search for connection is at the heart of what animates such aid activities in the first place. This resonates with what Ilan Kapoor has identified as the key role of 'desire in international development' (2020), which runs deep, but tends to be unacknowledged: 'the theory and practice of development, in this sense, are replete with unconscious social passions' (Kapoor 2020:4). Similarly, Bornstein notes, in the context of foreigners' charity work in Delhi, how 'empathising with persons or contexts radically different from one's own becomes desirable' (Bornstein 2012:121). At the core of this is that 'volunteering asserts distinction – I am not this – and strives to efface these divides through the potential of emphatic experience' (Bornstein 2012:122).

In many everyday humanitarian activities, a moment of connection becomes a starting point and a motivation for donors to become involved in more comprehensive forms of assistance. One example were Al and Donna, a retired couple from Australia, who used to run their own farm, and whose grown-up children had left home. According to their own account, at this stage they were actively looking to 'do something'. As Donna searched the internet, initially for volunteering opportunities, she came across a YouTube clip about a small village school in Cambodia. The village leader who had posted the video was hoping to raise funds through inviting people to become involved. In Donna's words, *'when I saw this, I was hooked. It was the kids – definitely the kids.'* On the strength of this sentiment, they travelled to Cambodia, and after an abortive stint of volunteering at an NGO, they visited the school, decided to get involved, and *'that was it'*. It turned out to be the start of an ongoing engagement, first fundraising for the school, then leading to a wider approach including health and livelihood support, as well as a greater role – in collaboration with village residents – in planning, financing and delivering assistance.

The 'spark' of spontaneous connection is often the beginning of a longer-term relationship, where assistance is provided in the context of more personal relationships. Significantly, these are sometimes couched in kinship terms. Ailish for example, a retired woman from Ireland, 'adopted' a Cambodian young man as her godson, including the obligations of support that this entailed. As her friend Jenny explains:

> *It's about human relations – something clicks. My friend Ailish first came here nine years ago – she met a tuktuk driver, sponsored him to go to Ireland, and to buy land here. She's at the moment volunteering with another organisation, near where he is based in Kampong Chang. She made her own connection. There is some spark, and then it takes off from there.*

As in Ailish's case, some people initially make use of organisations to source a volunteering placements. Finding the personal relations that they are looking for, can be done informally and independently: Ailish had *'made her own connection'*. It is worth noting that drawing on kinship terminology for shaping and understanding social relations, such as adopting a godson, can accommodate existing socio-economic inequalities, as well as justify, or even call for ongoing support between a foreign older woman and a younger Cambodian man. How kin relations matter in everyday humanitarianism is the focus of Chapter 6.

In the cases described here, the desire for development and the search for connection can be difficult or impossible to disentangle. In others, the wish for continued personal involvement – with people, a project, a place – is more clearly foregrounded. Ongoing assistance can be a means of maintaining those relations, and provide a rationale to return. This was the situation for Anette, a retired teacher in her sixties from Denmark, who I met in Stephane's music school. Stephane's project combined a for-profit school, offering tuition for guitar and piano, with a non-profit section. The latter consisted of two educational projects in deprived areas, where children from the surrounding neighbourhoods took classes in English, IT and life skills. Several years ago, Anette had spent time as a volunteer there, and had got to know Stephane, his team and some of the children well. Following on from this, Anette kept returning, first twice, and now once a year. This time, she had come for a two-week visit with her daughter. When I asked her about her ongoing support for Stephane's project, she explained that *'it's all about having that personal connection'*. While some of her time was spent sightseeing with her daughter, they were both keen to visit the classrooms, participate in lessons, and wander through the area, greeting people and chatting to those that they recognised from previous visits.

The connection that Anette was referring to did not always relate to particular young people, but to the team and the project more broadly. In other cases, more fine-grained aspects of the relationships became evident. Al for example, found it important that many residents in the village whose school they supported, were rice farmers. He recounted how he and his wife were once invited to sit with some of the villagers under a tree during a break from working in the fields. He was particularly touched by how one older woman, knowing Al was a farmer too, took his palms to examine if they showed signs of hard work. *'Then she said that "we're similar". That's what makes it so fulfilling'*, Al explained, *'that we share the experience. We know what it's like to farm, we can talk about crops, we're coming from the same place.'* The role of such perceived affinities for everyday humanitarianism is discussed in Chapter 7.

Another time, they were looking at fields and talking to some of the farmers, when they asked Al and Donna if they wanted to share their breakfast. Al enthusiastically recounted that *'they've never sat down with a couple of white people before and had food with them. So we sat down together ... it's great to make that connection.'* Al felt that he and his wife had experienced the same enthusiasm in meeting someone very different, yet familiar among the group of local rice farmers. Significantly, the interest and desires that local Cambodians have to seek a connection, or a personal relationship with foreigners, tend to be much less explored in literatures of development, voluntourism or indeed everyday humanitarianism. While there is research on the roles and social relations among local aid workers (Yarrow 2011; Warne Peters 2016; Sundberg 2020) less is known to what extent the desire for connection may be one-sided, reciprocal or indeed asymmetrical. Heron found that in the context of a Zambian NGOs, some local NGO workers refuted the foreigners' search for connection, and intentionally 'assert boundaries in response to our insistence on relations' (Heron 2007: 85). Heron's material, however, was gathered in the context of formalised development, among established NGOs. In contrast, among those involved in everyday humanitarianism, the valuing of relationships takes on a different significance.

Cosmopolitan connections

In fact, the question of what kind of desires might animate the 'subjects of development', as Kapoor puts it, constitutes something of a blind spot in his account of the role of desire in development. Desire is mostly attributed to the 'West' and its drive to intervene elsewhere (Kapoor 2020). As evident from Munny's house sketched at the beginning of this chapter, however, there was a keen desire to be connected to others in far-flung corners, to people in Asia, Africa and Europe. A difference to the reluctant national NGO workers described by Heron is that being connected to foreigners can be seen by Cambodian as desirable, for example to help them realise their own visions of development. (Some of these collaborations between Cambodians project founders and supportive foreigners are discussed in Chapter 7.) Their desire for development, on their own terms, may chime with what Tania Li has called the 'will to improve' (Li 2007). Nevertheless, while a desire for connection may include potential financial and resource benefits, it cannot be reduced to these.

In some cases, Cambodian founders of aid projects appreciate not just the potential funding streams for their project that are opened up by making connections with foreigners, but what might be described as cosmopolitan capital. As highlighted earlier, in Munny's house, mementos and material evidence of the students' transnational connections were prominently displayed. There were pictures of volunteer visits and shared meals; images of symbolic cheques that had been presented; drawings and cards sent from afar. Rather than putting up barriers to foreigners' insistence on contact, a more complex picture emerges where such contacts are purposefully sought and managed for a particular project, as well as benefiting local founders or facilitators of citizen aid in more personal capacities. Munny illustrated some of the connections:

> Last month, Steve from Manchester came, he comes every year, twice. He brings clothes and donations for the children. The children like the volunteers, to practise their English. They like to share their culture, how it's different, Cambodian culture. Steve has his own charity, it's called Sofia's children of the world.

Expanding on this theme, Munny illustrated in what ways he benefited from connections with foreigners:

> We always talk together with Steve. 'I want to see your place and what is going on', he said. I was still doing my hotel work. My English friend told me to stop the hotel work. How can I stop? If I stop, the kids have nothing to eat. My friends say, don't work like that, if you die, the kids have nobody. I borrowed money from a friend to build a house. English gave 2000, build a house, same with US, 2500, Switzerland family, visited last year. They work for a real estate company. I met him in the Lao border. At a poor school, he followed me to Cambodia. They're interested in Cambodia. They become donors and supporters.

These do not only matter for overseas supporters or locally based everyday humanitarians. The walls of Munny's house were a vivid illustration of how much connections were valued and cultivated by him and the students. This can be traced back to the history of Munny's project. As he recounted, he was working as a translator for the UN when he met a Japanese journalist, Akito, who was covering Cambodia for a Japanese newspaper. Munny began accompanying him on his assignments and, towards the end of his stay, the journalist pledged to support Munny in his vision to set up an after-school care facility for underprivileged children. From this friendship connection grew a partnership, which over several years helped Munny set up his school, and channel support, while Akito would come regularly to visit. This kind of connection helped Munny to realise his idea, much in the way that becoming acquainted with Leslie helped Rachana set up her own project (as discussed in Chapter 7).

Beyond the financial benefits they brought, Munny valued these connections for other reasons. He talked animatedly about the modest dinners they hosted, and recounted the names of the group of schoolgirls that had travelled from Ghana one year. He remembered the sponsors from the UK, some of whom had their names displayed on equipment they helped finance, a common practice across the projects I visited. While Munny had not been able to travel internationally himself as a result of these connections, their visits, letters and images connected his modest school at the end of a dirt track with other parts of the world.

Others have been able to travel as a result of their transnational connections. Vannak, a Cambodian in his fifties (who I turn to in Chapter 7), collaborated with an American family, setting up a primary school in a semi-rural area. At least once a year, Vannak accompanied Danny on a trip to the USA. On such a fundraising tour, he brought the stories of Khmer Rouge survivors to audiences there, rendering them tangible, and fundraised for the project. Similarly, Ponnleu, the Cambodian project partner of Markus, spent time in Germany with Markus's family some years into their collaborative ventures. These trips do not fundamentally challenge the mobility inequality that often characterises their relationships. They illustrate, however, that connections with foreigners are sought not just as a tool for fundraising, or for cosmopolitan capital as in Mr Ross's school, but to enable travel for local project founders and partners. Such connections can also transform people's lives, as the story of Visal illustrates.

Visal, a Cambodian in his forties who led a small aid project, described his sense of amazement when, in 1992,

> the UN was here, to look and observe. They were a big inspiration. They were the reason they sent me from that village to high school ... and it was dangerous at the time to come to Cambodia. But they still came, all the way, it was very rural and remote. It makes my dream come true. The UN was the first stranger I saw. They came to my school in my village, to observe elections. I was like, wow – I want to talk like that. They were so tall and blue eyes and golden hair. They said 'hello', I didn't know how to say hello. I didn't know what it means! Learning English, yes was very useful for me. I can find a job, I can change my life.

Having been picked up by Mabel, and becoming an NGO staff member prior to starting his project with Leo, Visal felt that his life had been transformed through the encounter and ongoing connections with foreigners:

> I speak in English, I work with internationals! I fly! I have a nice house, for someone my generation, my background. It's because you have models, like the UN guy, like Mabel. You have more choice, you can pick your life. Take the black door, take the blue door ... it's up to you. I would not have had the opportunities without the foreigners. They made me speak English. Before, I only speak Khmei, very limited. So meeting foreigner, being with foreigners, was a big inspiration.

To present these relationships solely in terms of their usefulness for humanitarian projects would be inaccurate. In the context of such initiatives, relationships are formed which turn into friendships across cultural and linguistic differences. One example was Sophea, a Cambodian who had been working for several years with a cafe supporting a small NGO, which regularly received foreign volunteers. One year, Sophea struck up a friendship with a young Dutch woman, Sandra. Sophea recounted how over the course of the year, they had lots of fun together, learnt from each other, ran the cafe and improved the project. They got on so well that after Sandra had returned to the Netherlands, she invited Sophea for a visit during the European winter months. At the time she was talking with me, more than five years later, Sophea pulled out a photo she had taken during that time, including one of Sandra's parents' front lawn covered in snow, with both of them throwing snowballs. Sophea spoke of their friendship with warmth, even though Sandra had not been back to Cambodia since, and had gone on to pursue her university studies. They kept in intermittent contact. Perhaps out of necessity, it turned out to be temporary and marked by asymmetries, such as Sophea's limited ability to travel and choose her livelihood, in contrast to the educational opportunities available to Sandra.

Considering the relevance of relationships for everyday humanitarians, a further aspect is the role of similarities, or shared experiences among supporters and beneficiaries, in providing an impetus for intervention (I expand on these as recognised affinity ties in Chapter 7). The recognition of shared experiences or similarities provided a base for some of the connections discussed here. Mitra, for example, was a naturalised Canadian citizen. She had grown up in Iran, but had to leave after her early childhood years due to the political situation. She had been working in international development as a consultant for several years, but found this most rewarding on the occasions when she knew the stories of the individual women to whom a project was directed. For example, the objective of one private sector development project she was involved in was to encourage women who had been forcibly evicted from their settlements to set up their own businesses in Cambodia's Northeastern region. What Mitra loved about it, was *'the satisfaction of knowing every woman ... explaining to them, this is how you do it, you need to get orders ... that motivates me'*. In particular, she found that:

> *listening to these women's stories, we have the same experience. I lost all of my roots. These women lost their homes in front of their eyes. My dad died of cancer four years ago, and I couldn't go and see him* [as she was unable to enter the country]. *Even now, I can't see my grandmother. So there is a shared experience with the evicted women. For them, through economic empowerment they can escape abuse* [after losing their livelihoods through eviction], *and I can help them with that.*

What put her off her work with international aid agencies, she declared emphatically, was that these connections were dismissed in her professional sphere, especially by one consultant and teacher whom she initially revered. Personal relations were not to be encouraged, she was told, as they provided merely instant gratification without changing policy. '*He said, "you shouldn't get any satisfaction because development is beyond these things"*', expressing perhaps an enlightenment emphasis on reason and denial of affect. In her view, though, '*we're all part of humanity, we fled a country – so it cannot be that this, dealing with forced evictions, does not matter. He told us that we were not meant to be part of the story.*' One might detect here an emphasis on reason and denial of the passions driving development, as visible in the desire for connection. In due course, Mitra set up her own online handicraft business, organising training for disadvantaged women in urban neighbourhoods, providing them with a more stable source of income. In these activities, Mitra found that she felt '*much more connected; I was so ready to do this full time*'. Nevertheless, this set-up, at the time, still relied on her earning an income through occasional consulting jobs in order to raise funds to grow her handicraft project. Relationships based on construction of a shared past, however symbolic, may thus provide both motivation and direction for citizen aid activities in the way that large-scale, formalised development would not allow for. Drawing on their own biographies enables supporters to become, in their words, 'part of the story' in more ways than one.

Conclusion

This chapter has taken as its starting point the observation that relationships matter for aid. It has argued that while the desire to help has often been foregrounded, especially in development studies, an equally important role is played by the desire to connect – that is, to establish meaningful personal relations with those being supported. The case of everyday humanitarians demonstrates that the shorthand of 'making a connection' includes physical presence, face-to-face contact with people, direct experience of aid activities and their tangible efficacy. The examples also demonstrate that 'thick' person-to-person connections are being sought, furnished with first-hand knowledge of the projects. Personal knowledge here stands for trust and accountability both towards donors, as well as local communities. A key aspect for choosing to provide support, as well as where to direct it, is the creation of personal relationships between those involved. Perceived differences offer as much incentive as constructed similarities, such as shared past experiences. A complex picture emerges which supports the argument that rather than the desire to help being a primary incentive, the desire to connect matters just as much. This, I suggest, holds for Cambodians involved in these projects as well as for visiting foreigners: the rewards of these connections extend beyond practical benefits, but include desired transnational connections, opportunities for travel, and friendships.

What are some of the implications of such a search for connection for aid theory and practice? At the very least, it implies that the impulse of philanthropy (Bornstein 2009) has been foregrounded, and perhaps unduly narrowed the range of imagined reasons why individuals support others. In addition, an equivalent 'anthropological impulse' comes into view: that is the desire to establish connections with others who are very different from oneself. Rather than pure exotic attraction to a needy other – a distant stranger, as it were – the material here suggests that this is inextricably twinned with a desire to find commonalities and sameness. While, as Heron suggests, the difference of the other both justifies intervention and creates attraction, identifying similarities provide a rationale for where to intervene, that is, supporting someone whom one knows personally, and feels close or connected to. The tension between similarity and difference, making these relationships challenging as well as desirable, is inherent in making such connections in the context of everyday humanitarianism. Such tensions complicate and question the well-rehearsed notion of a 'distant stranger' being the object of individual charity donations. On evidence from everyday humanitarianism, the wish for familiarity and closeness is a central element in directing assistance to others. This holds for overseas donors, visiting supporters, and for both foreign and Cambodian founders and facilitators. It is less clear, and needs exploring, how such connections matter for the people and communities who are being supported. As a way of differentiating existing notions of what drives individual development activities, it is an important first step.

6

Humanitarian kinship

Lizzie, who was heading an international aid agency in Phnom Penh, remembered about how she had met Sophorn, their adopted daughter:

> *We didn't choose her, she chose us. She was working down at the market, doing hair, and one day when I was in a rush I went to get my hair done there. We talked, and she practically adopted us. She lives with her mum and her sister but had not finished school. We got her onto an English course; she dropped out, now she's doing photography. Mike just bought her this expensive camera. But it's never quite enough! Things get messy, of course. Why did we not expect it to get messy?*

Lizzie was describing a form of relating to others that appeared frequently in conversations, and was woven through everyday humanitarian practices, namely the idiom of kinship. Her relationship with Sophorn was a result of both chance and choice, and it bore the hallmarks of families: there was emotional attachment, financial and other support, tempestuous fallouts, reconciliations, and ongoing engagement with each other. In other cases, these could also fizzle out over time, or be abandoned by either side. Given how frequently kin relations were invoked among foreigners and Cambodians, this chapter argues that the making of humanitarian kin, that is, a particular form of relations between practitioners and those they support, is a key modality of scaling close social relations.

Chapter 5 argued that a key motivation that drives support for others is the desire to create personal relationships with them. The twin desires to support and to establish bonds are often interlinked and occur simultaneously. The exact nature of these relationships may be blurred; often, those involved described them as making a 'connection'. The multiple differences that are entailed in these relationships, such as ethnic, socio-economic and linguistic ones, can make them attractive, while posing challenges in equal measure.

Whatever their qualities, the desire for these connections provides further impetus to query the trope of the distant stranger, even though it remains partly this distance that makes such connections attractive. This chapter foregrounds how social relations in the idiom of kinship result from, and shape, humanitarian practices. These are not necessarily separate from social relationships described in Chapter 5, and there may be overlaps between the two. Making visible how, and to what ends, participants choose to describe them as kin relations, is indicative of how people construct relationships and responsibilities to others. This chapter links to previous strands of discussion about the social closeness and distance of those we are responsible for. It asks what directs our decisions about whom to help among the 'sea of humanity', and how acts of support shape the resulting relationships in return. The answer provided by this chapter revolves around kinship ties as moulding humanitarian acts, while the final chapter explores the role of affinities and shared biographies in this process.

Relational humanitarianism

This insights presented here challenge humanitarian studies as they reveal that a relational rather than abstract-liberal humanitarianism animates supporters from the Global North, too. Critically examining Western strands of moral philosophy, Bornstein argues that Western moral philosophy and popular imagination are fixated on the 'distant stranger' as a key figure of humanitarianism. In her work on charity in Delhi, Bornstein makes a distinction between a liberal humanitarianism characteristic of a 'Western' tradition, and practices of charity and philanthropy in India. A 'relational humanitarianism' attributed to the Indian context is subtly contrasted with a disinterested, 'liberal humanitarianism' more typically found in Western societies. Bornstein proposes that such a model 'differs from relational empathy and a kinship of humanitarianism that are built through dynamics of social obligation' (2012:150). As a result, she finds that 'humanitarians that practice liberal altruism eschew the relational model by turning to abstract others in need, while those who practice relational empathy turn strangers into kin' (2012:170). Everyday humanitarianism in Cambodia suggests that these distinctions are more blurred in practice. While initially attracted to 'saving strangers', I have shown in previous chapters that a desire to turn strangers into known individuals and eventually kin, can be just as strong. Humanitarians from the Global North, as well as other Asian countries, are passionately engaged in exactly the kind of relational humanitarianism that Bornstein attributes to the Indian context. This is likely not unique to Cambodia either, as Chika Watanabe shows how a Japanese NGO presents itself as 'being like family' for Japanese and Burmese staff and volunteers (2019:144).

Kinning, in the context of transnational adoption where this concept originated, as well as in everyday humanitarianism, is about making strangers into kin. This matters both empirically and analytically: among and between Cambodians and foreigners, evidence of kinning practices, tightly interwoven with supporting others, abound. One might argue that this is prefigured in the long-established form of child sponsorship (Bornstein 2001) and as such not an unexpected form of humanitarianism. However, not much literature engages with how such idioms of kinship are deployed to produce a simile of kinship between a physically and socially distant sponsor, and a recipient. In the context of everyday humanitarianism, where bonds tend to be more intimate if still mediated by brokers (Fechter 2020), the purposes and rationales for using kinship idioms, as well as the tensions arising from them, deserve closer attention. This will provide a fuller understanding about how relationships and responsibilities are co-created or, conversely, abandoned in the context of supporting others.

Central to this reasoning is the assumption that all kinship is made. This follows from Schneider's argument (2014 [1984]) that Euro-American understandings of kinship have historically relied on a shared bio-genetic substance, or blood, as the basis for constructing kinship. However, this is merely one modus among many. Other forms include sharing substances such as rice or breastmilk (Carsten 2000). Kinship is made through acts of choice, emotions and practices (Weston 1991). All human kinship results from constructing and valorising particular acts, substances or emotions, and positing them as the fabric which defines and sustains kin relations. The distinction between biological and what has been called 'fictive' kinship (Gubrium and Buckold 1982; Macintyre 1993) is immaterial. The different ways in which kinship is made matter, but none is more natural or valid than another. They are social constructs. For the present purposes, and to express the notion that all kinship is made, I use the term 'kinning', or making kin (Howell 2003). This describes the process of 'making strangers into kin' (Howell 2003, 2006), such as parental care that turns an adopted child from another country into a family member (Modell 1994; Weismantel 1995).

Highlighting the relational nature of everyday humanitarianism means disrupting not just notions of the distant stranger, but also the dominance of the liberal-abstract forms of humanitarianism so prevalent in historic and philosophical debates. These relations can take different forms, such as the spontaneous connections described in Chapter 5, or the kin relations examined here. This chapter shows in what ways humanitarianism is infused with, and relies on, idioms and practices of kinship. This may be obvious as we take for granted that kin relations so often function as a mechanism for social protection. They also interlink with humanitarian agencies and support in less visible, but impactful ways. As Carruth shows in the case of displaced Somalis living in Ethiopia, kin relations and access to humanitarian services and employment can be intricately linked, and affect health and livelihoods (2018, 2021). She suggests that 'organisations would benefit from explicitly drawing on kinship-based forms of social organisation to guide their needs assessments, aid distributions, and mechanisms of triage such that existing support systems are strengthened while individuals without adequate kinship support are recognised and otherwise cared for' (Carruth 2018:166).

This chapter explores the role of kin for everyday humanitarianism; beyond this, how kinship and development interconnect is worthy of a wider investigation. Models of 'twinning' church communities, towns or even toilets, are long established; invocations of NGOs or the UN being a 'family' are common, and more recently this has been discussed in private refugee sponsorship in Canada (Macklin et al. 2020). I suggest that one reason why kinship lends itself, and is drawn on for development purposes is that it accepts rather than eradicates social and economic inequalities. It can also offer a sense of belonging for foreigners who may be unmoored abroad. Finally, this chapter illustrates how humanitarianism is not just shaped by, but productive of, kinship. Ekatherina Zhukova has explored this among children from Chernobyl being sent for recuperation to Italian families. She proposes that kinning means that 'the outcomes of disaster response, such as humanitarian assistance or migration' have a 'surprising potential to create new human relations transnationally' (Zhukova 2019:16). This chapter also shows how humanitarianism is productive of kin relations. I define humanitarian kinship here as social relations, cast in the idiom of kin, that are deriving from support acts, as well as relations struck up to create a framework that demands and enables acts of support to flow as a result of the relation. The first instance of this are humanitarian families.

Humanitarian families

Even though forms of institutional child care are not central to the humanitarian kinship that I want to discuss, they are a starting point for recognising how pervasive idioms of kinship are in aid. Such relevance has been documented in the context of formal residential child care, including how children themselves use such terminology (Kendrick 2013). In humanitarian contexts, kin terminology can become part of the official description of children's homes, for example those run by international charities and NGOs. One case are the international 'SOS children's villages' (Gmeiner 1960), located in twenty-nine countries. These are residential care homes in low-income countries, moulded in the shape of families. This includes dividing the children into small groups, each occupying one house, headed by a 'house mother', and sometimes a couple as 'parents'. Such institutions existed in Cambodia, run by local, national and international NGOs.

The problems posed by the model of residential children's homes, their potential for abuse, and the question about whether they should be dismantled, had become an increasingly live issue over the years during which I carried out fieldwork from 2013 onwards (Guiney and Mostafanezhad 2014; Reas 2013). Prompted by instances of orphanages which manifestly exploited children for the financial gain of the directors, such as through performances for tourists, a large-scale campaign was initiated by the ChildSafe Movement (n.d.) to discourage this practice, among others. This prompted serious consideration among the founders of some care facilities, and some switched to a day-care model, rather than a residential one, as a result. I also engaged with informal projects run by Cambodians, which did not necessarily consider themselves as running a formal children's home, but nevertheless provided accommodation, food and help with education for local children; these often maintained their residential support model.

Mindful of the ethical concerns regarding residential child care, I here argue that social relations resulting from supportive intervention were often couched in kinship terminology. This is more appropriately illustrated by small-scale, privately financed children's homes which are run by everyday humanitarians and tightly knit groups of individual donors, rather than by local municipalities or international NGOs. This setting illustrates the argument that humanitarian action can create kin relations, and strangers become kin through acts of care. 'Our Children's Village' was one such case. I first came across this small project looking after around twenty-five children in a southern province while travelling with Anya, a Danish staff member of an international aid agency. In her free time, she occasionally took representatives from philanthropic organisations to visit charity projects in her local area, which they might consider supporting financially. Our Children's Village had originally been set up by an Austrian family with the aim of 'improving the lives of orphaned Cambodian children'. The family resided in Austria, though their portrait adorned the wall of the main assembly room. Central to implementing their mission was Dieter, from Germany and in his sixties. With his Cambodian wife Nim, they referred to themselves as the 'parents' of the village. Each of the traditional-style wooden houses in village was headed by a 'house mother'. Dieter had travelled to Cambodia while the village was in its early stages of being established, at the behest of the Austrian founding family he was close to. Not having a partner or children of his own in Austria, he was free to relocate to Cambodia to help out at first, while gradually taking over the running of the home. As he told me with some contentment,

> it is really hard work ... there are always problems and challenges coming your way. But after such long days, in the evening, I sit here with a beer, and I look over the site and I think, this is my family, this is my home.

A couple of years after I first visited, I learned that Dieter had sadly and unexpectedly died of a heart attack. As the children's village already had a Cambodian deputy director, he subsequently took over responsibility for the home. It was thus entirely run by a Cambodian team, an outcome which had been the professed aim of the Austrian family.

Using the idiom of family may be considered especially desirable in institutional settings, precisely in order to make them appear less formal and more intimate. The use of kin and family idioms also abound in more informal settings, offering day care, rather than residential one. One such setting was RiceFirst, an after-school educational centre, in the outskirts of a provincial town. Through working with children who were living in their family homes, these day-care centres avoided the institutionalisation of children, a problem for which residential homes have long been criticised. It founder, Abby, had arrived in Cambodia as a young single professional on a career break from the USA. She was looking to take her life in a different direction, and had been 'hooked' by the children when she first became involved as a volunteer in a children's home. Having spent some time there, she set up RiceFirst, which offered free after-school classes, focused on English and IT lessons, to supplement the children's state-school curriculum. A key principle of their project was to incentivise the children's attendance at lessons with the provision of rice packets for their families. This helped families to not rely on children's wage-labour to supplement the family's needs. Caring for these children thus included intagible as well as tangible benefits in the form of a key substance, rice. Abby, well aware that each of these children were part of their own families, nevertheless spoke of them as 'her children'. As she explained it, '*all my life I've wanted kids, and now I've got 200! When I have fifty kids with smelly breath clambering all over me, then I know I'm in the right place.*'

Despite the fact that they were providing assistance to more than 200 children, Tammy insisted that '*we are small enough to be a family, but big enough to have a real impact*'. Their responsibility was to help these children secure a better livelihood in the future:

> the kids we are looking after ... they are one million times closer to getting their human rights! When they graduate from our place they will have some English, which is pretty much a mandatory life skill here. You can make $100 in the tourist industry, it makes the difference to earning $1 day in the rice field.

Even when RiceFirst were thinking of expanding their project by adding a second site, Abby insisted that the children would *'still be part of the family'*. Similarly, Tanya, a co-founder of what initially was a residential children's home, drew on a parent idiom to render her relationship to the former street children in their project. This is described in an interview for a book about 'unsung heroes' in Cambodia: 'Tanya is anxious to get back to the kids but is happy to answer one final question: "What is your dream for these kids?" She smiles as she answers, "The same as any other mum – just times seventy"' (Anderson, Griffin and Hartley 2013:86). Incidentally, this echoes questions of scale and social relations, raised in Chapters 2 and 3. Both Abby and Tanya insisted that familial relations were paramount, even as they multiplied to an extent which surpassed that of many ordinary families.

Such narratives of being a parent to Cambodian children, in numbers such as 50, 70 or 200, abounded. I discussed this with Sina, an Australian citizen and long-time resident in Cambodia, who was wholly dismissive of the idea that such projects even remotely resembled a family: *'How can you be the mother of one hundred children? That is just preposterous.'* Another friend thought that like many other everyday humanitarians, it was Abby, not just the children, who was having her own needs met. Abby sometimes commented that she would *'never go back to the Western world'*. Having married a Canadian working in the NGO sector, she explained that they had adopted *'three kids with fetal alcohol syndrome, with all kinds of behaviour issues'*. She added that at the beginning it had been *'difficult, really difficult, but they are terrific kids now'*.

As Abby's example shows, boundaries between considering two hundred children as one's own, and one's adopted children, may be fluid. I often witnessed everyday humanitarians supporting children in different capacities. They included members of their extended family, such as nieces and nephews; formally adopted children; and children they were looking after in their projects. Humanitarian action can thus generate families, both in institutional and informal child-care setting. At the same time, using kinship idioms, such as being 'parent' to relatively large groups of children suggests an intimacy that is more invoked than manifest in everyday life.

Child sponsorship and adoption

Me and Cambodia, it was like a mother and baby breastfeeding relationship. I didn't want to leave!

Such exuberant declaration was made by François, who first worked in the refugee camps along the Thai–Cambodia border in the 1980s, and had since made Cambodia his home. Working for several INGOs and later as an independent consultant, he had also set up an informal, child sponsorship scheme. This involved him travelling around villages in his local area, talking to people to identify the 'very poorest', in his words, who also had to be 'very bright', to qualify for his scheme. Through his social networks, François endeavoured to find a sponsor for each student, ensuring their school attendance, and to be offered further opportunities once they completed secondary school. Once, he was discussing with a friend the case of a local student from an ethnic minority group who he thought should be attending medical school rather than the provincial midwife training, because *'she would be wasted there'*. With donors in short supply at that time, his friend suggested financing the school fees through an ethnic-minority development project he was involved with so some costs would be covered and less sponsorship money needed. When donations were tight, his friend on occasion provided accommodation for one of these students in the household he shared with his Cambodian partner, while they were attending college or university in the capital.

Formal child sponsorship schemes have been the subject of extensive critical debate. They are charged with increasing the inequalities they aim to address, and causing jealousy and tension by favouring one child over their siblings, or others in the community. Further, they can be misleading, as the funds nominally allocated to a child are often channelled into wider community benefits; the scheme may fulfil the emotional needs of the sponsor, rather than the child; and they can create dependencies (Bornstein 2001). Some of these critiques undoubtedly also hold for informal arrangements such as initiated by François and others. I was told by Visal, in charge of an after-school club, how one former street child had been championed by an 'expat lady':

> *we had one lady, she bought so many things ... she buy him things in the mall, they go to Pizza Express, everything .... so he went back to his family and says, why was I not born with this lady, why I born with you? She can give me more and a better life.*

This had caused much tension among those he was living with, only for her to leave the country and sever their relationship. This had left the boy despondent, to the extent that he *'wished she had never come here in the first place'*. As Visal explained, *'he doesn't know, this is not the real life, you should be with your parents. We had to talk to him. It's not safe for the child, you get spoilt kids.'* At the same time, such informal arrangements face other challenges, such as the sustainability of donations, and risks to the continuity of support to sponsored children.

These debates notwithstanding, such informal child sponsorship arrangements demonstrate that support practices can generate, and be cast in the idiom of kinship. Humanitarianism can be productive of kin relations, as the relationships between François, his friend, and the sponsored students show. François proudly showed me the high school graduation pictures of 'his boys', as he called them, adding weight to the argument that 'Western' humanitarian practice is deeply relational, rather than liberal-abstract, casting support relationships in the idiom of kin. Such kin relations, specifically in the form of adoptions, also played out in the case of Leo and Visal. Together with Visal, his Cambodian partner in their project, he set up an after-school club. While they did not self-consciously present themselves as parents, kinship still mattered. Among the group of children who regularly attended their club, Leo had a special relationship with one of them, Lo. He called him his 'little brother', drawing on Khmer kin terminology. He was talking with pride about his progress at school and his success at football. A promising young player, he gained a place in a football academy run by an NGO. Once, after a day helping in Mabel's soup kitchen, Leo left earlier than the others, explaining that he needed to watch Lo at football practice. Around the same time, Visal, who Leo was also referring to as his 'brother', took responsibility for Pisey, another boy who was a regular at the after-school club.

They had met Pisey when an 'expat lady' had approached Visal for help, after Pisey had been seen wandering the streets and kept dropping into the woman's shop. Visal tried to find a foster family, but placing him proved difficult: '*nobody wanted him, but when we saw him, he looked so sad! He said he wanted to go to school, we couldn't leave him in the street.*' It turned out he had gone through four sets of foster parents, being a child '*out of wedlock, his mother died and his father disappeared*'. After spending time in several orphanages, at least one of which was abusive, Pisey had lived on the streets for two years. Estimated to be around 12 years old, Visal decided to adopt him. As he explained,

> *It wasn't very complicated, it cost about $37 for document fees. In the first six weeks, he ran away twice, but not any more since then. His face is happy. Three months ago, there was a real change, he asked me if he could call me dad. He says, you are my real dad. So the other kids, they can call me uncle or brother, it doesn't matter what, but not dad. That's just Pisey.*

On a return visit, a couple of years after this conversation, I asked after Pisey. Visal explained that he had moved out from their home, and taken residence in the local Buddhist temple complex, the *pagoda*. This was not an uncommon practice for young men, and Visal had done the same several years previously, to overcome a lean period in his own family. When I asked Visal what his family thought of him adopting Pisey, he explained that,

> *my mum liked it, my brother didn't say much. Actually, my older brother took in three neighbourhood kids. The parents packed up and one evening said, we're leaving for Thailand, can you have an eye on the three kids in the house? They were 5, 10, and 13, in a shack that was falling down. The father has come back once. He gave them $15. The kids were just so scared. So we pay for them to go to school.*

Visal's biggest concern in his work with the Life Project was that *'the children are not used to any rules. For me, the big challenge is to look after them – not being a dad, but being an uncle or brother. In a way, we have 16 sisters and brothers … we never planned to have a whole family!'* Such practices of kinship, where supporting people and making them into kin in the process, go hand in hand, are common. Another case was Ponnleu, a middle-aged Cambodian owner of a successful English language school. Together with Markus and Elke, whom she had got to know as neighbours, she co-founded a small NGO offering vocational training for disadvantaged students. When I talked with her about her charity work, both in the school and on their project, she explained some of the ways in which her family had been supporting adopted and native kin:

> *I have this feeling here and here* [pointing to her head and heart], *that's what I learned … we support people who are on a lower level, who are poorer. So we often donate, go to the Pagoda, to the countryside, and bring something. We also have two adopted sons. They are 19 and 16, we support them. We had nieces and nephews we help. From the beginning, we start from a low level too. Their parents were poor and sick and die, so we help them.*

Similarly, Federico, an Italian who had been working for an INGO in Cambodia for several years, told me that he and his Cambodian girlfriend,

> *we want kids too. But we've practically adopted her younger sister, who is only 12. She is going to a good school here, and lives with my girlfriend, but that's why we can't just move abroad, because her sister's English is not good enough to survive at an international school yet.*

As these examples show, supporting others can involve making them kin in the process, such as describing them as 'family', as 'having children' as well as formally adopting children. All this queries the 'distant stranger' narrative, and demonstrates how Cambodians and foreigners practise humanitarianism involving people they have (made) relations with. The stories told here contribute to kinship theory, in so far as they show humanitarianism is productive of kinship. Finally, hybrid kin practices which blend native, informally and formally adopted families abound, displaying how supporting and making others kin, are closely interlinked.

Inequality and belonging

The intense interweaving of differently made families and kin among foreigners and Cambodians can serve a range of purposes. As mentioned, some of those familiar with these practices found the use of kinship terminology irritating or ridiculous, especially in claiming to be the mother or father of dozens of children. What work does the kinship idiom do, such as the semiotics of scaling to closeness? In her work on child sponsorship, Bornstein argued that such relations can exacerbate existing socio-economic inequalities. In the context of everyday humanitarianism, such inequalities are one of the reasons why such relationships are instigated, both by possible sponsors or adopters, and those seeking assistance. While the previous sections dealt with kin relations that were created in the wake of giving support, humanitarian kinship practices also incorporate the desire to relate to others. Supporting them offers one modality of establishing these relationships. I argue that inequality is key to these relationships, not just as a reason to initiate the relationship. Rather, drawing on the idiom of kinship enables social relations – the purpose of which is not, or not only, to reduce socio-economic inequalities. Precisely because kinship itself is inherently unequal, couching one's social relations in an idiom of kin leaves room for existing inequalities, allowing the relationship to continue nevertheless. This sets it apart from friendship, which presupposes a greater level of equality and lack of hierarchy in order to function (Macklin et al. 2020).

The semiotic labour of kinship may gloss over such differences if necessary. To some extent, it takes inequalities for granted; it may alleviate them, but not ultimately aim to redress them. We know that 'families have built-in inequalities', not just in the Indian context (Bornstein 2012:150). The dynamics of inequality between giver and recipient is not necessarily reversed through a kinship idiom, but it can be accommodated. This form of humanitarian kinship bears strong resemblance to a patron–client relation. The differences are not necessarily clear-cut, and at times may be understood as both. The Cambodian patronage system was invoked by several foreigners who found themselves entangled in such relations, even though it may not have been fully understood by them. While such patronage has been mainly discussed in relation to politics and business (Un 2005; Kimchoeun et al. 2007; Chandler 2008; Springer 2010), it arguably pervades much of Cambodian society. Verver and Dahles argue that the 'inequality between patron and client and the proximity of their interrelation' are particularly evident in the Cambodian context (2015:54). Not coincidentally, these traits resonate with the humanitarian kin relations examined here. When I asked her about the Cambodian family members they supported, Lizzie for example exclaimed,

> Oh, they are so materialistic! My adopted daughter – money is the most important thing in her life. It's a patron–client relationship. Some of us at least know that were are a patron. Many expats ask for fictive kinship. Jim at Open House for example, they call him 'papa' – he doesn't even know the name of them all. But it's all relationship-based, once you've been drawn in. We wanted to resist going into the fictive kinship thing. There's a Khmer word for cord or string. They get your back, and then they are your patron. They all need it for their job. Having 'strings' is vitally important. I need a 'string' for this or for that. 'Papa' Jim is a patron.

But then again, Lizzie added,

> the grandmother [of Sophorn] said to me, 'you are a wonderful mother to Sophorn'. Her own daughter was such a mess. Is it kinship, is it a patron-client relationship? It's like world vision, you know, the child sponsorships. It feels good. You don't get that kind of feeling from sanitation reform in Koh Kong!

The last comment reflected on her sense of reward from these activities, compared to the more policy-oriented tasks that formed the mainstay of her paid work at aid agencies. Rather than the kinship idiom masking a patron–client relationship, in Lizzie's view, both were valid ways of understanding such a situation. She still reserved scorn for those foreigners who were thinking of themselves as a parent, with the emotional surplus this suggested, rather than a patron, who is chosen for their power, protection and resources offered. Inequalities can thus be accommodated in a framework that can be simultaneously understood as a patron–client, and an adopted parent–child relationship.

Those relations are not always clear-cut between those coming from the Global North and South, however. Amy and Jacob, for example, a couple in their late twenties, university graduates from the UK, were working in the tourism industry in Cambodia. They are had been based in Southeast Asia for several years, and Jacob explained that working in the region, though by choice, had not put them on a stable financial footing:

> when we talk to our friends in the UK, we tell them, we're living in Asia, we have nothing, no savings. And our friends say, we have less than nothing, we have debts! Basically, we've been advised to ignore all letters from the student loan company while we're in Asia. Our contact person at the bank said, they're just selling on the credit, safely ignore it, and when you come back, just say that you have nothing.

While definitions of what 'nothing' is vary, their perceived precarity meant that in Cambodia, Amy and Jacob sometimes resented the fact that they were considered wealthy foreigners. Once, Amy told me with some indignation,

> *I think it's absolutely gross to adopt a person, like sponsoring an individual. It's really wrong, these handouts. Tuktuk drivers get given stuff by foreigners – like the landlord who rents the apartment to us! He met this foreigner, and they are always wringing out some kind of story, they make a connection, and the foreigner gives them money.*

In their case, the foreigner helped a tuktuk driver to buy land and build a house. On reflection, she added, '*I guess ok, he's given him money to invest, and he's done something with it and now has an income.*' She resented that this income was now provided by foreigners such as Jacob and herself, whose own situation felt precarious due to their unstable income and student debt. To round things off, Amy concluded, '*our landlord calls him 'papa' – that is quite common because that fits into the Cambodian patronage system*'.

Humanitarian kin relations, whether emerging from a support function or creating responsibilities in their wake, can also generate ties of belonging to a place or social fabric which may not be available to people otherwise. Bornstein similarly observes that 'perhaps foreigners in India who practise liberal altruism are social orphans, so they seek family with strangers'. As argued here, many of the foreigners whose work I witnessed engaged in humanitarian practice were not driven by an abstract rationality, but by a desire to support people they knew. Nevertheless, the observation about seeking family with strangers holds in that humanitarian kinship practices can create a sense of belonging that some foreigners may be actively seeking. The role of humanitarian kinning and its cultivation of local embeddedness was acknowledged by Pierre, an international civil servant based in a Cambodian ministry. As he once remarked, '*I haven't got a Khmer wife, I haven't adopted a kid, I'm not embedded or connected to the place the way that some people are.*' This was not a particular regret for him; he was divorced, but living with his partner, a fellow aid worker, and did not seek closer relationships of other kinds.

For others, however, carrying out everyday humanitarianism, meant belonging 'to a humanitarian family in the kinship of humanitarianism' (Bornstein 2012:170). This could also take more official forms. François, for example, was awarded Cambodian citizenship, not easily available to foreigners. In his view, his long-term residence and engagement with Cambodia helped with his citizenship application, as well as his student sponsorship programme, which was highlighted by the government official at the award ceremony. François's services to the Cambodian people, and the honourable mention he received every year at the local high school for his sponsorship programme, generated national belonging in the form of citizenship. Some may regard this as a dubious honour, given the Cambodian government's flawed record on human rights and democracy. In order to ensure future cooperation with the government, however, becoming a citizen was a sign of trustful relations, and bode well for the safe maintenance of their everyday humanitarian projects.

Balancing responsibilities

Humanitarian kinship offered informal and formal belonging to some, who may have felt 'orphaned' or otherwise unmoored. Humanitarian kinship ties and resulting responsibilities sometimes sat alongside, or in tension with, ties to people's non-humanitarian families. Such balancing of responsibilities could be an ongoing process. Some foreign humanitarians spoke with warmth and enthusiasm about their Cambodian family, such as young people who they were looking after, or elderly Cambodians into whose family they had been adopted. When I enquired about their ties with, or the well-being of, their own family in their home countries, their responses occasionally lacked interest or passion. Jim, for example, a committed Christian from the USA, had been working with his wife in Cambodia for more than ten years, setting up projects to support young people living with HIV/Aids. When I enquired about family members in the USA, he explained that he had five children, none of whom had ever visited them in Cambodia. By way of explanation, he suggested; *'They've got busy lives. You know in America, they're in their thirties, it's all about career, families, and making money. They have little holidays; they have not got round to come yet. Actually, though, one grandson is scheduled to come soon.'*

This affected him differently from his wife. As Jim commented,

that's the hardest thing for my wife about being here – not seeing the grandkids. We are going home for a week this summer, and she doesn't want me to do any fundraising or speaking, very strict, this time is just for the grandchildren.

Having reflected on this matter, he added a little while later,

I actually hate my children ... just joking! But they say once you have grandchildren, if you knew how much fun that was, then you'd skip the bit having children! No ... it's just like, you don't have much money then, when you have kids. And when you have grandchildren, you can spoil them ... and then give them back to their parents.

Jim had clearly felt burdened by the financial obligations when raising their own family. In relation to Cambodia, however, he described to me at length the range of schemes, and the very successful fundraising he was carrying out on behalf of his project and the Cambodian children affected by HIV/Aids. He also spoke with delight about the children involved in their project, and emphatically referred to them as 'our children', and that they called him 'papa', a term he very much relished.

A similar emotional ambivalence towards their own families was evident when I explored this with Terence, a soft-spoken teacher for deaf people from the USA. After taking retirement from a decades-long career in specialist schools for the hearing impaired, he went travelling in Southeast Asia. Like others, he was looking to embark on a new life stage. Having provisionally settled in a Florida retirement residence, he found that he could not contemplate such a lifestyle in the long term. Realising that *'sitting back in Florida was not an option for me'*, he set off to travel. During a stint in Cambodia, he started volunteering, kept returning, and then settled there on a semi-permanent basis. He became responsible for curriculum design in a school set up by a US family, who offered free tuition to Cambodian children from disadvantaged backgrounds. Terence was fully committed to this voluntary role, as well as teaching a group of young deaf people in a charity project. In our conversations, the matter of family in the USA did not emerge spontaneously. When I asked, he mentioned that they had lost their adult son to cancer several years earlier. He was separated from his wife, who still lived in the USA. Terence would not have been described as a misfit; but certainly, when I met him, his commitment and care was oriented towards the Cambodian children he was working with in the school; the sponsoring family in the USA, and the group of volunteers he helped coordinate, rather than the diminished family ties he had left behind.

Similarly, Abby told me that *'when I'm in Canada, I miss my family here, the team, the kids. The kids here are really my immediate family.'* Aiko, originally from Japan, also mentioned that *'when I go back to Japan, I see my family. One sister, we don't talk, but the other sister, she support me. They have not been to Cambodia. My family think that I'm a bit crazy.'*

One accusation that has been levelled specifically at international aid workers is that they are 'misfits' in their home countries, and that this constitutes one of the reasons for seeking work abroad (Stirrat 2008). Being a 'misfit' means being socially awkward and not fitting in, but also having cut ties with or abandoned their own families. While this may be common among people travelling for a living, the sting in Stirrat's claim is that the heroism and self-sacrifice attributed to aid workers must be seen in a context where these people, ostensibly committed to 'saving strangers', are disconnecting from their biological families. The perspective I offer here is more nuanced, in so far as some balance responsibilities between native and humanitarian kin, while some prioritise one over the other at different stages in their life course.

The case of Trevor illustrates the ways in which kinship ties that are chosen, and those that are not, may still differ – in how the person decides, to some extent, how they matter in their lives. Trevor, originally from the Isle of Man, had taken early retirement from his job in the UK. He had left home at the age of 15, and joined the merchant navy at 17. He settled and got married, but later got divorced. He did not feel close to his birth family, most of whom still lived on the Isle of Man:

> I don't like their parochialism, the inward looking, nationalist outlook. Bashing immigrants. It's actually my sister's birthday today, so I've sent her a message on Facebook. But I don't like all this Isle of Man stuff on her page. My dad died last year, and I went to the funeral, but we weren't close. I'm not really close to any of them.

Trevor had not cut ties with them completely, acknowledging birthdays, and attending his father's funeral. At the same time, he told me of how during his first visit to Cambodia, in 2007, he took a photo of a girl whom he had met at the temples, as she approached him to try and sell him a soft drink. After their first encounter, he returned the following year, visited the area where he remembered their huts stood, and brought them a photo he had taken of her. A neighbour recognised the image, and led him to her family's house. Since then they had been in touch, a period spanning seven year at that stage, from when the girl was 7 years old. Steve commented that they were *'like an adopted family. Even if I only go there a couple of times a year, and bring a picture or little things.'* Her older brother used to translate, but even though he was attending high school in town and was not around as much, Trevor found that *'it's nice when you can see them develop, as they go along, and now she speaks some English'*.

Trevor stressed his sense of belonging created through the giving relationship. He felt he played a role in Leap attending school and doing well. This was less so for his nieces and nephews living in the UK. At the same time, the informal kinship ties that he established with Leap and her family, in the form of a visiting relative or patron, were to a large extent at his discretion. He decided when to visit, what to bring and how tight or loose he wanted these connections to be. If he could not afford to sponsor them any more, his health deteriorated or if he had to return to the UK for another reason such as visa requirement, these ties would be lessened or cut, without Leap and her family being able to make demands on Trevor. The degree of agency and control that he had in the family he chose was thus considerable. This is not entirely dissimilar, however, from the relations he maintained with his birth family. Trevor's case illustrates which family people choose to engage with, and how these decisions interweave with practices of supporting them, highlighting the temporalities of commitments to different categories of families.

Obligations and rewards

Responsibilities to kin, and to those who are not considered kin, are often very differently understood. In the Indian context, Bornstein argues that 'the obligations and responsibilities that one has toward kin and friends are not considered to be humanitarian', but rather acts of duty (2012:150). Supporting one's family members is an obligation; supporting those who one is not related to is a voluntary act of charity. Even though such differences may occasionally be blurred, they matter because of how these activities are valorised, and the merit they carry in the eyes of wider society. As Bornstein observes, 'the unmarked tasks that, when written about in the context of family, would be considered usual acts or required acts become heroic acts when liberal humanitarians do them for others with whom they have no connection' (2012:151).

I suggest that families that are 'made' – humanitarian families – also incur obligations and as such are no different from duties to native kin. Nevertheless, discharging those obligations may bring a greater sense of reward, and thus orientate people towards their humanitarian kin. Some, over time, became more involved with their Cambodian-based, rather than home country families. Rob, for example, was distinctly leaning towards his 'Cambodian family', people with disabilities, in addition to his children living back in Canada. As he explained, this engagement had a longer history:

> In high school, I was already involved. I used to go to disability camp every summer. And we adopted a girl who had cerebral palsy, she was hard to adopt at 4 months. We already had two healthy sons.

His sons were now in their thirties and had started their own families. He did not want to live in Canada, though. '*Yes, I could be a dad and a granddad, as my kids are starting to have their own families. I could see them every weekend, or every other weekend.*' However, this did not hold particular appeal for him. Rather, he was preoccupied at that time with Nuon, who had come into the 'family' of people with disabilities at his project. He stated, '*This disabled girl here, Nuon, she's part of my Cambodian family now. It's so dehumanising what has happened to her. I really want to make a difference here.*' Rob's sense of the difference he could make for this family is experienced as more rewarding than the obligations posed by native kin, such as being a father or grandfather.

The prospect of greater rewards, because helping someone unrelated is considered exceptional, explains some of the desires animating everyday humanitarianism. By extension, this is true of kin work such as parenting. This requires an enormous amount of time, care work and effort over many years to raise children to be self-sufficient and live fulfilled lives. In a low-resource environment, such as Cambodian-run day-care centres, there are no such easy gains either. For Munny, who was running an informal day-care centre for disadvantaged children mentioned in Chapter 5, there were no quick rewards, spurred on by the difference in resources commanded by well-off foreigners. Although his team enjoyed regular successes, they were moderate in scale – a girl not dropping out of school to work in a massage parlour, high-school exams being passed or entry gained to a hospitality training course. Small gains might be seen as more significant at the lower end of the socio-economic scale than apparently larger gains at the already higher end of the scale. Modest ones may be life-changing in the long run, but they were achieved through Munny putting his physical and mental well-being at risk. His limited personal resources and time were often so stretched that he was on the brink of exhaustion a good deal of the time. There may be no brownie points for raising one's own children in a decent manner, but there may well be in helping to 'raise strangers' – although, as shown, they may be made into kin in the process.

Does it mean that assisting those who are non-native kin accrues more merit, since it is done as a voluntary act, rather than as a form of duty? Richard was such a case in question. Originally from the USA, Richard came to Cambodia in the late 1990s, when the country was emerging from civil war, and the first elections overseen by the UN had been held in 1993. Richard was working for an NGO which specialised in the detection and removal of land mines. He was on the frontline of their work, operating in rural areas to remove land mines and make areas around villages safe for people to start farming their land, and making paths safe to use. The work was high-risk and stressful, the living conditions difficult, and yet Richard looked back on that time in his life as intensely rewarding. He made close connections with Cambodian friends and colleagues and keeps in contact with them, visiting regularly, many years after returning to USA. The rewards were camaraderie, but also the heroism of the dangerous de-mining work.

At the same time, when I spoke with him, it emerged that he had become the father of two children during his time in Cambodia. Both mothers were foreigners, and returned to their home countries in mutual agreement, as neither had planned to remain in a relationship with him. Initially, in their early years, the children were living with the mothers abroad, and had only irregular contact with him. This eventually changed, Richard returned to the USA and settled in a place close to where they lived. The time I first spoke with him, his commitments seemed to be divided: a deep care for his life-endangering work in removing land mines, for the sake of Cambodian villagers with whom had no particular affiliations with to start with, and which left him with a permanent health condition. At the same time, he engaged in relationships with women he was only very partially committed to at the time.

When he talked about his early years in the chaotic and dangerous times which Cambodian people found themselves in, there was a sense of purpose and excitement that animated his account of working in land-mine removal. Speaking of his casual romantic relationships, they appeared as something that had happened along the way, but not of enormous consequence. The mundane and tedious tasks of everyday relationship building, compounded by the stresses of early parenthood, possibly shackled to a desk-based job in the Global North, held no appeal for him. As I caught up with him several years later, Richard's priorities had changed; he was living near both of his children, looked after them regularly and relished their relationships.

Richard's case shows that the rewards from helping those unrelated to oneself, such as Cambodian villagers, can at times carry rewards that are different from looking after one's biological children. His work on de-mining, while stressful and dangerous, also carried notions of heroic masculinity and potentially life-saving acts on a daily basis, while endangering his own. In comparison, the mundane tasks of looking after small children in a country of the Global North offered less dramatic recognition, not least in the eyes of the public. The rewards of helping strangers are thus different from those from helping kin, and partly explains why some everyday humanitarians are drawn to the former more than the latter, even though this may change depending on their life course stage.

Unmaking responsibilities

Sometimes, as in Richard's case, balancing the obligations between one's humanitarian and 'biological' kin, at some point tilted towards the latter. As Marilyn Strathern reminds us, kinship ties, and the responsibilities associated with them, can be made and unmade (1996). Or, as Rob put it more prosaically in the context of observing everyday humanitarians come and go over a number of years, *'many of these projects are just one relationship break-up away from being dropped'*. He referred to the fact that in many projects, a moment appeared where commitments to children, grandchildren or partners were given priority over those to Cambodian families whom they were supporting. Stories of responsibilities to humanitarian families that were being suspended or cut were not uncommon.

Glenys was an Australian in her sixties and full of energy. She was committed to a project which supported women in a squatter area to train in sewing skills, marketing and selling their products. After several years of travelling back and forth between Australia and Cambodia, I spoke to Glenys at the point when she was about to become a grandmother, as her daughter was expecting her first child in Australia. Having returned for a short visit, Glenys explained how she decided to scale back her activities in Cambodia for the time being, in order to be present for her daughter and the grandchild. Notably, she took care to find a friend to take over her role on the women's project in the meanwhile. Indeed, after a couple of years' absence, having engaged with and supported the project from afar via social media, she subsequently returned, and re-engaged with the community of single mothers that she had been working with. By finding a temporary replacement, this hiatus had not been severed, but temporarily put on hold her responsibilities to them.

In other cases, such a hiatus can become permanent, with support relations more seriously undermined. This can happen when marital relations, which were central to a project, disintegrate. 'Sun House', for exampl,e was a modest project which provided support for children with disabilities. It had been transformed and had grown from its origins as a volunteer placement taken by Jill and David, a retired couple originally from the UK. Over the course of each year, they divided their time between the UK and Cambodia, and together helped the Cambodian staff operating the project, even when they were not in the country. At some point, however, they separated. David began a relationship with a Cambodian woman, while Jill felt that her grandchildren in the UK required more of her time than she was able to give them while away. She therefore shifted her residence back to the UK, while David remained in Cambodia, albeit also withdrawing from the project. Jill remained supportive of Sun House from afar, but eventually the main responsibility was transferred to its Cambodian deputy director. The fact that this infrastructure had been built over a number of years thus ensured that the project continued, even if the pull of biological kin back home prevailed.

In some cases, the outcomes are more drastic, and more unsettling for those who used to rely on the support that was first established. Sonya, for example, from Australia, had become heavily involved in sponsoring individual children through a traineeship at a local NGO. She was able raise substantial sums in Australia over three or four years. At one point, however, she fell out with one of the key Cambodian partners in the sponsorship scheme, and eventually 'pulled the plug', in the words of a staff member. As he explained, '*Sonya did a lot for those kids and their training with us, but she just dropped it, and now all that hangs in doubt. We found a solution for the next few months, but then what? Who is going to continue?*' The break-up of relationships, such as with co-founders, can thus cause lasting damage if dependencies have been created without any fallback positions. This can happen especially when projects are very focused on the person, or personality of the sponsor. Amy for example, from the USA, came to Cambodia 'in a bit of a crisis', and took in a boy as a foster child. She had just retired, and eventually adopted the boy, but without her, there would be no alternative network to care of him.

While precarious for the sponsored or adopted child, such heavy reliance on an adopter may be precisely what attracts some, namely that it is possible, in Markus's words, '*to achieve so much with so little means*'. While raising children in the USA or Australia may be experienced as financially burdensome and laborious, ensuring a more stable future for a Cambodian child is a comparatively easy target to achieve, with the risk that that entailed for the child if this support was withdrawn.

Finally, everyday humanitarians who found or co-found a project might start a non-humanitarian family and return to their home country with the purpose of raising that family there. Scott, for example, whom I mentioned earlier, had come to Cambodia from the USA in the aftermath of a divorce, and a decision to leave his corporate career. After several years of establishing his project, he began a relationship with Sokha, a Cambodian woman. They married and had two small children. When I met him, he was increasingly struggling to provide for the time and financial needs of his family while juggling to keep the project afloat. He was drawing a modest salary, and having less time available compared to when he was single, equipped with savings and looking for a purpose. Scott eventually decided to relocate to the USA, again taking care to identify a successor to lead the project. When asked later on a social media site what he was up to in Denver, Colorado, having left his project behind, he stated that his aim was '*just going to work and raising a family*'. He illustrated this with pictures of him and Sokha, celebrating their son's success at a local swimming gala. For Scott, leaving the high stakes of supporting marginalised children in an impoverished area in Phnom Penh behind, for a comparatively mundane life in an American suburb furnished with swimming pools, a regular job and nearby grandparents, was the appropriate choice. Sometimes, after a spell abroad the responsibilities towards biological kin come to the fore, while those towards one's humanitarian families are transferred, or undone.

Conclusion

This chapter has explored how kin relations shape and are created through everyday humanitarian practices. It began with the assertion that human kinship and structures of support and care are inextricably woven together, including across geographical distances. It is not always clearly defined who is considered kin, on what basis, and what obligations and responsibilities follow or are constructed as a result of that. Bornstein's suggestion that relational humanitarianism – based on existing social relations – which is characteristic of Indian, rather than 'Western' supporters, does not hold in the Cambodian context, nor possibly more widely. As discussed in Chapter 1, indeed all humanitarianism is 'relational' in the sense that social relations are deeply enmeshed in and drive its practice. In particular, this chapter shows that everyday humanitarians who are active in Cambodia, including foreigners from other parts of Asia, the Global North and Cambodians themselves, draw on kinship idioms to construct humanitarian kinship. This is an entwined process, where the desire to support exists alongside the desire to make strangers into kin, and supporting them is one way of achieving this. In the first instance, the chapter argues that relationships of support, such as with young people in residential or non-residential care, can be couched in idioms of family. Humanitarian action can be productive of kinship, a notable contribution to kinship theory which is in many ways evident, though it lacks formal recognition in either field.

I also suggest that everyday humanitarian practices such as supporting a young person are often conceived of through the idiom of kin and specifically through adoption, be that informally or formally. While there is substantial literature on making strangers into kin in the context of formal adoption practices, these are not necessarily or primarily viewed as humanitarian acts. Viewing these practices in Cambodia through the lens of humanitarianism raises the question what work the semiotics of kinship does. Research on child sponsorship has stressed that the inequalities that motivate sponsorship can also perpetuate them. I suggest that a main reason for couching support relationships in kinship idioms is that they accommodate inequalities, rather than seeking to remove or overcome them entirely, while continuing to justify interventions. A further motivation for conceiving of humanitarian families is that they offer a form of social belonging which some foreigners, as well as some Cambodians, seek out and appreciate.

The second part of the chapter takes a closer look at how responsibilities are constructed and implemented in the context of 'biological' and humanitarian kin. While balancing these is not unusual, the question arises what motivations come into play when deciding on how to support or care for others. While their life stage definitely makes a difference to people's involvement in care for others, this does not play out in straightforward ways. For some, becoming a grandparent or even parent implies a shift in their responsibilities towards own kin, while for others, this holds less appeal than becoming involved with humanitarian kin in Cambodia. While many people balance support for biological kin and humanitarian kin, some are distinctly more drawn towards engaging with the latter. One reason for this may be that support for the latter may be considered more heroic than that provided to one's own family members, which is framed as an obligation. Finally, while families and kin ties can be made and unmade at any time, the question here is how humanitarian practices are affected by such relationship dynamics, demonstrating how ruptures such as marital breakdown, or conversely, intensified kin ties, such as becoming a parent or grandparent, can shape and disrupt humanitarian support relationships. This plays out in a more pronounced form among non-Cambodians, as their transnational mobility means that they can engage and disengage from their support relationships differently than those humanitarians who stay local.

7

Affinities and shared biographies

For me, it's about everyone should have what I was fortunate enough to have, that is, going to school. When the kids come to us after school, I see their smiling faces when they see, there is rice! Food! When I was a child, I came home from school, there was nothing. No rice, no food, nothing. I had a childhood like that. But these kids, they are born to be a child. So in a way, it's about me. I wish I had a childhood like that. I want them to have it.

This was the view of Visal, now in his early thirties. One of six siblings, his father died when he was small. He had to leave his family to stay in a pagoda for several years, in order to be able to go to school. Having to support some of his nieces and nephews, he tried running a market stall, without much success. At that time, he met Simona, an Italian local resident who kept dropping by and buying things. Eventually, he asked her, *'why do you buy so much?'* She replied, *'Because you're not selling well!'*

They started talking, and he began volunteering in her small charity and working at a cocktail bar at night to make ends meet. He barely slept until he became a paid staff member at the charity. One evening at the cocktail bar, he met Leo, from Australia, who had dropped out of a sponsored volunteer stint at a 'bogus orphanage'. Having met Visal, Leo decided to stay on in Cambodia, and they set up a small after-school club that they were running collaboratively when I first spoke to them.

Visal's trajectory from a struggling school student, to a paid charity worker, to project co-founder may be remarkable. More broadly, it is not uncommon that erstwhile beneficiaries of everyday humanitarian initiatives become volunteers, staff members or found such projects themselves. Chapter 6 illustrated how humanitarian kin relations underpin practices of supporting others. It also suggested that acts of everyday humanitarianism are not necessarily aimed at distant strangers, but many are framed as obligations to kin. This chapter attends to the role of collective and personal histories and experiences, such as illustrated by Visal's story. They can become a driver as well as a conduit for action.

As discussed in Chapter 2, debates in moral philosophy have attempted to identify who humans are responsible for. In the view of Singer (1996), everyone is responsible for everyone else, no matter how geographically distant or close, or how socially near or far they are. In a similar fashion, established forms of humanitarianism are governed by principles of neutrality, professionalism and impartiality, among others (Barnett and Weiss 2008). The principle of impartiality mandates helping anyone solely based on their need, independent of their national, ethnic, political or religious affiliation. As established previously, this constitutes an impossible situation, as it is not feasible to equally support everyone in need (Williams 2006). In contrast, one might argue that partiality – prioritising some humans over others – is not a flaw, but a precondition for any kind of intervention. In Chapter 6, the criteria for prioritising the needs of some people over others were based on humanitarian kinship. This entailed kin relations that brought with them responsibilities to intervene, and support practices that created kin relations in their wake.

This chapter discusses how people make choices about whom they will help through their everyday humanitarianism, other than from a sense of 'connection' and kinship ties. Chapter 4 complicated the narrative of the distant stranger. Rather than distance (and difference) being a sole incentive to intervene, oscillating between proximity and distance was more characteristic of everyday humanitarian engagements. Chapters 5 and 6 argued that instead of helping strangers, supporting those with whom people make a connection, whether spontaneously personal, or in the form of humanitarian kin relations, is a key modality of humanitarian intervention. This chapter proposes that another vector along which support is channelled, are collective and individual biographies, and affinities created by shared experiences. People mobilise narratives of affinity (and difference) to justify intervention, while such affinities also create responsibilities to begin with. A perspective highlighting affinities nuances the debate on the 'white saviour industrial complex' (Cole 2012), which has dominated humanitarian and development studies. Examining affinities unsettles the centrality of the 'white saviour' discourse, critical and otherwise, as it radically widens our understanding of who is involved in everyday humanitarianism, and what this means for its theorisation.

Being attentive to the partialities of everyday humanitarianism makes different patterns visible. A comprehensive look at who is supporting whom in Cambodia shows that those from the Global North are but one among many groups of 'saviours'. This includes a constituency that is obvious and overlooked in popular and academic accounts of the Global North. These are everyday humanitarians from neighbouring countries in the region, and other parts of Asia. Together with Cambodians, they are central to many humanitarian initiatives. The analytical tools to render these everyday humanitarians visible are affinities or affinity ties (Ho 2017; Oliff 2022) as a driver for supporting particular groups of people. These are based on collective histories, and biographical trajectories and experiences.

The notion of affinity is drawn from Elaine Ho's analysis of the humanitarian aid that members of the ethnic Jingpo, who are Chinese nationals, extend to ethnically related groups of Kachin people across the border between Myanmar and China. Ho describes affinity ties as 'connections emanating from a dynamic constellation of cultural attributes to do with history, ethnicity, religion and place among other malleable identity constructs' (Ho 2016:1). This aid is directed at ethnic Kachin by the Jingpo community, Chinese citizens and fellow Christians, who live across the border from the camps of displaced Kachin. Because the latter do not receive support from international NGOs, they rely on donations of food and resources from their co-ethnics, and fellow Christians, across the border. These kinds of affinity ties are a catalyst for informal resource distribution, functioning both as an imperative, and a criterion, for whom to support.

Affinities can be constituted along a wide range of characteristics and experiences that matter to people. Borne out of their particular ethnographic contexts, the affinity ties identified by Ho and others (Horstmann 2017; Watanabe 2019; Ong and Steinmüller 2020; McCarthy 2020; Carruth 2021; Olliff 2022) often concern ethnicity and religion. For everyday humanitarianism in Cambodia, the most prominent ones were affinities of shared nationality and history; an ethnic-based notion of pan-Asianness; and individual shared biographies and life experiences. This temporal perspective, in terms of collective and individual histories, recognises the diversity of resource distribution motivations and patterns, in Cambodia and other parts of the world. It also disrupts established accounts of the centrality of the 'white saviour' in everyday humanitarianism, and brings into view a more nuanced account of who is supporting whom.

The dividend resulting from a focus on affinities is an awareness of those constituencies who often remain excluded from humanitarian narratives, many of which are analytically fixated on a North–South axis of intervention. In bringing into view a wide range of practitioners, this chapter delivers a broader account of who engages in everyday humanitarianism in Cambodia. It demonstrates that this does not necessarily revolve around a North–South axis carried by forms of 'white saviourism'. On the contrary, a multi-polar humanitarian landscape emerges, where nationals of other Asian countries, neighbouring and those further afield, become visible (Watanabe 2019; Ong and Steinmüller 2020). This chapter addresses the question of who people single out for support – not necessarily the most needy according to abstract definitions, but those with whose experience they have an affinity.

Such ties become incentives, as well as modalities, that shape everyday humanitarianism.

The affinities and shared biographies discussed here provide a rationale for intervention, as well as being mobilised in interventions that are already underway. They provide a narrative framework in which these choices about what cause, and which people to support – are being rendered meaningful. The semiotic labour of carving out these affinities resembles the 'logic of the one', described in Chapter 3. First, some of these affinities arise from a sense of collective histories, invoked by everyday humanitarians from other Asian countries and their trajectory from impoverished post-war nations to prosperous ones. This framework situates Cambodia on an earlier point of a developmental scale, and their aim to assist Cambodians in achieving progress along that scale, in the way that they have experienced themselves, is sometimes embedded with reference to shared 'Asian values'. Second, affinities arise from shared biographical experiences of migration and poverty, finding resonance in the displacement und deprivation among Cambodians in the aftermath of the genocide and civil war. Finally, many consider such affinities enable better and more effective interventions in the context of their humanitarian projects – a question that remains open to debate.

Considering affinity ties also brings another reality to the fore. This book has not explicitly focused on 'beneficiaries', as they are routinely classified in institutional humanitarianism. In the first instance, the perspectives of recipients are not being foregrounded here as the aim of the book is to understand everyday humanitarianism as a set of imaginations and tools for social change. An important next stage will be an analysis of recipients' experiences of these practices (see also Kinsbergen, Schulpen and Rueben 2017). Second, and perhaps more significantly, this study argues that conventional categories of donor, supporter and beneficiary are not distinct; they obscure the fact that people can move through these categories, and inhabit more than one at a time. This chapter provides detailed examples of how some beneficiaries become project founders. This is not incidental, but highlights a key rationale for intervention: people's biographies, and affinity with others in similar situations, constitutes a driving motivation for supporting them. It has also become clear in the preceding chapters that among those who benefit from everyday humanitarianism are practitioners and supporters themselves.

As I document throughout, people were often keen to point out to me how much they benefited from, and enjoyed supporting others. Rather than framing this as a 'need' to help (Malkki 2015), I suggest that we radically widen our understanding of who benefits from humanitarianism. No longer confined to 'recipient', the notion of 'beneficiary' can be flipped to similarly include donors, brokers and supporters. In this sense, the voice of beneficiaries is present throughout the book; less so in terms of recipients, but through

Cambodians who are beneficiaries-cum-founders, and founders who experience humanitarian practice as enormously beneficial for themselves. This echoes with what Roth (2015) describes as 'alternating activities' through the life courses and careers of professional aid workers. Some of these might have started out as participants or volunteers, and include aid workers from neighbouring countries. Such border-crossing between different forms of humanitarianism underscore fuzzy boundaries between 'beneficiary', volunteer and professional aid worker, while also highlighting that the experienced meaningfulness of their work underwrites its sustainability (de Jong 2011; Taylor and Roth 2019).

Collective affinities

One of the more prominent affinities evident in the literature is an ethnic or racial similarity: a shared Asianness, or pan-Asian sensibility (Watanabe 2019). In Amrith's study of medical workers from the Philippines working in Singapore she finds that this matters to both the migrant workers as well as the people they are caring for. A sense of being fellow Asian can facilitate communication and personal connection, including invoking a set of shared 'Asian values' such as 'hard work, thrift, communitarianism, a strong family orientation' (Amrith 2017:15 and 108; Chua 1999; Milner 2001). However, despite all this, other tensions and resentments surface based on national (and ethnic) differences, such as Indian nurses being 'submissive' to authority or Chinese ones being fast workers, but less caring (Amrith 2017). Such tensions were also visible in Watanabe's study of a Japanese organisation, the Organization for Industrial, Spiritual and Cultural Advancement (OISCA), and their work in Myanmar (Watanabe 2019). They trained young Burmese volunteers in organic agriculture through a strict, military-style communal regime. Watanabe shows this is predicated on a dominance of Japanese-style hierarchies and ultimately, their assumed superiority. Invoking affinities does not on its own engender equality; as Watanabe explains, 'the idea of pan-Asian solidarity promoted by OISCA is firmly rooted in ideological visions of 'Japaneseness' reminiscent of the imperialist aspirations of the past' (Watanabe 2019).

Several everyday humanitarians from other Asian countries as well as Cambodia, mentioned a shared Asian identity facilitating interventions, though not as a sole catalyst for support. As I discuss, some supporters had explored sites in other Asian countries to set up projects, and ended up in Cambodia for a number of reasons. Like the medical workers studied by Amrith, those Cambodians who worked with them, or received support from them, occasionally remarked that there was greater ease interacting with fellow Asians, but this did not erase other tensions or difficulties. It deserves closer scrutiny, rather than assuming a blanket sense of similarity or unity with everyday humanitarians from Asian countries. The most important factor in spurring on interventions were more specific affinities, in particular shared national histories and individual life trajectories. This resonates with Ho's insights, who found that between members of the Kachin and Jingpo people, 'webs of connections [were] forged through shared biographies or spatial sensibilities that produce affinity ties' (Ho 2017:91). Finally, in many accounts (Fountain 2013, 2015; Horstmann 2017; McCarthy 2020), religion emerges as a motivating factor for humanitarian intervention, such as in the Christian 'Free Burma Rangers' (Horstmann 2017). This undoubtedly played a role in some forms of everyday humanitarianism in Cambodia. As discussed in the introduction, I did not include groups that undertook humanitarian aid with an explicitly religious or proselytising mission, such as South Korean Christians which were active in Cambodia.

One evening, I was talking with Harun in the compound where he lived with his Cambodian wife, Nary, and their three children. Having grown up in Malaysia, Harun talked about being 'hot-housed' at school, driven by his Indian-heritage parents' emphasis on education. He subsequently attended university in Singapore, emerging into a high-pressured, but successful career as an IT professional. When he came to Cambodia on holiday as a young person, travelling across the countryside on motorbike, his first impressions were that *'the Cambodians were living like my grandparents in Malaysia ... I remember it so well, having pigs in the backyard.'* Cambodia, for him, was like travelling backwards in time, to a rural-dominated, agrarian society into which IT work and urban high-rises had not yet found entry. Such sentiments surfaced repeatedly among those everyday humanitarians from neighbouring countries, especially Malaysia and Singapore, who had set up aid initiatives. It spoke of an affinity between them and Cambodia in the form of a shared, national trajectory. As Southeast Asian neighbouring countries, they saw themselves as having moved from humble beginnings, non-industrialised and farming-based livelihoods, to a presence in the twenty-first century where their economies and societies had undergone rapid modernisation and industrialisation, furnished with transport and technology infrastructures, and able to compete with 'developed', or high-income Northern or Western countries. In contrast, the travel in time that Harun experienced when arriving in Cambodia, corresponded to something more rudimentary than their level of industrialisation and technology (see also Watanabe 2019 on Japanese development aid to Myanmar).

Placing Cambodia on an earlier point on a linear, temporal trajectory, on which their own country or society had moved further along, provided an incentive for setting up projects in Cambodia. This would, they hoped, provide Cambodians with opportunities for personal and national development that they themselves had been able to take advantage of. The connection or affinity here coalesced around an imaginary shared past, combined with an imperative to propel Cambodia into a modern, developed present. This chapter considers how constructions of similarity and difference unfold along a temporal axis, in contrast to a spatial one, as explored in Chapter 4. This is perhaps not technically a shared inhabited past, as Cambodians are living in that as their 'present', in Harun's view. Rather, it is a case of a perceived shared teleological trajectory, and Harun and Cambodians being in different places – in a combination of sharedness and difference – that motivates the intervention here. It resonates with Johannes Fabian's argument that one way of constructing an Other is through placing them in a different, past time frame, and denying them 'coevalness' (Fabian 1983): a shared present. Temporal distance is also a scale that is being made and deployed in the context of everyday humanitarian efforts.

This became visible in the work of Carol and Daniel, a couple from Singapore in their early sixties. Carol was a trained textile designer, who had, among other jobs, worked for a large NGO in Singapore, whereas Daniel had worked in corporate banking for many years. Although he was now formally retired, he managed some of his business interests without having to be based in Singapore, so he often travelled with Carol to Cambodia. I met them in what they called a 'slum community', where they ran a small enterprise project with a group of local women. Carol was sitting on the tiled floor of a small room, examining the latest products that some of the women had made. She looked with a critical eye through the bracelets, bags and jewellery that had been fashioned from recycled materials such as ringpulls from drink cans, string and beads. A group of four women sat around her, each busy finishing pieces such as an elephant soft toy, a shoulder bag, and small brooches in the form of insects made from wire and beads. Carol and Daniel were both practising Christians, and part of the set-up which they established with these women was that during the hours that they produced these handicrafts, which Carol helped to market, and for which they received sales income, their children were attending the nearby Christian school, run by Singaporean-based missionaries.

When I asked Carol and Daniel about their activities in Cambodia, Carol explained that she had been involved in projects with recovering drug addicts in Singapore. The mood was somewhat sombre at the time, as the death of the founding father and long-time ruler of modern Singapore, Lee Kuan Yew had just been announced. Following from this news, Daniel explained that part of their motivation to get involved in Cambodia, is that *'we have benefited from development ourselves – we were a poor country, in Singapore,* but through better government, and better leadership, things can improve a lot'. As one consequence of what he considers to be Singapore's model journey from a poor country to a first-world, high-income one, Daniel suggested that *'our leaders have encouraged us to go beyond our shores'*. This meant trying to spread 'modernity', for example, in surrounding countries in Southeast Asia that were less advanced on what he saw as a desirable political and social trajectory. Consequently, he and Carol started their charitable work in Singapore, where Carol used to work for a large NGO, as well as setting up her own project, focusing on recovering drug addicts. *'For us, it's a way of giving back'*, says Daniel – an attitude which had been further cemented by a life-changing illness that Carol had gone through, which encouraged her turn towards Christianity.

This chimes with observations of how becoming a donor can be key for a nation's sense of where they are in the world. Becoming a donor means, for example, that 'informed by the memory of the Polish experience as an aid recipient [...] Poles can now share their experiences with other nations' (Drążkiewicz-Grodzicka 2013:72). Nilima Gulrajani and Liam Swiss argue that for new donors, 'an important driver is the desire to legitimise one's reputation as an advanced and influential state' (2017:4). Meanwhile, Asian donors allocate a substantial share to their neighbours, because 'foreign aid is deployed as a key tool of commercial, diplomatic as well as development goals' (Dole et al. 2021:1).

Carol and Daniel did not consider themselves and this particular project in Cambodia as part of the aid sector, though. As Carol stressed, using their private funds, *'gives us the freedom to do what and how we want it'*. At the same time, more importantly, she emphasised that: *'it demonstrates to people that it can be done. We've done it in Singapore, the social work, helping drug addicts, and now we are doing it here.'* What Carol meant with 'it can be done' was, in their case, teaching people how to lift themselves out of poverty through a training, hard work and Christian faith. This training consisted for example in getting the women to check their products carefully, picking up an ear of a hand-sewn elephant that was about to come loose, and being reminded that *'it is worth putting effort in to get it just right – you'll get a better price for it. It's your choice, but doing this properly will be worth it.'* Carol saw them as a beacon from a neighbouring country: *'for Cambodians, it's good you hear so many inspiring stories, that captivates you – and you want to be part of that'*. As she emphatically explained,

> we've seen how it works, in Singapore, and here in this village they can benefit from that. We are not activists, we're not telling the Cambodians what to do. There are Western ideas of democracy ... their approach to engaging is different. They are always telling the others, Cambodians, what to do!

Elaborating on Carol's explanation, Daniel added: *'the Western approach, it's like, straight from here* [marking a point on his far left] *to there* [spread his arms out]. *They try to impose things … but they haven't been through this themselves.'* From their perspective, coming from a country which ascended from a low to a high income status relatively recently gave them legitimacy. They could show the women 'how it is done', in the way that Singapore, as a nation, had achieved this. At the same time, the shared history of coming from a poor country characterised their approach to small-scale development. As Daniel explained, on the one hand, *'we are also Asians … having been exposed to other things, we've got a more conscious, nurturing, positive environment'* – more than, he suggested, those from non-Asian countries who were imposing their ideas in Cambodia in ways that might be inappropriate and not as successful, due to the lack of shared history and understanding that this provides. Daniel conceded that *'whether we do it well, bringing this here, is another matter'*.

One might argue that Daniel's view masked another form of hierarchy and paternalism. As Watanabe (2019) describes in the case of the Japanese in Myanmar, there was a sense of Singaporeans considering themselves superior to Southeast Asian countries in terms of its development. While this does not necessarily replicate a North–South axis of paternalism, its forms of South–South humanitarianism, whether formal or grassroots, are not by their very nature free of hierarchies and power imbalances (Pacitto and Fiddian-Qasmiyeh 2013).

Founders of small projects from other Asian countries hailed from Singapore and Malaysia, Japan and South Korea. Among them was Sawa, a Japanese national, who ran a creative educational project. Although she did not explicitly draw on a shared historical trajectory, Sawa invoked an 'Asian affinity' that mattered for her initiatives in Cambodia. She had trained as a teacher in Japan, and had founded a non-profit school in Siem Reap nearly a decade ago. Whereas her reasons for wanting to start a school outside of Japan were complex, she was clear that her chosen site would have to be in Asia. While scouting different possible locations, she made a first start in Nepal and bought a plot of land. She found that owing to the communist regime at the time, however, it was politically too unstable to be viable. She then considered India, but found the inequalities ingrained by the caste system too difficult to deal with. It was only while talking with a Cambodian friend in Tokyo who worked for the embassy, that she found that *'their story is real for me'*, and *'it's a very similar way of thinking here'*. Sawa attributes these affinities both to a shared Buddhist background, as well as to histories of poverty that both countries have gone through. As she recalled her own background,

Affinities and shared biographies

> *I wanted to work with poor children. I was born in 1948 ... I lived in a poor country, then. When I grow up ... I was in a poor country but I had a happy childhood anyway. I want to support the poor children, to enjoy their childhood through art making.*

Even though Sawa had wanted to start a school in Japan, the reasons for doing so in Cambodia were compelling, including the fact that

> *in this country, there is no art education system. When you go to the village here, it is a very new world for them. Often the parents had to stop learning art because they had to support their family. When the Khmer Rouge occupied this country, Pol Pot killed the artists and teachers in their regime. And Cambodia had no support from other countries.*

She originally wanted to do it in Japan, then looked at other countries in Asia and finally settled on Cambodia. The main reason for not implementing this in Japan were, apart from Cambodian people's needs being evidently much greater, that it proved too expensive: '*I had the same vision to do this with Japanese kids but it was too expensive to set it up in Japan. So I looked to somewhere cheaper, and my friends said, you can do this in Cambodia!*' For Sawa, having a shared history of poverty did not translate into having a shared notion of the creative process. She herself, as she explains, '*learnt art the European way, and the Japanese way, but I threw that away! I threw my way away. I start with nothing*', in the sense that she had to recognise that particular conventions of drawing, for example, were not immediately accessible to Cambodian children. In Sawa's view,

> *the European way is not so good for the children to express their emotion. In the beginning, the kids can't do anything! But they have a thought in their heart ... and they find a way to express themselves. Some said, 'I don't know what to draw'; often they start with two mountains and the sun, that's how they do it here.*

In due course, she found that she was often able to nurture them into finding their own way of expressing themselves. Sawa's conviction that art was central for a child's well-being very much stemmed from her own childhood experience, an issue to which I return.

Histories of loss

The shared experience of a country emerging from poverty, such as post-war Japan and Singapore, shaped the motivations of Carol and Daniel, as well as Sawa, to become involved or set up projects in Cambodia. In contrast to Carol and Daniel's optimistic, forward-looking attitude, however, for others a significant affinity strand also evolved around shared experiences of traumatic recent history. A feature that usually elicited strong reactions from foreigners coming to Cambodia was its history of genocide, civil war and the experience of being a refugee. In the aftermath of the destructive Khmer Rouge regime, and the civil war that followed, many Cambodians fled – either to refugee camps over the border in Thailand, or to overseas destinations (Kiernan 2002; Ong 2003). For those foreigners who had such experiences themselves, or with family histories of forced migration, this sometimes meant that they felt particular affinities with Cambodia. This held for Europeans, North-Americans and Australians in ways that were different from Cambodians who had direct experiences of the Khmer Rouge regime and whose stories I turn to. In some cases, such experienced affinity might be merely a diffuse sense of displacement, stemming from a family history of forced migration.

Boris, whom I mentioned earlier, was a naturalised Australian in his sixties. The origins of his Jewish family were in Ukraine, from where, via Austria, his parents had fled from the Nazi regime, eventually settling in Australia. A dark, brooding figure with an occasionally explosive temper, Boris had never quite felt at home there, and identified as a European more than anything else. When I spoke with him, he had spent some time living in Austria (a transit location of his parents), but he was now resident in Cambodia, which suited him. He felt that lack of a sense of belonging forged an affinity with CambodiansI whom had experienced displacement during and after the times of the Khmer Rouge. Boris had been instrumental in setting up sports activities for people with disabilities, aiming to improve confidence as well as their livelihoods. While the basis of his perceived affinity – feeling out of place – did not link directly to the kinds of humanitarian causes he engaged in, they mattered as they turned Cambodia into a place where he felt he belonged, even in the form of shared experience of displacement.

Even migration journeys that people had undertaken in a more distant past could engender such affinities. Griet, whom I met during one of her frequent trips to Cambodia with her husband, described herself as a 'lifelong activist', a title which humorously graced her home-made business card. Griet's parents were Jewish, living in the Netherlands, and escaped the Nazi occupation by fleeing to Canada. This trajectory was similar to her husband's family, who originated from Russia. Once established in Canada, she met her husband and they had raised a family. During the 1970s, as a result of both the Vietnam War and the Khmer Rouge regime, refugees had been arriving in Canada from Cambodia and Vietnam. At that time, and together with their neighbours, they had formed 'welcome committees', and had taken responsibility for families that had been allocated to them (Hyndman, Payne and Jimenez 2017).

Griet recounted in detail who they were, what challenges they faced and how they had fared since that time. As they had remained in touch with the children of these first refugee families, she was now travelling to Cambodia and Vietnam in order to catch up with their extended family members who had not fled, and some of their children who had returned to Vietnam in order to set up businesses there. This confluence of migration and mobility, past and present, forced as well as voluntary, speaks of the significance of shared affinities around migration experiences. In the case of Griet and her husband, their own status as refugees from Nazi occupation had spurred them into offering assistance to more recent arrivals in Canada, as well as building close connections with their extended families, with whom she was reconnecting at the time we met.

While their story suggests how important shared refugee histories are in motivation and support, this is neither necessary nor sufficient: many people with refugee histories do not turn to helping others with similar experiences, while many of those who are helping do not share those histories (Yarris et al. 2020). For example, one volunteer at the Life Project was Dunja, whose family had fled the war in Bosnia in the 1990s and had been able to settle in Sweden. Dunja had been travelling in Australia and on her way back stayed in in Cambodia. She especially enjoyed helping out on her friends' after-school care programme. This was much to the dismay and incomprehension of her mother, who was asking, as Dunja recounted, *'why on earth do you want to live in Cambodia? Because we came to Sweden fleeing the conflict in Bosnia – so you could be living in the nicest place on earth, so why choose to go to Cambodia instead?'* Having or making affinity ties, therefore, is neither a necessary nor a sufficient condition for offering humanitarian support in the same vein.

The parallels drawn between events that fundamentally shaped a country's trajectory, and the attendant experiences of living through it, can sometimes be less obvious. While first-hand accounts of the violence that families suffered during the Khmer Rouge regime inevitably leave strong impressions with many visitors, this can resonate with people in different ways. This was the case for Jamie, from the USA, who was travelling around Southeast Asia. She crossed paths with a Cambodian genocide survivor, Kunthea. Jamie, a businesswoman then in her fifties, had met Kunthea while she was working as a tour guide at the temples. When Jamie learnt of Kunthea's private support initiatives for local schools, she joined her on a trip to drop off supplies. As they spent time together, in early 2003, Jamie felt that they *'really connected in a 9/11 world'*, referring to her own experience in the

USA at the time of the terrorist attacks in September 2001, which had left a deep impression on her. As Jamie remembers, *'the Cambodian history spoke to me in the ways the genocide was turned around; how the Cambodians dealt with trauma on their own soil. It was pretty powerful.'* The approach of 'turning the genocide around' also specifically referred to Kunthea's focusing of her educational support on the children of genocide perpetrators, which I turn to in the following section. It is worth noting that Jamie's experience of 9/11 did not lead to her undertake an initiative based in the USA, but it was the 'shared trauma' she identified in Cambodia that prompted her to become involved in everyday humanitarianism there.

Shared biographical experiences

In addition and alongside affinities based on collective or national trajectories, humanitarians from Asian and European countries as well as Cambodians constructed affinities through shared life histories and experiences. These affinities related to a wide range of life events, including childhood trauma, living with a disability or poverty. A traumatic early life experience, for example, lay at the heart of Aiko's commitment to teaching children art. In the first instance, Aiko, having grown up in post-war Japan, felt affinity with children living in impoverished Cambodian communities. One of her art school's key objectives was to enable poor children to enjoy their childhood despite their challenging circumstances. In her words, *'childhood is such a short period in a human's life. I like to see their happy faces.'* She emphasised that *'these should be joyful days for Khmer children; they are drawing: they are enjoying their "own time", they really focus, and they express themselves'*. Furthermore, despite her insistence of having had a happy childhood, it emerged later on that Aiko had lost her own mother at the age of seven. In the aftermath, she took drawing classes which, she said, woke her up from the numbness of pain. In her words, *'I found the power of life through painting – blossoming trees. It helped me through the sadness of my mother's death.'*

Subsequently, her own past made her determined that Cambodian children should receive a similar lessening of their burdens. When I asked her how art makes a difference in Cambodian childrens' lives, she explained that *'when they focus on art, when they are face-to-face with their own artworks, they feel less about their troubles. The children have lots of problems. But doing art is good for their mind'*. When Aiko was 18 years old, she decided that she would open her own school: *'I had all the choices, doctor, engineer … but I said, when I finish work in Japan, I want to go to a poor country and support poor children in Asia.'* Affinities in Aiko's case matter in several ways. The deprivation of her post-war childhood, which links her to the poverty of the Cambodian children that her art activities are aimed at; a traumatic early childhood event, for which art practice provided a remedy; and an affinity with Asia in that as she was keen that any aid initiative she was going to set up would be located in Asia, not anywhere else.

Such affinities could also stem from less overtly traumatic, but nevertheless biographically, significant circumstances. Carol for example, whose project was aimed at the disadvantaged women in the village, explained why the situation of these women mattered to her:

> my mother was a single mother. I know what it is like. I have a different perspective on their situation, because I've been there myself. So trust levels are better. Sokhom, for example [one of the women they are supporting], her husband just left. He promised he would take the kids to school but he didn't. She has to bike them to school every morning. It's very hard for them and she's under a lot of stress. Her son is sick. They are all under a lot of stress, I can relate to that.

The affinities discussed so far were invoked by foreigners from neighbouring Asian nations or further abroad, who felt they had gone through similar experiences in their own countries or personal lives. Such biographical affinities were also central for many Cambodians who founded humanitarian projects. This is not unique to Cambodia or everyday humanitarianism, but a further analytical tool to make visible how, and in what modes, people decide whom to support. Such motivation for helping others like oneself has been documented in other contexts, such as among palliative care patients, students from minority backgrounds or women who have left prison (Gysels, Shipman and Higginson 2008; Rhoads, Buenavista and Maldonado 2004). In the Cambodian case, experiences of poverty, deprivation and lack of access to education loomed large, but also of abandonment, violence and disrupted family relationships. There were many stories of Cambodians who went through such events and subsequently dedicated their work to preventing others from going through similar experiences. Sothy, a Cambodian in his fifties, is one such case where biographical affinities guided humanitarian initiatives.

Sothy worked for a donation-financed school affiliated with the Cambodian state school system. Formally established by a US-based family, it was driven by Sothy's vision of quality education made accessible to disadvantaged communities. When I spoke with Sothy, in his role as deputy director in the school office, I asked him about his trajectory. He told me that,

> it started in 2005. I was working as a tour guide in Angkor Wat. I tell the people stories about Cambodia. I'm from Banthey Manchey province, but we fled Cambodia and into the camps. I actually lived in the border camps near

> Thailand until 1992, for 12 years spent time in a Thai camp. I stayed in an orphanage centre – my mum and siblings are still alive, but I was not sure where they were during that time. I learned to speak Thai and English, and a bit of Japanese. Then the peacekeepers sent me home, to my birth province, but I had nothing to do there ... I forgot how to grow rice.

Subsequently he decided to *'stick to the townspeople'*, and stayed in the capital, Phnom Penh, for ten years. When he was still young, he worked during the day, and went to school at night. He was employed by Khmer families to teach Thai language to their children, which enabled him to put himself through school until, in 1997, after the coup, foreign investors again left the country: *'like in 1975, because they thought bad things would happen'*. After one month, life returned more or less back to normal, so Sothy joined the tourism industry. With a high school certificate, and six months' study to become a tour guide, friends helped him establish himself in Siem Reap. After he had got married and started a family, he met an American businessman, and was employed as a tour guide at their travel company. During one long drive to a temple complex further away, the American visitor spotted a donated water well near the road. As Sothy remembers,

> he saw the sign, and ask, what is the point with it. I explain. It's about helping the Cambodians with what they need. Water, education, healthcare. So back to the hotel, and on the way to the airport, he said, 'Sothy, here is $300, build some wells with it.'

After Sothy had done as suggested, he remembered that

> we drilled the third well in this community, it was bad looking. Full of people who were former Khmer Rouge soldier. So the families, they were born around 1974–76, and 35 years on, still can't write or read. They don't give any value to the children. Just send them to collect the recycling. So I met 60 of them ... and I think, I have that experience. That is the concept, that I have experience of the same situation, just poor. Because I saw the kids and I was the same. The people at the orphanage centre [at the refugee camp], they feed me, they send me to school. So the kids there can do the same. In my mind, I want to develop the country. For the future, I would like to get Cambodian children to be as good as the ASEAN ones.

Sothy's account picks up on the issue of modernisation, chiming with the 'will to improve' (Li 2007), aiming to bring Cambodia in line with other ASEAN countries who were considered success stories. Sothy was drawing parallels between his experience of being a refugee child and, paradoxically, the children of former Khmer Rouge soldiers. He saw them as trapped, for different reasons, by illiteracy and neglect as he once was, and from which he was rescued by the staff at the refugee camp.

The connection between living through the Khmer Rouge regime, and its destruction of the Cambodian education system, was a driver for another survivor-turned-founder, who set up an NGO focused on supporting state primary schools with extra-curricular programmes, including teaching of English and IT. Her life story is recounted on their project website, Ponheary Ly Foundation (PLF 2021), extracts of which I present here. The importance of biographical affinities is foregrounded in this narrative:

> Ponheary grew up in a family where education was important. Her father was a teacher, and she and her siblings knew the value of education. Early in life she took advantage of opportunities to learn and expand her knowledge, but all of that changed when the Khmer Rouge took power. The Khmer Rouge abolished education and killed many ... including Ponheary's father and thirteen of her family members. In the aftermath of the regime, Ponheary and her surviving family members worked to rebuild their lives. Ponheary became a teacher. It is during her teaching years that she began supporting students and extra programmes at the schools where she worked. After working as a teacher, Ponheary then became a tour guide. It was here that she began to secure funding for poor children to attend school. At the Temples of Angkor where she took tourists, Ponheary came into contact with numerous children who spent their days selling trinkets to tourists rather than attending school. Moved by what she saw, Ponheary decided to use her tips to support a better education system for Cambodia's children [...] After living through the brutal rule of the Khmer Rouge, Ponheary [...] is working to move past her own struggles as well as to move her country beyond the traumatizing memories of the past.

In this case, everyday humanitarianism can help survivors work through their own traumatic experiences. In my conversations with her, however, most of the narrative was focused on the shared experiences as a driver for action, and much less as a therapeutic practice. When I asked her about how she set up PLF, she explained,

> in 2001, I start out alone. I had no supplies. Then when I was working as a tour guide, I met Linda. From 2001 to 2005, I got money from my tour guiding. So at the beginning of the school year, I buy uniforms and supplies, but I work alone, just with my family. The poor kids, they are too shy to tell if they need something. So when I pass by Banthey Srey temple, I spy in the school: are the teachers in school, where is the class? What about the kids that are not at school? And the kids at the temple, they make more money than the tour guides. So I thought, if I could get the tourists to get money to support kids' education, that was the idea for PLF [their NGO]. And there is so much to do in this province, it's rich in tourism but a poor province.

Ponheary was 'turning it around' by metaphorically taking revenge on the families of Khmer Rouge perpetrators by engaging their children in education. As she put it, '*the tree is dead, but there is growth on the branch. PLF is* targeting children of perpetrators.' Her project partner quipped, 'that's Ponheary's revenge on the Khmer rouge: to turn their children against them. Don't let them poison the minds of the people.' A key driver for where and why they operated was that Ponheary's family came from an area which had been a Khmer Rouge stronghold, a community of perpetrators. Such 'punishing' worked not through educating their children about the horrors of the regime. Rather, they offered them an educatiIn, aiming to reverse the attitude of many of their parents which, in line with Khmer Rouge ideology, demonised this.

I recounted the story of Visal, who helped set up an after-school club, at the beginning of this chapter. His journey from beneficiary to staff member and project founder resonated with that of others who had become involved in such humanitarian initiatives. At Ponheary's foundation, I met Boupha, a young woman in her early twenties, who worked as a media trainer for the foundation. She was herself a graduate of the extracurricular programme which PLF offered. As she remembered of her childhood in a rural area and the reluctance to send her to school: '*my family was scared about animals ... they thought it was not safe to go to school*'. Boupha only started school at the age of 13, but still often lacked transportation, such as a bike, to get to school in the first place. In 1996, her father became sick, and a few years later left the family. She started living in one of the dormitories that PLF supports and stayed there for eight years until she finished school. During that time, she says, '*I see a lot of people who need help ... and I want to work with NGO as well. Now, my family are proud of me because of that*' since she joined PLF first as a volunteer and media trainer, then as a social worker. From her experience with in the countryside, Boupha was aware that,

> the girls are very shy ... very quiet. My family are farmers. Most of them can't read and write. School is far; their house is in the forest; and like my parents, the family doesn't want to risk sending kids to school. The family want the kids to stop going to school. They don't have enough to eat. So we work with the government, and do extra classes in English, computer, health, and get them breakfast.

Boupha said that what she likes about her current role as a social worker was that '*I'm so happy that I can help someone with a problem ... a person like me*', adding with a bemused giggle, '*I'm a student counsellor for over 2,500 people – that's over 2500 problems!*' As Ponheary later pointed out, Boupha was not alone in moving from being a student on their programme, to becoming a staff member. Indeed, she emphasised that, '*you have to keep your eyes out among the students that you support, which ones you want to keep!*' This practice of internal recruitment is common, especially among small-scale projects with their informal ways of engaging, and a firm commitment to the cause, having gone from beneficiary to staff member.

'It can be done'

Shared experiences were seen by everyday humanitarians as creating better understanding, and more effective interventions. Leo pointed out that their collaboration very much depended on a division of labour. Specifically, being small afforded them possibilities that larger organisations did not have: *'big organisations, they have big money, but they don't have the personal experience to relate to the people in poverty, effectively, to the people they are working with'*. He pointed out that Visal had a wealth of informal experience as a social worker because,

> he lived in the pagoda for five years, and he was always going out into the communities. I don't actually know what it's like to work with them. So when we go out into the villages and to the families, Visal does the talking, I'm there, but in the background.

Leo was taken aback by the lack of entitlement among poor communities: *'it's a totally different mentality, they don't feel they're entitled to anything'*. He remembers how one of their students, Chek, a shy young person, wanted to register for a nursing course at the local university. When they suggested he approach people there to get information, he returned only with a phone number scribbled on a piece of paper, because he had not dared to talk to anyone. Leo and Visal accompanied him on his next visit, and encouraged him to speak for himself, so he eventually got hold of the forms that he was looking for. When Visal asked another of their students to pick up a visitor from an upmarket hotel in town, the student later returned empty-handed and alone. He had missed the visitor, having waited in a side street, because he did not feel confident to approach the hotel's front entrance. This 'mentality', as Leo called it, also surfaced in relation to skin whitening practices. As he recounted,

> the boys have grown up in the village, they are dark! But it's a class thing, it's just so removed from my own experience. Like in Australia, you don't have this constant bleaching of skin, so we are trying to get them past it. But it's not possible to do it from the outside. You have to be able to relate to all this – the lack of entitlement, the embarrassment, and the hang-ups about dark skin.

This remark may speak of Leo's lack of concern with existing race and inequalities in Australia. Visal, however, was considered to be in a much better able position to engage with students on these issues, owing to his intimate awareness of growing up in rural, deprived communities, and stigmatisation based on dark skin colour. It is important to bear in mind, of course, that such similarity is neither necessary nor sufficient for motivating intervention.

Carol and Daniel reckoned that seeing a person achieve, who is 'like you', provided a highly encouraging role model. Carol encouraged the women from the village to sell their handmade crafts at a local artisan market at weekends. The market was situated near a large hotel, and aimed mostly at international tourists. Their limited ability to speak English, and in some cases lack of confidence engaging with foreigners, made it difficult for some women to be effective sellers. When I asked Carol one day how the selling had gone, she noted how the overall project products did much better than the women's own designs, partly because they found it difficult to engage with customers: '*I don't expect them to speak the perfect English … but it is tough for them*'. In those situations, it can make a huge difference if the women observe someone 'like them', who has managed to negotiate these situations successfully. On one occasion a Cambodian woman dropped by the women's stall, and told them her story. At 26 years old, and speaking excellent English, she told them how she had gone to Singapore to work as a domestic worker for a foreign family. They asked her to accompany them to Canada for two years, and while there, sponsored her English classes. After her return to Cambodia, she set up her own business and was doing very well. As Carol thought, '*it was so good to see for the Khmei ladies, Saroeun and the others, that it can be done, that is was a fellow Khmei lady who had done so well and how confident she was*'. Carol realised that the most effective way of teaching the women English was through a Cambodian returnee, who visited Cambodia regularly from their home in the USA. In Carol's words,

> *she does a good job, and they enjoy her. It's so much better with a local teacher; with foreigners it can be intimidating. She's very patient, and she's inspiring, because she's Khmei herself and her English is great, so it shows them it can be done.*

The effect of 'showing that it can be done', based on shared past experience and positionality, holds for many of those described, who have transitioned from survivor to project founder, or from project beneficiary to staff member. The examples are numerous, and include Rin, who was suffering from diabetes. He had completed a peer-to-peer education programme, and worked as the deputy to the project founder, Maxim. Together, they pioneered peer-to-peer diabetes education in rural areas, a public model made possible partly because the educators were recruited from the pool of patients. Similarly, recalling the story of Boupha earlier, the fact that she graduated from the social work programme strengthened her authority and impact now working for this programme herself.

The efficacy of 'showing people how it is done' also resonates with the logic of 'paying it forward'. This was discussed in Chapter 3 as one way in which a focus on an individual could create changes in wider society. This is the idea that those receiving support should respond not by repaying those who provided them with assistance, but instead extend it to those who are in greater need than themselves. Many of the stories recounted involve people who survived genocide, fled their country and experienced poverty. Some of them were given a helping hand, either by staff, such as at a refugee camp, or by their employers, such as Rin, or by foreigners who they crossed paths with. I have explored the practice of 'paying forward' in Chapter 3, on how people envisage change through focusing on individuals.

Finally, one issue needs to be raised to put the above discussion into context. The stories of the people recounted here are not representative, as not everyone who suffers hardship decides later, when they are in a position to do so, to support others. As has become evident throughout this chapter, having shared biographies or affinities ties is neither necessary nor sufficient to engage in everyday humanitarianism. The 'desire to connect' discussed in Chapter 5 means that some people make strangers familiar in the process of helping them, but not necessarily on the basis of substantive shared histories. There is thus a more pervasive tension between difference and similarity running throughout this book. I have encountered those who consider themselves survivors, having been 'saved', and who were still supporting extended family. They were looking after themselves financially, for example though starting a business, but without intending to 'take others with them' beyond their immediate kin.

In one case, Malis, a Cambodian who had suffered discrimination and bullying when she was young, distanced herself from the activities of the disability-focused NGO for whom she had been working. Living with the impact of having suffered polio as a child, Malis had been a 'target group' for a disability NGO, and had worked hard for several years in their office, in their programmes and running their cafe. When I asked her if she had felt supported by them, she rejected this outright and explained that, in her view, she had been exploited over many years. She was therefore not at all inclined to become involved with disability activities supporting others, at least not with this NGO. Rather, she was grateful that she had been given the opportunity to manage a small local guesthouse by the owner, a job which she found more satisfactory, and where she was able to work more independently, than when she was with the disability NGO. Her main aim was to provide for herself, her mother and her younger sister, with the vision of one day setting up her own business. While Malis's rejection of the way the NGO had treated her may seem stark, it is a reminder that not all beneficiaries who turn staff members eventually turn into project founders or donors. Some simply define their responsibilities not to others who are living with a disability, but focus on their own, and their family members' livelihoods.

Conclusion

As Malis's case shows, affinities are neither necessary nor sufficient to engender interventions. Nevertheless, this chapter shows that similarities between people, however conceived, have been unduly neglected as drivers of everyday humanitarian intervention. Chapters 5 and 6 illustrated the relations that underpin everyday humanitarian action. Chapter 5 foregrounded spontaneous personal connections that were sought across national, ethnic and cultural differences, while Chapter 6 highlighted social relations that took the form of humanitarian kin. In these cases, this worked in both directions, as the relations became a conduit for support, as well as resulting from supportive action in the first place. A similar dynamics is evident in this chapter, where people draw on collective and personal shared histories, providing a framework in which their humanitarian interventions are made meaningful. At the same time, affinities are seized on in the context of ongoing support.

The benefit of a relational lens is that it makes visible a wider range of people involved. In much of critical humanitarian and development studies, the assistance nexus from the Global North to the South remains central. This is slowly shifting and being challenged, not least through acknowledging forms of South–South cooperation on the level of state actors. Looking at ground-level practices of development, such as everyday humanitarianism, further reveals a much more diverse and nuanced picture of who is intervening where, how, why and in what contexts. This matters because one might argue that even the critique of the 'white saviour industrial complex' (Cole 2012), reiterates the centrality of white saviours for development. Highlighting the myriad affinities that extend beyond and across, unsettles the North–South axis that has been dominating debates. It generates a multi-polar rather than bi-polar account of where global support and intervention flows. This matters because it disrupts conventional narratives of development, which despite growing evidence, persistently foreground 'white' saviours and Global–North-led initiatives, even in their critiques. Tracing the efficacy of affinity ties, in contrast, allows for a de-centring of how development happens, who is involved and what difference that makes.

While standard narratives foreground distance and difference, embodied in the tropes of the distant stranger, or the white saviour, this chapter shows that similarity and closeness are just as important. Humanitarian efforts may be characterised by constant tension and negotiations between distance and proximity, difference and sameness. It is worth noting that affinities as a basis for humanitarian action may well be imbued with the same kind of 'saviourist' attitude that has been amply criticised in North–South interventions. As examples from among Singaporean or Malaysian nationals show, just because these are fellow Asians, does not imply that their actions avoid the pitfalls and paternalism of 'white' saviourism; they might rather recreate them in other forms. Finally, recognising and acknowledging how affinities matter, has benefits beyond disrupting the prevailing Global North–South assistance nexus, and the centrality of the 'white saviour' narrative. It challenges normative ethics put forward by moral philosophers, as well as standards of institutionalised humanitarian action. These decree that humanitarian support must be extended to others impartially, based on need only. This chapter shows, in contrast, the profoundly partiality underpinning humanitarian efforts. Studying everyday moralities and decision-making reveals that in real life, rather than in normative ethics, people often choose to support those they are partial to, with whom they have a connection, similarity, or affinity. Rather than being an obstacle to implementing development, partiality emerges as a key driver and motivator of humanitarian action. This does not necessarily result in fair or equitable distribution of support across the world. Like remittances, which are given on the basis of kinship ties, these may exacerbate existing inequalities. Without passing judgement, it is useful to recognise what kind of moral decisions people make and on what grounds, to enable more inclusive everyday humanitarian action.

Conclusion

Why does all this matter? Everyday humanitarianism is just one example of people seeking to bring about social change. What drew me to their activities in the first place was a sense of exasperation: what was the point of the multitude of small gestures and seemingly minute interventions? This seemed especially pressing at this particular moment, where global challenges were not just long-entrenched, such as poverty and inequality, but the climate crisis was eminently time-sensitive. While there has long been the imperative to 'think global, act local', the link between the two has remained elusive for many. The insights gained from everyday humanitarianism matter because they relate precisely to the sense of futility that engulf many who are trying to catalyse local action, in their home communities or elsewhere, while being aware of the broader challenges that they are facing.

Scaling social change

The approach of making scales that I have developed here speaks to the potential sense of futility in two ways. In the first instance, it is a reminder that there is nothing small, micro or mere as such: these are scales made and deployed by people as they navigate this terrain, and as they position themselves and their activities. What counts as small, and how that is valued, is a process with a range of outcomes, as illustrated in Chapters 1–3. Insistence on remaining small does not preclude being aware of the broader contexts of one's work. People are mindful of the gains and weary of the losses they anticipate if they 'scaled up'. Second, the scales that they make ultimately fold into each other in myriad ways. The approach of scaling makes visible how people, through their semiotic labour and in their humanitarian actions, link together the 'small' and the 'big'. They think of themselves as part of collective action, a division of labour where they take a chunk out of a shared problem. They also envisage the link through temporal scales, where the logic of 'one at a time' enables a focus on the immediate, the present and the singular, while opening a path to the future and the multiple.

What is the empirical and theoretical significance of this ethnographic material? One might argue that not least because its protagonists, everyday humanitarians, can lend themselves to ridicule and dismissal, the potential for their contribution to theoretical debates becomes more visible. The ethnographic case presented here is an example of creating social change. The fact that it can be understood as a form of development is to some extent incidental; this is not about the merits (or demerits), or the latest forms of development and humanitarianism as such. Instead, it asks how those initiating social change envisage and enact this process, and how they negotiate challenges. This book raises pertinent questions, answering them to some extent and exploring the tensions which remain inherent to many such endeavours. These are how to make and use one's own scales, and upending existing ones in the process. Challenging scales and the values associated with them, has wider applicability in relation to bringing about social change, whether addressing inequality, environmental justice or the climate crisis. As Newell, Daley and Twena (2021) remind us, how to scale behavioural change remains central for addressing the climate crisis. This book has shown that there are many ways in which individual, 'small' acts can be linked – through imaginatively connecting scales, and practical action – to the bigger picture and 'larger' outcomes.

Beyond the upending of scales, this book offers an ethnographic account of moral reasoning and practice. As discussed in the Introduction, debates in moral philosophy had come to an 'impasse' in determining people's responsibilities towards fellow humans. There seemed to be no agreement on what role social or geographical distance should play for an imperative to save others. This book confronts such prescriptive but diverging accounts with empirical insights. It tells us how some people, everyday humanitarians, think about and make decisions about intervening in others' lives. While not making generic claims, it suggests that rather than being neutral, impartial and addressing any form of suffering, people act on the basis of commonalities, shared affinities and histories. The role and nature of social relations emerges as central for how some people construct their responsibility for others. It is not just the fact of their partiality, but also the nature of these connections, that offers a more profound and nuanced understanding of what makes some people support others.

Such inherent partiality of people's interventions speaks to another quandary facing those seeking social change. This is a possible sense of paralysis when faced with where to start. If one can only take one chunk out of the problem, which should one choose? In the context of everyday humanitarianism, such partialities are fundamentally governed by the kinds of social relations that people seek out and value. These may be spontaneous personal connections as in Chapter 5, or humanitarian kin, or shared affinities, as in Chapters 6 and 7. They give direction and meaning to whom to support, and why. The principle of directing one's effort towards a singular issue one cares about, still holds. It mitigates paralysis in the face of options, and a sense of being overwhelmed by the 'bigger picture', further illustrating the link between the 'small' and the 'large'. This book documents some of the dilemmas that inevitably trouble those seeking social change. These are not just choices between addressing the seemingly small and the large, but also between the personal on the one hand, and the structural or collective on the other. How people attempt to resolve these dilemmas is shown in Chapter 2, through linking the part and the whole; and in Chapter 3, on how social change is achieved through individuals, branching out to the collective and the future over time.

A lay approach

Everyday humanitarianism matters in a wider social context. Its insistence on the local, the singular and the particular in the face of substantial challenges, are a driving factor in what could be described as a 'lay approach' to a wide range of issues. It can be understood as part of a movement of individual or citizen-led, do-it-yourself ways of facilitating change. The growing prominence of everyday humanitarians is a bellwether of broader shifts in citizen engagement. There is much evidence of such do-it-yourself campaigns, and a groundswell of actions at local and translocal levels. Not least during and after the COVID-19 pandemic, neighbourhood support, mutual aid and volunteering have been resurgent. The same holds for transnational crowdfunding. Humanitarians in Cambodia reported that they 'never felt alone' or abandoned during pandemic times. Despite, or perhaps because supporters from other countries were facing similar challenges, their engagement in Cambodia has been steady. If anything, an intensification, rather than waning of concern was apparent locally and across borders. Being a 'lay' humanitarian is just one example of activities and initiatives that are built from the bottom up. They include peacebuilding (Autessere 2021); citizen science (Aristeidou et al. 2021) and journalism (Nah and Chung 2019). They extend to data mapping, legal challenges, financing medical treatment for individuals where health systems fall short (Brkovic 2016), or new drug trials (Nutt and Masters 2017). They take the form of guerrilla gardening (Hardman, Larkham and Adams 2018) and community seed banks (Francis 2015). Their more recognised forms include citizens' assemblies (Fournier et al 2011; Gastil and Richards 2013) and, not least, crowdsourced aid (Banerjee 2020) and digital humanitarianism (Meier 2015). Without either endorsing or dismissing them, these indicate sectors of society where lay approaches have taken root, or have existed all along.

A key objection concerns the ability of such movements to bring about 'systemic' rather than small-scale and individual change. They stand accused of merely addressing symptoms, rather than what are considered root causes. This brings us back to the earlier debate regarding the logic of the 'single life' bemoaned by Fassin, and the apolitical nature of the 'mere' which characterises domestic humanitarianism, according to Malkki. Berman, among others, regrets the failure among everyday humanitarians to even consider systemic injustices leading to poverty in countries of the Global South (2017). We can, of course, categorise their activities as development, judging their efficacy and legitimacy, and gauge if they are a viable way to making things better. Or one might eventually come to the conclusion, as Schnable (2021) and others have, that if American citizens really wanted to make a difference to African farmers, their best bet would be to vote wisely in elections, and scrutinise their government's subsidies for American peanut growers.

While such judgement is entirely reasonable, I have tried to show in this book how the two practices – being an astute citizen and voter, and an everyday humanitarian, are not mutually exclusive. The small, the mere, or the amateurish are not disconnected from the professional, the political and the big picture. Everyday humanitarians do not necessarily understand themselves to be 'doing development', at least not conceived of in this term. Ostensibly clear distinctions between amateurs and professionals blur in so far as it is not uncommon for full-time aid agency staff to be aid amateurs in their spare time. Furthermore, the charge of not tackling root causes also applies to overseas state aid. Institutional development has long been accused of 'rendering technical' what are essentially political problems, and ignoring the latter (Escobar and Ferguson 1985). Neither lack of scale, in the sense of quantity or volume, nor failure to address 'root causes' and effect systemic change therefore sets everyday humanitarianism apart, in principle, from its institutional forms.

Everyday humanitarianism in the aid ecosystem

Presenting my research on everyday humanitarianism has often resulted in no more than raised eyebrows among aid practitioners or development experts. Seen as a niche practice, it was considered of no real consequence to the business of the formal aid sector. I suggest that this attitude is misguided, and prevents us from a much more comprehensive understanding of what constitutes aid. It is more appropriate to conceive of aid not as a sector, but an ecosystem which is populated by different groups of people, institutions and organisations. What is the role of everyday humanitarianism in this ecosystem? What difference does its existence make for the broader understanding and practice of aid? What can be done with this knowledge, and how can it be made productive? What are the implications for policymakers and aid professionals? At this stage, answers to these questions are provisional rather than authoritative. They feed into an ongoing debate about the existing humanitarian system which, a recent reports claims, is 'on the brink' (Parker 2022). Widening the scope to recognise aid and humanitarianism's diversity is therefore a much-needed step forward, and potentially out of the current impasse. Several issues come to the fore here. In the first instance, there is need for better data on the volume and impact of everyday humanitarianism. It is also imperative to challenge prevailing attitudes towards 'aid amateurs' within the sector; to better understand the interface between formal and informal aid; and to appreciate how everyday humanitarianism points the way to localising aid more broadly.

Volume and impact

While everyday humanitarian activities seem to be a 'drop in the ocean' of need, the private aid which they facilitate has yet to be systematically quantified. The sense that they are not alone in their endeavours, and are indeed taking a 'chunk' out of a problem alongside others, is not fanciful, and has some grounding in the available data. In the USA, a detailed register exists in the form of the inland revenue system, as in the UK. These account for the numbers and size of the grassroots NGOs, but such information is less readily available in other countries, where it continues to rely on estimates. The sheer number of such 'grassroots international NGOs' has increased tenfold since about 2010 in the USA, the UK and Europe (Kinsbergen and Schulpen 2010; Clifford 2016; Schnable 2021), as stated at the outset. They offer sufficiently robust evidence that such small organisations are indeed a growing force in the third sector. This holds even though they may appear marginal to it, by virtue of their informal ways of operating. Moreover, charity registers do not account for those projects which are not formally registered as non-profit organisations. Until there is a clearer picture of how much financial and other resources flow through these informal channels, their precise impact is harder to capture (Hénon 2014).

As we consider measurements of scale in relation to state-funded overseas development aid, we are reminded of where this is positioned in the grander scheme of things. The volume of overseas state aid is minimal compared to the next largest resource flows into countries of the Global South, namely remittances by migrants. These, in turn, are dwarfed by foreign direct investment into these countries. As Berman points out, 'remittances, private philanthropy, and private investment are more consequential to the economies of poor countries than the aid extended by the governments of rich countries' (Berman 2017:145). Indeed, a recent estimate by the World Bank puts the volume of remittances to low- and middle-income countries as triple that of overseas development assistance, as well as surpassing foreign direct investment by a third (World Bank 2019). Such support, transferred across borders by individuals to families, like in everyday humanitarianism, cannot therefore be discounted on the basis of being 'small scale'. Considering remittances, small streams do indeed make big rivers. To what extent this also holds for private aid flows, and if they might even be larger in scope than formal humanitarianism needs to be determined. It is urgent to start accounting for these flows, by including quantitative measurement of private aid flows into research designs. While we can trace the volume and impact of prominent, large-scale philanthropy much better, this is not the case for these dispersed, and harder-to-track resource flows.

While the quantitative volume of resources channelled through everyday humanitarianism has yet to be detailed, this also raises the question of their impact on the ground. What are such initiatives contributing; how do they matter, and for whom? Few studies assess the impact of grassroots aid systematically (e.g. Kinsbergen, Schulpen and Ruben 2017). Swidler and Watkins, in their study of HIV/Aids projects in Malawi, find that in concrete terms, 'amateur altruists make more of a difference than do the professionals, both symbolically and practically' (2017:36). The reason for their positive estimate is that unlike most projects funded by large donors, they find that 'the amateurs usually provide material help' (2017:36). Given the ethnographic material discussed in this book, their claim of aid amateurs providing material support, presumably instead of policy advice, training or government collaboration that the larger NGOs undertake, needs to be critically considered.

Conversely, in their critical account of the role of large NGOs, Swidler and Watkins argue that their main impact, deviating from their stated intentions, is having created a labour market in Malawi, where formal employment opportunities are otherwise very limited. This chimes with the views of some international aid workers I spoke with. One of them concluded, after many years' work with a multilateral agency in Cambodia, about his impact: *'the only thing we have done here is to train up people'*. The same could be said of grassroots initiatives, given that many of their activities consist of investing in people, as discussed in Chapter 2. From the examples I have presented throughout the book, it is clear that the impact of everyday humanitarianism is achieved through interventions that are more varied than simply offering material assistance. In order to supersede conjecture and anecdotal evidence, however, there is a clear need to provide a more detailed and evidence-based analysis on the volume, and differences that everyday humanitarianism is making on the ground.

Challenging attitudes

In spite of favourable impressions suggesting that 'amateurs make more of an impact than the professionals' (Swidler and Watkins 2017), the attitudes towards these amateurs are often steeped in distrust or ridicule. They are branded as 'contraband humanitarians' (Berman 2017) or 'freelance altruists' (Swidler and Watkins 2017). They are considered not legitimate in the sense of not having formal development-related qualifications. They can be seen as self-serving saviour figures, not versed in policy or practice of what constitutes 'good aid' in the rulebook of international organisations. There is undoubtedly potential for abuse and real harm that can be done by those 'amateurs'. Nevertheless, one outcome from the study of everyday humanitarianism could be a dose of humility, rather than superiority by professional aid workers and organisations. This is because charges usually levelled at 'freelance altruists' often similarly apply to established organisations. The following issues offer some examples.

One concern raised repeatedly is the tenuous and limited time commitment of freelance altruists. Swidler and Watkins describe them as 'butterflies' who parachute in, dwell for a moment on a project, and depart (2017). Extrapolating from my research, there is some truth in the relative fragility of their commitments. As I have discussed, some everyday humanitarians' projects are only 'one relationship break-up away from being abandoned', as one participant described it. This can be the case when a marriage ends, or grandchildren arrive and take precedence. There is also counterevidence, however. Based on my long-term observations over a decade of visits to Cambodia, I found, sometimes to my surprise, just how many of the aid projects I knew of were still running two, five or more years later. Many of the supportive overseas participants that I talked with returned annually, sometimes twice a year, to engage with projects. Quite a few decided to relocate to Cambodia after years of travelling back and forth, for example after taking early retirement from jobs in their country of origin. Other foreigners made Cambodia their home early on, and continued to raise their families there. Those everyday humanitarians who are Cambodian tend to not just disappear. Although it does of course occur, obligations have been created particularly when they are involved with local communities or individuals that are not easily abandoned.

At the same time, institutional and formal aid does not necessarily constitute a stable presence. The office of the UK's (now defunct) Department of International Development in Cambodia, for example, was closed down at an early stage in my research, as their priorities shifted towards other countries. Many aid agencies which had been active in Cambodia in the 2000s, started to move their staff and operations to Myanmar from 2012 onwards, as the political situation there changed, and international aid agencies were able to operate there. When discussing their work professional aid workers, not infrequently, complained about how one of their cherished projects or programmes, in which they had invested time and effort, had prematurely been terminated, despite, they said, their favourable track record. It is well documented that aid policy undergoes continuous shifts and changes. While they are not directly comparable, it is unreasonable to state that only freelance altruists flit around like unaccountable 'butterflies'. Institutionalised altruism is similarly characterised by constant policy changes, programme terminations, staff turnover and office closures. Some of the most enduring aid relationships may indeed be between those everyday humanitarians, Cambodians and foreigners, who have made a commitment to local residents or communities.

A further concern is the risk of abuse and a lack of accountability and relevant qualifications among the 'freelance amateurs'. There is undeniably the potential for abuse and damage caused by not being 'professional', and without institutional mechanisms to control this. A case in point was the US missionary Renee Bach, posing as a medical doctor, who harmed young children and their mothers in Uganda who came to her 'clinic' to seek care. Unfortunately, the existence of safeguarding protocols, even rudimentary ones, is not always sufficient to prevent sexual abuse and harassment by 'professional' aid staff. Another case in point is the exploitation of Haitian earthquake survivors by senior international aid workers (Charity Commission 2019). A recent report found that despite organisational commitments to change, not enough had been achieved to reduce these risks, or to hold those responsible accountable. All of these issues, including tenuous commitments and risk of abuse, are undeniably real concerns when it comes to the role of everyday humanitarianism and I suggest that they deserve greater scrutiny and vigilance. The formal sector also needs to engage with informal actors to develop shared protocols with regard to safeguarding and good practice. This has happened in Cambodia, for example, in the form of the 'Childsafe' campaign. There, a coalition of groups, supported by UNICEF, devised a programme to raise awareness and establish safeguarding protocols to reduce orphanage tourism, and support formal and informal aid projects in upholding child welfare in their work. Rather than reserving suspicion for 'aid amateurs', good practice needs to extend across all those active in this area.

It is helpful here to consider the critical debates around the 'professionalisation' of humanitarian work. Arguably, the increasing presence of 'amateur' humanitarians in disaster situations was a driver for employing more accredited and formally qualified staff. While this has been changing employment in the formal sector, it has also acted as a barrier to entry for practitioners from countries of the Global South. In further research, it would therefore be important to draw on the professionalisation debate to critically evaluate the strength and weaknesses of such everyday humanitarian practice in relation to institutional, formalised ones – bearing in mind that some everyday humanitarians may act in their capacity as professionals (if unpaid), and that professional staff may moonlight as 'everyday humanitarians' in their spare time. In relation to this, questions of effectiveness, accountability and, not least, legitimacy of everyday humanitarians will have to be addressed.

Barriers to collaboration

The Childsafe campaign is a good example of how collaboration between formal aid organisations and informal aid initiatives can produce successful outcomes. Generally, collaboration between them can be more complicated, and can be seen as lacking. Members of the public as much as 'professional' aid workers often query why there is not more interaction between formal and informal aid projects, given that they should have broadly similar objectives. Notably, the lack of collaboration is often highlighted even between organisations which are all part of the same formal sector, instead competing for resources through 'competitive humanitarianism' (Stirrat 2006). While there is mutual support between grassroots founders who are, in the words of one informant, 'trying to do the same thing', there is less interaction between informal and formal aid than there could be. The reasons for this are multiple. Simply bemoaning a lack of cooperation betrays a misrecognition of their respective intentions, of what they want to achieve and how they want to go about it.

In the first place, there is a misconception that everyday humanitarians would want to formalise their activities, take them 'upstream' and maximise their reach and impact. As I have detailed in Chapter 2, this is not necessarily, or not at all, the case. Many are keen to keep their activities in a steady state, wary of the consequences of 'scaling up'. These may include relinquishing control over their projects, having to change their ways of operating or losing touch with those who they want to support. Others, such as Schnable (2021) have argued that a key motivations for many aid amateurs is to be able to 'invent their own wheel'. This is a shorthand for a process of learning and problem-solving which is not based on formal qualifications and training, but relies on their own ingenuity and creativity. Many enjoy a process of trial and error in devising solutions for an aid or development challenge. They relish the challenge and reward of 'owning' the process, rather than resorting to existing solutions or responses by others. Becoming part of a formal sector might inhibit such possibilities, and so can present a major obstacle to closer interaction or collaboration.

While such attitude might appear self-serving and not in the best interests of those receiving support, there are other reasons why everyday humanitarians might be hesitant. As discussed in Chapter 1, there are concerns that institutionalised humanitarianism can be used as a form of control, for example through the management of displaced people. Informal humanitarian initiatives, like those providing support in makeshift refugee camps, are keen to avoid becoming involved in such forms of governmentality, preferring pro-migrant activism instead. There are further barriers, such as the fear or being co-opted by larger operators; losing control over one's project; or not being able to innovate. Others prefer staying under the radar to enable them to continue their work without political interference, keeping local or national authorities at a careful distance. Addressing these concerns and avoiding the pitfalls of NGO-isation, or incorporation into larger organisations, will be key to making collaboration more likely and productive. Understanding everyday humanitarians' intentions draws attention to the limits of these possibilities.

The barriers to greater collaboration listed here relate to the reluctance of everyday humanitarians, and have been further explored in relation to 'alternative humanitarianism' in Greece (Iskhanian and Shutes 2022). This is despite formal aid organisations positing other obstacles to collaboration. These are certain modes of operating, with regard to funding applications, report writing or governance structures, which informal aid initiatives may be unable or unwilling to engage in. Formal and informal aid projects may share some of the same objectives; in practice, however, they fall into a complementary, organic division of labour. This means accepting limits to cooperation owing to their different intentions, interventions and anticipated rewards. It also means that they may continue to inhabit different niches of an aid ecosystem across the Global North and South.

Localising aid?

Like voluntourism, everyday humanitarianism is often regarded as yet another manifestation of white saviourism, or the 'white saviour industrial complex'. Such critiques often reinscribe the centrality of a 'white' saviour, neglecting that unequal relationships and interactions can pervade all kinds of humanitarian interventions, including those initiated by those other than from the Global North. The evidence and arguments put forward in this book point towards a much wider range of humanitarian interactions than such critiques are usually trained on. This means recognising that everyday humanitarians are not by definition white, nor from the Global North, but comprise a wide range of local and regional actors which are often overlooked in accounts of humanitarianism. The contribution here is the recognition that everyday humanitarianism takes place in the Global North and South, and is being initiated by actors spanning local, regional and transnational contexts. The study of everyday humanitarians shifts perspectives on who is helping whom, under what circumstances and with what outcomes. Paying attention to everyday humanitarians makes visible much more diverse sets of people involved. Intervening in others' lives is not a prerogative of those from the Global North.

Widening our understanding of who is supporting whom should lead to an acknowledgement of how aid, and by extension social change, is driven by other than the usual, often institutional, suspects. Calls for 'localising aid' often mean transferring resources top–down from international, institutional actors to local or national ones. Such calls are problematic, since taking everyday humanitarianism seriously means acknowledging that much aid and development is local already. Even so, in many accounts, national and local humanitarians appear as mere brokers, gatekeepers and administrators. Regional and fellow ethnic actors often remain unacknowledged. It is time to recognise that nationals often drive projects, enlist foreigners to help, and collaborate. Examining everyday humanitarianism helps unsettle tropes such as the 'white saviour' or 'distant stranger', which have kept such actors less visible. Existing accounts reinscribe white dominance even through its critique. Unsettling these is not sufficient in itself for making humanitarian practices less 'saviourist', paternalistic or ridden by inequalities. At the very least, we can ask how power works in aid relationships from a vantage point that takes all those supporting others into view.

As such, everyday humanitarianism stages an important intervention in the debate about 'localising aid'. The wider context is a recognition that the current state of the humanitarian system, as mentioned, is considered untenable. Its state of crisis is partly attributed to a 'fractured, conflict-ridden international community' (Parker 2022), and an increasing number and duration of protracted crises worldwide. The formal humanitarian system is not best placed to improve its delivery of assistance, not least because despite formal pledges, it has not increased the amount of funding devolved to national and local actors. The commitment to a 'localisation agenda' made at the World Humanitarian Summit in 2016 stipulated that donors allocate a much greater share of their budgets to local actors such as civil society organisations. Contrary to their pledges, the relevant percentage in fact sank from 3.3 per cent in 2018 to 1.2 per cent in 2021. This is in spite of the ostensible recognition of 'the power of social and community responses and other organisations outside the formal system' (Parker 2022).

This book, invoking international development, claims the place of everyday humanitarians in this ecosystem, among a multitude of others. If members of the formal humanitarian system were genuinely interested in pulling back 'from the brink', a crucial first step would be to acknowledge what aid is being delivered from 'outside the formal system' – including by diaspora members, through remittances, regional neighbours, everyday humanitarians and the uncharted private aid flows they facilitate. The everyday humanitarianism described in this book points to the multitude of people, projects and initiatives which are operating at a grassroots level. The narrative that international aid needs to be 'localised', is based on a narrow and exclusive definition of 'humanitarianism' and clearly has had negligible impact so far. Instead, the study of everyday humanitarianism demonstrates just how much aid is local already, and what it can achieve.

References

Altman, Tess. 2020. 'Making the State Blush: Humanizing Relations in an Australian NGO Campaign for People Seeking Asylum'. *Social Analysis*. DOI: https://doi.org/10.3167/sa.2020.640101/

Altman, Tess. 2022. 'From Stranger to Neighbor: Gendered Voluntarism as Feminist Caring Politics against Australia's Hostile Borders', in Andria D. Timmer and Elizabeth Wirtz (eds), *Gender, Power, and Non-Governance: Is Female to Male as NGO Is to State?* Oxford: Berghahn Books, pp. 93–123.

Amrith, Megha. 2017. *Caring for Strangers: Filipino Medical Workers in Asia*. Copenhagen: Nias Press.

Anderson, Lee, Kerryan Griffin and Shawna Hartley. 2013. *Unsung Heroes Cambodia: People and Projects Making a Difference*. Potts Point, Australia: Unsung Heroes.

Andersson, Ruben. 2014. *Illegality, Inc.: Clandestine Migration and the Business of Bordering Europe*. Oakland: University of California Press.

Appe, Susan, and Allison Schnable. 2019. 'Don't Reinvent the Wheel: Possibilities for and Limits to Building Capacity of Grassroots International NGOs'. *Third World Quarterly* 40 (10): 1832–49.

Apthorpe, Raymond. 2011. 'Coda: With Alice in Aidland: A Seriously Satirical Allegory', in D. Mosse (ed.), *Adventures in Aidland: Anthropology of Professionals in International Development*. Oxford: Berghahn, pp. 199–219.

Aristeidou, Maria, Christothea Herodotou, Heidi L. Ballard, Alison N. Young, Annie E. Miller, Lila Higgins and Rebecca F. Johnson. 2021. 'Exploring the Participation of Young Citizen Scientists in Scientific Research: The Case of iNaturalist'. Edited by Christopher A. Lepczyk. *PLoS ONE* 16 (1): e0245682. https://doi.org/10.1371/journal.pone.0245682.

Autessere, Severine. 2021. *The Frontlines of Peace: An Insider's Guide to Changing the World*. Oxford University Press.

Banerjee, Shonali (2020) 'Intimate Technologies for Development: Micro-philanthropy, Crowdfunding Platforms, and NGO Fundraising in India'. Unpublished doctoral thesis, University of Sussex.

Barnett, Michael N. 2011. *Empire of Humanity: A History of Humanitarianism*. Ithaca, NY: Cornell University Press.

Barnett, Michael N., and Thomas G. Weiss. 2008. *Humanitarianism in Question: Politics, Power, Ethics*. Ithaca: Cornell University Press.

Barnett, Michael N., and Janice Gross Stein. 2012. *Sacred Aid: Faith and Humanitarianism*. New York: Oxford University Press.
Benthall, Jonathan. 2007. 'Islamic Charities, Faith-based Organizations and the International Aid System', in J. Alterman and K. van Hippel (eds), *Islamic Charities*, Washington, DC: Center for Strategic and International Studies.
Berman, Nina. 2017. *Germans on the Kenyan Coast: Land, Charity, and Romance*. Bloomington, IN: Indiana University Press.
Biehl, João Guilherme, and Torben Eskerod. 2013. *Vita: Life in a Zone of Social Abandonment*. Berkeley, CA; London: University of California Press.
Boltanski, Luc. 1999. *Suffering and Distance*. Cambridge: Cambridge University Press.
The Borgen Project. 2013. 'History of the Peace Corps'. https://borgenproject.org/history-of-the-peace-corps/The Borgen project.
Bornstein, Erica. 2001. 'Child Sponsorship, Evangelism, and Belonging in the Work of World Vision Zimbabwe'. *American Ethnologist* 28 (3): 595–622.
Bornstein, Erica. 2009. 'The Impulse of Philanthrophy'. *Cultural Anthropology* 24 (4): 622–51.
Bornstein, Erica, and Peter Redfield. 2011. *Forces of Compassion: Humanitarianism between Ethics and Politics*. Santa Fe, N.M.: SAR Press.
Bornstein, Erica. 2012. *Disquieting Gifts: Humanitarianism in New Delhi*. New Delhi: Foundation Books.
Bristley, Joseph. 2020 'Scale and Number: Framing an Ideology of Pastoral Plenty in Rural Mongolia'. *Social Analysis* 64 (1): 63–79.
Brkovic, Carna. 2016a. 'Depoliticization "From Below": Everyday Humanitarianism in Bosnia and Herzegovina'. *Narodna umjetnost* 53 (1): 97–115.
Brkovic, Carna. 2016b. 'Scaling Humanitarianism: Humanitarian Actions in a Bosnian Town,. *Ethnos: Journal of Anthropology* 81 (1): 99–124.
Brkovic, Carna. 2019. 'Vernacular Humanitarianism', in Antonio di Lauri (ed.), *Humanitarian Keywords*. Leiden: Brill.
Cabot, Heath. 2016. '"Contagious" Solidarity: Reconfiguring Care and Citizenship in Greece's Social Clinics'. *Social Anthropology* 24 (2): 152–66.
Calhoun, Craig. 2012. 'The Imperative to Reduce Suffering: Charity, Progress, and Emergencies in the Field of Humanitarian Action', in M. Barnett, *Humanitarianism in Question*. Ithaca: Cornell University Press.
Carr, E. Summerson, and Michael Lempert. 2016. *Scale: Discourse and Dimensions of Social Life*. Oakland, CA: University of California Press.
Carruth, L. 2018. 'Kinship, Nomadism, and Humanitarian Aid among Somalis in Ethiopia'. *Disasters* 42 (1): 149–68.
Carruth, L. 2021. *Love and Liberation*. Ithaca: Cornell University Press.
Carsten, Janet. 2000. *Cultures of Relatedness: New Approaches to the Study of Kinship*. Cambridge: Cambridge University Press.
Chambers, R. 2007. *Who Counts? The Quiet Revolution of Participation and Numbers*. IDS Working Paper 296. Brighton: IDS.
Chandler, David. 2008. *A History of Cambodia*, 4th edn. Boulder, CO: Westview Press.
Charity Commission. 2019. *Charity Inquiry: Oxfam GB*, www.gov.uk/government/publications/charity-inquiry-oxfam-gb.

ChildSafe Movement. n.d. 'Children are not Tourist Attractions', https://thinkchildsafe.org/children-are-not-tourist-attractions/.

Chouliaraki, Lilie. 2010. 'Post-humanitarianism: humanitarian communication beyond a politics of pity', *International Journal of Cultural Studies* 13 (2): 107–126.

Chouliaraki, Lilie. 2012. *The Ironic Spectator: Solidarity in the Age of Post-Humanitarianism.* Cambridge, UK: Polity Press.

Chouliaraki, Lilie and Shani Orgad. 2011. 'Proper Distance: Mediation, Ethics, Otherness'. *International Journal of Cultural Studies* 14 (4): 341–45.

Chua, Beng Huat. 1999. '"Asian-Values": Discourse and the Resurrection of the Social Positions'. *East Asia Cultures Critique* 7 (2): 573–92.

Chua, Liana. 2018. 'Small Acts and Personal Politics: On Helping to Save the Orangutan via Social Media'. *Anthropology Today* 34 (3): 7–11.

Clifford, David. 2016. 'International Charitable Connections: The Growth in Number, and the Countries of Operation, of English and Welsh Charities Working Overseas'. *Journal of Social Policy* 45 (3): 453–86.

Collinson Sarah, and Samir Elhawary. 2012. *Humanitarian Space: A Review of Trends and Issues.* HPG Report 32. London: Humanitarian Policy Group.

Cole, Teju. 2012. *The White Saviour Industrial Complex*, www.theatlantic.com/international/archive/2012/03/the-white-savior-industrial-complex/254843/.

Cole, Tomas. 2019. '"Power-Hurt": The Pains of Kindness among Disabled Karen Refugees in Thailand'. *Ethnos* 85 (2): 224–40.

Comaroff, Jean, and John Comaroff. 2003. 'Ethnography on an Awkward Scale'. *Ethnography* 4 (2): 147–79.

Cooper, Frederick, and Ann Laura Stoler. 1997. *Tensions of Empire Colonial Cultures in a Bourgeois World.* Berkeley, CA; London: University of California Press.

Curley, Melissa. 2018. 'Governing Civil Society in Cambodia: Implications of the NGO Law for the "Rule of Law"'. *Asian Studies Review* 42 (2): 247–67.

Davis, John-Michael. 2020. 'Canada's GINGOs: Who Are They, What Are They Doing, and What Role for the Future?' *Development in Practice* 30 (6): 738–50.

Dean, Hartley. 1999. *Begging Questions: Street-Level Economic Activity and Social Policy Failure.* Bristol, UK: Policy Press.

De Jong, Sara. 2011. 'False Binaries: Altruism and Selfishness in NGO Work', in Anne-Meike Fechter (ed.), *The Personal and the Professional in Aid Work.* Boulder, CO: Kumarian Press.

De Jong, Sara. 2014. *Complicit Sisters: Gender and Women's Issues Across North-South Divides.* Oxford: Oxford University Press.

Dessewffy, Tibor, and Zsofia Nagy. 2016. 'Born in Facebook: The Refugee Crisis and Grassroots Connective Action in Hungary'. *International Journal of Communication* (10): 2872–94.

Dickens, Charles. 1996. *Bleak House*, ed. Nicola Bradbury, Harmondsworth: Penguin.

Doidge, Mark, and Elisa Sandri. 2018. '"Friends That Last a Lifetime": The Importance of Emotions amongst Volunteers Working with Refugees in Calais'. *The British Journal of Sociology* 70 (2): 463–80.

Dole, David, Steven Lewis-Workman, Dennis D. Trinidad and Xianbin Yao. 2021. 'The Rise of Asian Aid Donors: Recipient-To-Donor Transition and Implications for International Aid Regime'. *Global Journal of Emerging Market Economies* 13 (1): 58–80.

Drążkiewicz-Grodzicka, Elżbieta. 2013. 'From Recipient to Donor: The Case of Polish Developmental Cooperation'. *Human Organization* 72 (1): 65–75.

Duchâteau-Arminjon, Benoit. 2013. *Healing Cambodia: One Child at a Time: The Story of Krousar Thmey, a New Family.* Singapore: Editions Didier Millet.

Ear, Sophal. 2013. *Aid Dependence in Cambodia: How Foreign Assistance Undermines Democracy.* New York: Columbia University Press.

Eiseley, Loren C. 1969. *The Unexpected Universe.* Boston: Harvest Books.

Eltringham, Nigel. 2019. *Genocide Never Sleeps: Living Law at the International Criminal Tribunal for Rwanda.* Cambridge: Cambridge University Press.

Escobar, Arturo, and Dianne Rocheleau. 2008. *Territories of Difference: Place, Movements, Life, Redes.* Durham, NC: Duke University Press.

Eyben, Rosalind. 2006. *Relationships for Aid.* London: Earthscan.

Eyben, Rosalind. 2011a. 'Fellow Travellers in Development", *Third World Quarterly* 33 (8): 1405–21.

Eyben, Rosalind. 2011b. 'The Sociality of International Aid and Policy Convergence', in David Mosse (ed.), *Adventures in Aidland: The Anthropology of Professionals in International Development.* Oxford: Berghahn.

Fabian, Johannes. 2014 [1983] *Time and the Other: How Anthropology Makes its Object.* New York, NY: Columbia University Press.

Fassin, Didier. 2012. *Humanitarian Reason: A Moral History of the Present Times.* Berkeley: University of California Press.

Fassin, Didier. 2018. *Life: A Critical User's Manual.* London: Polity.

Fechter, Anne-Meike. 2007. *Transnational Lives: Expatriates in Indonesia.* Aldershot: Ashgate.

Fechter, Anne-Meike. 2009. 'Living in the Gap: Foreigners in Yogyakarta, Java'. *iNtergraph: Journal for Dialogic Anthropology* 2 (1). ISSN 1469–7947.

Fechter, Anne-Meike. 2011. (ed.), *The Personal and the Professional in Aid Work.* London: Routledge.

Fechter, Anne-Meike. 2016. 'Aid Work as Moral Labour'. *Critique of Anthropology* 36 (3): 228–43.

Fechter, Anne-Meike 2018. 'An Excess of Goodness? Volunteering among Aid Professionals in Cambodia'. *South East Asia Research* 25 (3): 268–83.

Fechter, Anne-Meike, and Anke Schwittay. 2019. 'Citizen Aid: Grassroots Interventions in Development and Humanitarianism'. Introduction to Special Issue, *Third World Quarterly* 40 (10): 1769–80.

Fechter, Anne-Meike. 2020a. 'Transnationalising the "Moral Neoliberal": Private Aid Initiatives in Cambodia'. *Southeast Asia Research* 28 (1): 87–102.

Fechter, Anne-Meike. 2020b. 'Brokering Transnational Flows of Care: The Case of Citizen Aid'. *Ethnos* 85 (2): 293–308.

Fechter, Anne-Meike. 2023. 'Citizen Aid Celebrities? The Role of Charismatic Founders', in L. Schulpen, H. Haaland, H. Wallevik and S. Kinsbergen (eds), *The Rise of Small-scale Development Organisations: Citizen Aid Actors and their Role in Civil Society.* London: Routledge.

Feener, Michael, and Keping Wu. 2020. 'The Ethics of Religious Giving in Asia: Introduction'. *Journal of Contemporary Religion* 35 (1): 1–12.

Fekete, Liz. 2018. 'Migrants, Borders and the Criminalisation of Solidarity in the EU'. *Race & Class* 59 (4): 65–83.

Feldman, Ilana, and Miriam Iris Ticktin. 2010. *In the Name of Humanity: The Government of Threat and Care*. Durham, NC: Duke University Press.

Fiddian-Qasmiyeh, Elena, A. Ager and A. Greatrick. 2021. 'Understanding Local Responses to Displacement': Refugee Hosts Project Recommendation for Research and Practice #1.

Finn, Jeremy. 2016. *The Beggar Dilemma: A Practical Search into an Often Overlooked Question*. CreateSpace: Independent Publishing Platform.

Fleischmann, Larissa, and Elias Steinhilper. 2017. 'The Myth of Apolitical Volunteering for Refugees: German Welcome Culture and a New Dispositif of Helping'. *Social Inclusion* 5 (3): 17–27.

Fleischmann, L. 2020. *Contested Solidarity: Practices of Refugee Support between Humanitarian Help and Political Activism*. Bielefeld: Transcript Verlag.

Fountain, Philip. 2013. 'The Myth of Religious NGOs: Development Studies and the Return of Religion'. *Revue internationale de politique de développement: Religion and Development* 4: 9–30.

Fountain, Philip. 2015. 'Religious Actors in Disaster Relief in Asia'. *Journal of Mass Emergencies and Disasters* 33 (1): 1.

Fournier, Patrick, Henk van der Kolk, R. Kenneth Carty, André Blais and Jonathan Rose. 2011. *When Citizens Decide: Lessons from Citizen Assemblies on Electoral Reform*. Oxford: Oxford University Press.

Francis, Charles. 2015. 'Community Seed Banks: Origins, Evolution and Prospects'. *Crop Science* 55 (6): 2929.

Fylkesnes, June. 2016. 'Small Streams Make Big Rivers: Exploring Motivation and Idealism in Norwegian Personalised Aid Initiatives in the Gambia'. Unpublished MA thesis, University of Agder. https://uia.brage.unit.no/uia-xmlui/handle/2414518.

Gastil, John, and Robert Richards. 2013. 'Making Direct Democracy Deliberative Through Random Assemblies'. *Politics & Society* 41 (2): 253–81.

Gell, Alfred. 1992. *The Anthropology of Time: Cultural Constructions of Temporal Maps and Images*. Oxford: Berg.

Ghandeharian, Sacha, 2014. 'Moral Distanciation: Modernity, Distance, and the Ethics of Care'. MA thesis, Carleton University. https://curve.carleton.ca/ad90c3e8-d92d-4208-a93c-2151866b7a94.

Girgis, Mona. 2007. 'The Capacity-Building Paradox: Using Friendship to Build Capacity in the South'. *Development in Practice* 17 (3): 353–66.

Gmeiner, Hermann. 1988 [1960]. *Die SOS-Kinderdörfer: Moderne Erziehungsstätten für verlassene Kinder*. Innsbruck, Austria: SOS-Kinderdorf-Verlag.

Gubrium, Jaber F., and David R. Buckholdt. 1982. 'Fictive Family: Everyday Usage, Analytic, and Human Service Considerations'. *American Anthropologist* 84 (4): 878–85.

Guillou, Anne, and Silvia Vignato (eds). 2013. 'Helping and Being Helped'. *Southeast Asia Research* 21 (3): 371–79.

Guiney, T., and M. Mostafanezhad. 2014. 'The Political Economy of Orphanage Tourism in Cambodia'. *Tourist Studies* 15 (2): 132–55.

Gulrajani, Nilima, and Liam Swiss. 2017. *Why do Countries become Donors? Assessing the Drivers and Implications of Donor Proliferation*. Report, Overseas Development Institute (ODI): London.

Gysels, Marjolein, Cathy Shipman and Irene J. Higginson. 2008. '"I will do it if it will help others": Motivations among Patients Taking Part in Qualitative Studies in Palliative Care'. *Journal of Pain and Symptom Management* 35 (4): 347–55.

Hardman, Michael, Peter Larkham and David Adams. 2018. 'Exploring Guerrilla Gardening: Gauging Public Views on the Grassroots Activity', in *Urban Gardening as Politics*, Routledge: London, pp. 148–66.

Hayes, Michael. 2016. 'Homage to a Caring and Thoughtful American'. www.phnompenhpost.com/opinion/homage-caring-and-thoughtful-american (accessed 23 June 2021).

Hayes, Matthew F. 2018. *Gringolandia: Lifestyle Migration under Late Capitalism*. Minneapolis: University of Minnesota Press.

Hénon, Sarah. 2014. 'Measuring Private Development Assistance: Emerging Trends and Challenges'. *Development Initiatives*. http://devinit.org/wp-content/uploads/2014/08/Measuring-private-development-assistance1.pdf.

Heron, Barbara. 2007. *Desire for Development: Whiteness, Gender, and the Helping Imperative*. Waterloo: Wilfried Laurier Press.

Heuser, Eric Anton. 2011. 'Befriending the Field: Friendship and Culture in Development Worlds'. *Third World Quarterly* 33 (8): 1425–39.

Hilhorst, Dorothea, and Bram J. Jansen. 2010. 'Humanitarian Space as Arena: A Perspective on the Everyday Politics of Aid'. *Development and Change* 41(6): 1117–39.

Hinton, Alexander. 2005. *Why Did They Kill? Cambodia in the Shadow of Genocide*. Oakland: University of California Press.

Ho, Elaine Lynn-Ee. 2017. 'Mobilising Affinity Ties: Kachin Internal Displacement and the Geographies of Humanitarianism at the China-Myanmar Border'. *Transactions of the Institute of British Geographers* 42 (1): 84–97.

Holbraad, Martin, and Morten Axel Pedersen. 2009. 'Planet M'. *Anthropological Theory* 9 (4): 371–94.

Horstmann, Alexander. 2017. 'Plurality and Plasticity in Everyday Humanitarianism in the Karen Conflict', in Dan Smyer Yü and Jean Michaud (eds), *Trans-Himalayan Borderlands. Livelihoods, Territorialities, Modernities*. Amsterdam University Press: Amsterdam, pp. 167–88.

Howell, Signe. 2006. *The Kinning of Foreigners: Transnational Adoption in a Global Perspective*. New York: Berghahn Books.

Howell, Signe. 2003. 'Kinning: The Creation of Life Trajectories in Transnational Adoptive Families'. *Journal of the Royal Anthropological Institute* 9 (3): 465–84.

Hyndman, Jennifer, William Payne and Shauna Jimenez. 2017. 'Private Refugee Sponsorship in Canada'. *Forced Migration Review* 54: 56–9.

Irvine, Renwick, Robert Chambers and Rosalind Eyben. 2004. 'Learning from Poor People's Experience: Immersions', in *Lessons for Change in Policy and Organisations* 13. Brighton: Institute of Development Studies.

Irvine, Judith. 2016. 'Going Upscale: Scales and Scale-Climbing as Ideological Projects', in E. Summerson Carr and Michael Lempert (eds), *Scale: Discourse and Dimensions of Social Life*. Oakland, CA: University of California Press.

Ishkanian, A., and Shutes, I. 2022. 'Who Needs the Experts? The Politics and Practices of Alternative Humanitarianism and Its Relationship to NGOs'. *Voluntas*, 33: 397–407.

Jensen, Derrick. 2009. 'Forget Shorter Showers | Essays'. https://derrickjensen.org/2009/07/forget-shorter-showers/.

Jupp, Eleanor. 2022. *Care, Crisis and Activism*. Bristol: Bristol University Press.

Kamm, Frances. 1999. 'Famine Ethics: The Problem of Distance in Morality and Singer's Ethical Theory', in Dale Jamieson (ed.), *Singer and His Critics*. London: Blackwell, pp. 174–203.

Kapoor, Ilan. 2020. *Confronting Desire: Psychoanalysis and International Development*. Cornell: Cornell University Press.

Kendrick, Andrew. 2013. 'Relations, Relationships and Relatedness: Residential Child Care and the Family Metaphor'. *Child & Family Social Work* 18 (1): 77–86.

Kent, Alexandra, and David P. Chandler. 2008. *People of Virtue: Reconfiguring Religion, Power and Moral Order in Cambodia Today*. Copenhagen: Nias Press.

Kiernan, Ben (2002) [1996]. *The Pol Pot Regime: Race, Power and Genocide in Cambodia under the Khmer Rouge, 1975–1979*. New Haven, CT: Yale University Press.

Kimchoeun Pak, Horng Vuthy, Eng Netra, Ann Sovatha, Kim Sedara, Jenny Knowles and David Craig. 2007. *Accountability and Neo-Patrimonialism in Cambodia: A Critical Literature Review*. Phnom Penh: Cambodia Development Resource Institute.

Kinsbergen, Sara, and Lau Schulpen. 2010. *The Anatomy of the Private Initiative – The Results of Five Years of Research into Private Initiatives in the Field of Development Cooperation*. Nijmegen: CIDIN/NCDO.

Kinsbergen, Sara, Lau Schulpen and Ruerd Ruben, 2017. 'Understanding the Sustainability of Private Development Initiatives: What Kind of Difference Do They Make?' *Forum for Development Studies* 44 (2): 223–48.

Kinsbergen, Sara. 2019. 'The Legitimacy of Dutch Do-it-yourself Initiatives in Kwale County, Kenya'. *Third World Quarterly* 40(10): 1850–68.

Kristof, Nicholas. 2010. 'D.I.Y. Foreign-Aid Revolution'. *The New York Times Magazine*, 20 October. www.nytimes.com/2010/10/24/magazine/24volunteerism-t.html.

Kuon, Vannsy. 2011. 'The Pursuit of Authenticity in Tourist Experiences: The Case of Siem Reap-Angkor'. Unpublished Masters thesis, Lincoln University. https://researcharchive.lincoln.ac.nz/bitstream/handle/10182/4306/kuon_mtm.pdf?sequence=5&isAllowed=y.

Lakoff, George, and Mark Johnson. 1980. *Metaphors We Live By*. Chicago, IL. University Of Chicago Press.

Lambek, Michael. *Ordinary Ethics: Anthropology, Language, and Action*. New York: Fordham University Press.

Levy, Ariel. 2020. 'A Missionary on Trial'. *The New Yorker*, 6 April. www.newyorker.com/magazine/2020/04/13/a-missionary-on-trial.
Lewis, David, and Mark Schuller. 2017. 'Engagements with a Productively Unstable Category: Anthropologists and Nongovernmental Organizations'. *Current Anthropology* 58 (5): 634–51.
Li, Tania. 2007. *The Will to Improve: Governmentality, Development, and the Practice of Politics*. Durham: Duke University Press.
Lynch, Philip and Kristen Hilton. 2006. 'We Want Change: Understanding and Responding to Begging in Melbourne'. *Parity* 19 (1): 40–42.
Macintyre, Martha. 1993. 'Fictive Kinship or Mistaken Identity', in Diane Bell, Pat Kaplan and Wazir Jahan Karim (eds), *Gendered Fields: Women, Men and Ethnography*. Routledge, London.
Macklin, Audrey, Luin Goldring, Jennifer Hyndman, Anna Korteweg, Kathryn Barber and Jona Zyfi. 2020. 'The Kinship between Refugee and Family Sponsorship'. *Working Paper 4* (August). Ryerson Centre for Immigration and Settlement (RCIS) and the CERC in Migration and Integration.
Malkki, Liisa H. 2015. *The Need to Help: The Domestic Arts of International Humanitarianism*. Durham: Duke University Press.
Massey, Doreen. 2004: 'Geographies of Responsibility'. *Geogr. Annals* 86 B (1): 5–18.
Masters, Alexander, and Dominic Nutt. 2017. 'A Plutocratic Proposal: An Ethical Way for Rich Patients to Pay for a Place on a Clinical Trial'. *Journal of Medical Ethics* 43 (11): 730–6.
Meier, Patrick. 2015. *Digital Humanitarians: How Big Data Is Changing the Face of Humanitarian Response*. Boca Raton, FL: CRC Press, Taylor & Francis Group.
Mathers, Kathryn. 2010. *Travel, Humanitarianism, and Becoming American in Africa*. New York: Palgrave Macmillan.
Mauss, Marcel. 1954. *The Gift: Forms and Functions for Exchange in Archaic Societies*. London: Cohen & West.
Mawdsley, Emma, Janet G. Townsend and Gina Porter. 2005. 'Trust, accountability, and face-to-face interaction in North–South NGO relations'. *Development in Practice* 15 (1): 77–82.
Mawdsley, Emma. 2012a. *From Recipients to Donors: Emerging Powers and the Changing Development Landscape*. London: Zed Books.
Mawdsley, Emma. 2012b. 'The Changing Geographies of Foreign Aid and Development Cooperation: Contributions from Gift Theory'. *Transactions of the Institute of British Geographers* 37: 256–72.
McCarthy, Gerard. 2016. 'Buddhist Welfare, Informal Institutions & the Definition of "the Political" in Provincial Myanmar', in Nick Cheesman and Nicholas Farrelly (eds), *Making Sense of Conflict in Myanmar*. Singapore: ISEAS, pp. 314–32.
McCarthy, Gerard. 2020. 'Bounded Duty: Disasters, Moral Citizenship and Exclusion in Myanmar'. *South East Asia Research* 28 (1): 13–34.
McKay, Deirdre, and Padmapani Perez. 2019. 'Citizen Aid, Social Media and Brokerage after Disaster'. *Third World Quarterly* 40 (10): 1903–20.
McLennan, Sharon J. 2017. 'Passion, Paternalism, and Politics: DIY Development and Independent Volunteers in Honduras'. *Development in Practice* 27 (6): 880–91.

Meisler, Stanley. 2012. *When in the World Calls: The Inside Story of the Peace Corps and Its First Fifty Years*. Boston: Beacon.

Milner, Anthony. 2001. '"Asia" Consciousness and Asian Values', Faculty of Asian Studies, Australian National University. https://openresearch-repository.anu.edu.au/bitstream/1885/41906/1/cons_vals.html.

Modell, Judith. S. 1994. *Kinship with Strangers: Adoption and Interpretations of Kinship in American Culture*. Oakland, CA: University of California Press.

Mostowlansky, Till. 2020. 'Humanitarian Affect: Islam, Aid and Emotional Impulse in Northern Pakistan'. *History and Anthropology* (November): 1–21.

Nah, Seungahn and Deborah S. Chung. 2020. *Understanding Citizen Journalism as Civic Participation*. London: Routledge.

Nemiroff, Marc. 2018. 'Facing Moral Dilemmas and Beggars in the Street | Psychology Today United Kingdom'. www.psychologytoday.com/gb/blog/where-the-heart-is/201803/facing-moral-dilemmas-and-beggars-in-the-street (accessed 23 June 2021).

Newell, Peter, Freddie Daley and Michelle Twena. 2021. 'Changing our Ways? Behaviour Change and the Climate Crisis'. Report of the Cambridge Sustainability Commission on Scaling Behaviour Change.

Olliff, Louise. 2022. *Helping Familiar Strangers: Refugee Diaspora Organizations and Humanitarianism*. Indiana: Indiana University Press.

Ong, Aihwa. 2003. *Buddha is Hiding: Refugees, Citizenship, the New America*. Berkeley: University of California Press.

Ong, Andrew, and Hans Steinmüller. 2020. 'Communities of Care: Public Donations, Development Assistance, and Independent Philanthropy in the Wa State of Myanmar'. *Critique of Anthropology* 41 (1): 65–87.

Osella, Filippo and Tom Widger. 2018. '"You can give even if you only have ten rupees!": Muslim Charity in a Colombo Housing Scheme'. *Modern Asian Studies* 52 (1): 297–324.

Osner, Karl. 2007. 'With the Strength of the Powerless: Using Immersions for Processes of Structural Change, Participation, Learning and Action'. https://pubs.iied.org/sites/default/files/pdfs/migrate/G02900.pdf.

Otegui, D. 2022. 'Relational Humanitarianism', in *A Symbolic Approach to Humanitarian Action*. Contemporary Humanitarian Action and Emergency Management. Springer, Cham.

Ovesen, Jan, Ing-Britt Trankell, and Joakim Öjendal. 1996. *When Every Household Is an Island: Social Organization and Power Structures in Rural Cambodia*. Uppsala: Uppsala University, Department Of Cultural Anthropology.

Pachirat, Timothy. 2013. *Every Twelve Seconds: Industrialized Slaughter and the Politics of Sight*. New Haven, CT: Yale University Press.

Pacitto, Julia, and Elena Fiddian-Qasmiyeh. 2013. 'Writing the "other" into Humanitarian Discourse: Framing Theory and Practice in South-South Responses to Forced Displacement'. *Working Paper Series* 93. Refugee Studies Centre, University of Oxford.

Pallister-Wilkins, Polly. 2018. 'Hotspots and the Geographies of Humanitarianism'. *Environment and Planning D: Society and Space* 38 (6): 991–1008.

Papi, Daniela. 2016. 'Tackling Heropreneurship'. *Stanford Social Innovation Review*. https://ssir.org/articles/entry/tackling_heropreneurship.

Parker, Juliet. 2022. *The State of the Humanitarian System*. Report, ALNAP. https://sohs.alnap.org/.

Pedwell, Carolyn. 2012. 'Affective (Self-)Transformations: Empathy, Neoliberalism and International Development'. *Feminist Theory*: 163–79.

Pérez-Muñoz, Cristian. 2018. 'Beneficence, Street Begging, and Diverted Giving Schemes'. *Political Research Quarterly* 71 (4): 923–35.

Pollet, Ignace, Rik Habraken, Lau Schulpen and Huib Huyse. 2014. *The Accidental Aidworker: A Mapping of Citizen Initiatives for Global Solidarity in Europe*. Leuven: Katholike Universitet.

Polman, Linda. 2008. *The Crisis Caravan: What's Wrong with Humanitarian Aid*. New York: Picador.

Ponheary Ly Foundation. 2021. 'Ponheary's Story'. www.theplf.org/history-2/ (accessed 21 February 2019).

Rabbitts, Frances. 2012. 'Child Sponsorship, Ordinary Ethics and the Geographies of Charity'. *Geoforum* 43 (5): 926–36.

Reas, Jane. 2013. '"Boy, have we got a vacation for you": Orphanage Tourism in Cambodia and the Commodification and Objectification of the Orphaned Child'. *Thammasat Review* 16: 121–39.

Rhoads, Robert A., Tracy Lachica Buenavista and David E. Z. Maldonado. 2004. 'Students of Color Helping Others Stay in College: A Grassroots Effort'. *About Campus* 9 (3): 10–17.

Richey, Lisa Ann. 2018. 'Conceptualizing 'Everyday Humanitarianism': Ethics, Affects, and Practices of Contemporary Global Helping'. *New Political Science* 40 (4): 625–39.

Richner, Beat. 2010. *Ambassador Between Live and Survival*. Zurich: Elster-Verl.

Robbins, Bruce. 2019. 'The Politics of Life: Rethinking Humanitarianism in an Age of Planetary Inequality', *The Nation*. www.thenation.com/article/archive/didier-fassin-life-a-critical-user-manual-humanitarianism-aid-review/.

Roth, Silke. 2015. *The Paradoxes of Aid Work: Passionate Professionals*. London: Routledge.

Rozakou, Katerina. 2016. 'Socialities of Solidarity: Revisiting the Gift Taboo in Times of Crises'. *Social Anthropology* 24(2): 185–99.

Rozakou, Katerina. 2017. 'Solidarity Humanitarianism: The Blurred Boundaries of Humanitarianism in Greece'. *Etnofoor* 29(2): 99–104.

Rygiel, Kim. 2011. 'Bordering Solidarities: Migrant Activism and the Politics of Movement and Camps at Calais', *Citizenship Studies* 15(1): 1–19.

Salary.com. 2023. 'Writing through Grants Writer Salaries', www.salary.com/research/company/writing-through/grants-writer-salary?cjid=18295011.

Sandri, Elisa. 2018. '"Volunteer humanitarianism": Volunteers and Humanitarian Aid in the Jungle Refugee Camp of Calais'. *Journal of Ethnic and Migration Studies*, 44 (1): 65–80.

Schech, Susanne, Tracey Skelton and Anuradha Mundkur. 2016. 'Building Relationships and Negotiating Difference in International Development Volunteerism'. *The Geographical Journal* 184 (2): 148–57.

Scherz, China. 2013. '"Let Us Make God Our Banker': Ethics, Temporality, and Agency in a Ugandan Charity Home'. *American Ethnologist* 40 (4): 624–36.

Schnable, Allison Y. 2021. *Amateurs Without Borders: The Limits of Global Compassion*. Oakland: University of California Press.

Schneider, David. 1984. *A Critique of the Study of Kinship*. Ann Arbor: University of Michigan Press.

Schwittay, Anke. 2015. *New Media and International Development: Representation and Affect in Microfinance*. London: Routledge.

Schwittay, Anke. 2019. 'Digital Mediations of Everyday Humanitarianism: The Case of Kiva.org'. *Third World Quarterly* 40 (10): 1921–38.

Sezgin, Zeynep and Dennis Dijkzeul. 2015. *The New Humanitarians in International Practice Emerging Actors and Contested Principles*. London: Routledge.

Silk, John. 2000. 'Caring at a Distance: (Im)Partiality, Moral Motivation and the Ethics of Representation – Introduction'. *Ethics, Place & Environment* 3 (3): 303–9.

Singer, Peter. 1972. 'Famine, Affluence, and Morality'. *Philosophy & Public Affairs* 1 (3): 229–43.

Singer, Peter. 1996. *The Life You Can Save*. London: Macmillan.

Skinner, Rob, and Alan Lester. 2012. 'Humanitarianism and Empire: New Research Agendas'. *The Journal of Imperial and Commonwealth History* 40 (5): 729–47.

Smirl, Lisa. 2015. *Spaces of Aid: How Cars, Compounds and Hotels Shape Humanitarianism*. London: Zed Books.

Solnit, Rebecca. 2010. *A Paradise Built in Hell: The Extraordinary Communities That Arise in Disaster*. New York: Penguin.

Springer, Simon. 2010. *Cambodia's Neoliberal Order: Violence, Authoritarianism, and the Contestation of Public Space*. London: Routledge.

Springer, Simon. 2015. *Violent Neoliberalism: Development, Discourse, and Dispossession in Cambodia*. London: Palgrave Macmillan.

Springer, Simon. 2020. 'Caring Geographies: The COVID-19 Interregnum and a Return to Mutual Aid'. *Dialogues in Human Geography* 10 (2): 112–15.

Stafford, Charles. 2013. *Ordinary Ethics in China*. London: Bloomsbury.

Stamatov, Peter. 2010. 'Activist Religion, Empire, and the Emergence of Modern Long-Distance Advocacy Networks', *American Sociological Review* 75: 607–28.

Stirrat, Jock. 2006. 'Competitive humanitarianism: Relief and the tsunami in Sri Lanka'. *Anthropology Today* 22 (5): 11–16.

Stirrat, Roderick and Heiko Henkel. 1997. 'The Development Gift: The Problem of Reciprocity in the NGO World'. *ANNALS of the American Academy of Political and Social Science* 554 (1): 66–80.

Stirrat, Roderick. 2008. 'Mercenaries, Missionaries and Misfits: Representations of Development Personnel'. *Critique of Anthropology* 28 (4): 406–25.

Stoler, Ann Laura, and Frederick Cooper. 1997. 'Between Metropole and Colony: Rethinking a Research Agenda', in F. Cooper and A. Stoler (eds), *Tensions of Empire: Colonial Cultures in a Bourgeois World*. Oakland: University of California Press, pp. 1–56.

Strathern, Marilyn. 1995. *The Relation: Issues in Complexity and Scale*. Cambridge: Prickly Pear Press.

Strathern, Marilyn. 1996. 'Cutting the Network'. *Journal of the Royal Anthropological Institute* 2 (3): 517–35.

Strathern, Marilyn. 2018. 'Relations', in *The Cambridge Encyclopedia of Anthropology*. Open Access online resource, www.anthroencyclopedia.com/entry/relations.

Sundberg, Molly. 2020. 'Career Trajectories of Tanzanian Aid Workers: Structural Inequalities and New Management Practices in Public Foreign Aid', in Melina C. Kalfelis and Kathrin Knodel (eds), *NGO and Lifeworlds in Africa*, Oxford: Berghahn.

Swidler, Ann, and Susan Cotts Watkins. 2017. *A Fraught Embrace: The Romance and Reality of AIDS Altruism in Africa*. Princeton and Oxford: Princeton University Press.

Taithe, Bertrand. 2019. 'Demotic Humanitarians: Historical Perspectives on the Global Reach of Local Initiatives, 1940–2017'. *Third World Quarterly* 40 (10): 1781–98.

Talmud, *Mishnah Sanhedrin*, www.sefaria.org/Mishnah_Sanhedrin.4.5?lang=bi.

Taylor, Rebecca, and Silke Roth. 2019. 'Exploring Meaningful Work in the Third Sector', in Ruth Yeoman et al. (eds) *The Oxford Handbook of Meaningful Work*. Oxford: Oxford University Press, pp. 257–73.

Ticktin, Miriam. 2015. 'Humanitarianism's History of the Singular'. *Grey Room* 61: 81–5.

Ticktin, Miriam. 2019. 'From the Human to the Planetary: Speculative Futures of Care'. *Medicine Anthropology Theory* 6 (3): 133–60.

Trnka, Susana, and Catherine Trundle. 2017. *Competing Responsibilities: The Ethics and Politics of Contemporary Life*. Durham, NC: Duke University Press.

Tsing, Anna L. 2012. 'On Nonscalability: The Living World Is Not Amenable to Precision-Nested Scales'. *Common Knowledge* 18 (3): 505–24.

Un, Kheang. 2005. 'Patronage Politics and Hybrid Democracy: Political Change in Cambodia, 1993–2003'. *Asian Perspective* 29 (2): 203–30.

United Nations Conference on Development. 2020. 'The Least Developed Countries Report'. https://unctad.org/system/files/official-document/ldcr2020_en.pdf.

Vandevoordt, Robin. 2019. 'Subversive Humanitarianism: Rethinking Refugee Solidarity Through Grass-roots Initiatives'. *Refugee Survey Quarterly* 38 (3): 245–65.

Vandevoordt, R. and Verschraegen, G. 2019. 'Subversive Humanitarianism and its Challenges: Notes on the Political Ambiguities of Civil Refugee Support', in M. Feischmidt, L. Pries and C. Cantat (eds), *Refugee Protection and Civil Society in Europe*. Cham, Switzerland: Palgrave Macmillan.

Vandevoordt, R. 2021. 'A More Subversive Humanitarianism? The Political Strategies of Grassroots Initiatives Supporting Illegalised Migrants', in M. G. Jumbert and F. Pascucci (eds), *Citizen Humanitarianism at European Borders*. Milton Keynes: Taylor & Francis Group, pp. 99–113.

Vandevoordt, Robin, and Larissa Fleischmann. 2020. 'Impossible Futures? The Ambivalent Temporalities of Grassroots Humanitarian Action'. *Critical Sociology*, 47 (2), 187–202.

Vaux, Tony. 2001. *The Selfish Altruist: Relief Work in Famine and War*. London: Routledge.

Verver, Michiel and Heidi Dahles. 2015. 'The Institutionalisation of Oknha: Cambodian Entrepreneurship at the Interface of Business and Politics'. *Journal of Contemporary Asia* 45 (1): 48–70.

Vogt, Wendy. 2018. *Lives in Transit: Violence and Intimacy on the Migrant Journey*. Oakland: University of California Press.

Walsh, Katie. 2018. *Transnational Geographies of The Heart: Intimate Subjectivities in a Globalising City*. London: Wiley Blackwell.

Warne Peters, Rebecca. 2016. 'Local in Practice: Professional Distinctions in Angolan Development Work'. *American Anthropologist* 118 (3): 495–507.

Wastell, Sari. 2001. 'Presuming Scale, Making Diversity: On the Mischiefs of Measurement and the Global: Local Metonym in Theories of Law and Culture'. *Critique of Anthropology* 21 (2): 185–210.

Watanabe, Chika. 2015. 'Commitments of Debt: Temporality and the Meanings of Aid Work in a Japanese NGO in Myanmar'. *American Anthropologist* 117 (3): 468–79.

Watanabe, Chika. 2019. *Becoming One: Religion, Development, and Environmentalism in a Japanese NGO in Myanmar*. Honolulu: University of Hawai'i Press.

Watson, Brad 2015. 'The Origins of International Child Sponsorship'. *Development in Practice* 25 (6): 867–79.

Weismantel, Mary. 1995. 'Making Kin: Kinship Theory and Zumbagua Adoptions'. *American Ethnologist* 22 (4): 685–709.

Weston, Kath. 1991. *Families we Choose: Lesbian, Gays, Kinship*. New York: Columbia University Press.

Williams, Bernard. 2006 [1985]. *Ethics and the Limits of Philosophy*. London: Routledge.

Wilkinson-Maposa, Susan. 2005. *The Poor Philanthropist: How and Why the Poor Help Each Other*. Cape Town: Southern African-United States Centre for Leadership And Public Values, Graduate School Of Business, University of Cape Town.

World Bank, 2019. 'Money Sent Home by Workers now Largest Source of External Financing in Low- and Middle-Income Countries', https://blogs.worldbank.org/opendata/money-sent-home-workers-now-largest-source-external-financing-low-and-middle-income (accessed 1 July 2021).

Yarris, Kristin Elizabeth, Brenda Garcia-Millan and Karla Schmidt-Murillo. 2020. 'Motivations to Help: Local Volunteer Humanitarians in US Refugee Resettlement'. *Journal of Refugee Studies* 33 (2): 437–59.

Yarrow, Thomas. *Development Beyond Politics: Aid, Activism and NGOs in Ghana*. Palgrave Macmillan, 2011.

Zaman, Tahir. 2016. *Islamic Traditions of Refuge in the Crises of Iraq and Syria*. New York: Palgrave Macmillan.

Zhukova, Ekatherina. 2019. 'Kinning as Intimate Disaster Response: From Recuperation in Host Families to Educational Migration of the Chernobyl Children from Belarus to Italy'. *Identities: Global Studies in Culture and Power* 29 (2): 205–22.

Zhukova, Ekatherina. 2020. 'Private Humanitarian Responses to Disaster Vulnerabilities: The Chernobyl Children from Belarus in Italy'. *Childhood* 27 (2): 238–53.

Zucker, Eve Monique. 2013. *Forest of Struggle: Moralities of Remembrance in Upland Cambodia*. Honolulu: University of Hawai'i Press.

Index

abuse 41, 118, 125, 172–3
adoption 19, 36, 122, 127, 129, 142
affinity tie 3, 22, 24–5, 32, 40, 146–7, 149, 164
aid, localising 170, 175–6
altruism 105, 106, 122, 133, 173
amateur 7, 28, 30, 31, 33–4, 169–74

Barnett, M. 24, 27, 81–2, 145
beneficiary 9, 40, 41, 106, 147–8, 160–2
Bornstein, E. 21, 24, 32, 36, 67, 90, 105, 113, 120, 122–3, 128, 131, 133, 137, 142
business 6, 14, 20, 60, 69, 71–2, 74, 78, 84, 111, 118–9, 131, 150, 154–5, 162–3, 169

Carr, E.S. and M. Lempert 34–5, 39, 43, 64, 66–7, 74, 78–9
Christian 27, 32, 37, 50, 134, 146, 149–51
citizen aid 12, 17, 31, 116, 119
corruption 55–6, 85

democracy 55, 78, 134, 151
dilemma 89, 91–2, 102, 168
disability 2, 50, 67–8, 70, 72, 137, 156, 163–4
donation 2, 5, 18, 33, 47, 52, 57, 70, 108–9, 110, 116, 120, 128, 146
education 90, 107, 110–11, 125, 149, 153, 157, 159
ethical 4, 16, 27, 29, 99, 100, 102, 106, 125

Fassin, D. 24–6, 30, 169
fundraising 8, 18, 22, 46, 51, 77, 109–11, 113, 117, 134–5

genocide 41, 147, 154–6, 163
governmentality 25–6, 30, 103, 175

history 2, 27–8, 40, 64, 85, 116, 137, 146, 152–4, 156
human rights 55, 58, 99, 126, 134

impact 10, 43, 45, 51, 54, 57–8, 78, 89, 95, 110, 126, 163, 170–2, 174, 177
impartiality 3–4, 21–22, 27, 40, 145
imperative 11, 27, 29, 35, 39, 59, 104, 146, 150, 166–7, 17

leadership 2, 8, 52, 76–7, 151

Malkki, L. 19, 26, 33, 36, 40, 43, 48, 65, 88, 105, 169

orphanage 125, 129, 133, 145, 158, 173

philanthropy 15, 21, 32, 86–7, 90, 92, 105, 120, 122, 171
political 13, 19, 26, 33, 39, 43, 45, 55, 58–9, 65–6, 85, 87, 97, 102, 118, 145, 151, 169, 173
power 34, 41, 43, 59, 65, 75–6, 78, 84, 88, 102, 152, 156, 159, 176–7
privilege 16, 34, 41, 84, 88, 93–4, 98, 100, 102
professional 2, 4–8, 11–3, 15–16, 20–21, 28–31, 33–4, 38, 43, 56,

65, 78, 85–7, 91, 94, 96–7, 102, 119, 126, 145, 148–9, 170–4
public health 43, 57

recipient 10, 15, 17, 72, 105, 109, 123, 131, 147, 151
religion 40, 146, 149
rescue 13, 25, 30, 42, 64, 70, 79
responsibility 22, 38, 49–54

scales
   geographical 20, 56, 81–2
   temporal 45, 53–54, 61, 64–5, 73
Schnable, A. 7–8, 28, 31, 36, 38, 60, 169–70, 174

social enterprise 6, 85
social media 18, 22, 57, 140–1
sponsorship 46, 67, 108, 123–4, 127–9, 131–4, 141–2
suffering 19, 35,37, 39, 43,69, 81–2, 162
Swidler, A. and S. Watkins 7, 9, 171

trauma 60, 85, 154, 156–7, 159

vernacular 4, 26, 28, 31–4, 36

white saviour 9, 22, 24–5, 41, 145–6, 164–5, 175–6

EU authorised representative for GPSR:
Easy Access System Europe, Mustamäe tee 50,
10621 Tallinn, Estonia
gpsr.requests@easproject.com